Korean Studies of the Henry M. Jackson
School of International Studies

CLARK W. SORENSEN, EDITOR

OVER THE MOUNTAINS ARE MOUNTAINS

Korean Peasant Households and Their
Adaptations to Rapid Industrialization

CLARK W. SORENSEN

With a New Preface by the Author

University of Washington Press

Seattle & London

This publication was supported in part by the Korea Studies Program of the University of Washington in cooperation with the Henry M. Jackson School of International Studies.

UNIVERSITY OF WASHINGTON PRESS
PO Box 50096, Seattle, WA 98145, USA
www.washington.edu/uwpress

LIBRARY OF CONGRESS CATALOGING-IN-PUBLICATION DATA
ISBN 978-0-295-992765-1
Complete cataloguing information for this title
is available from the Library of Congress.

The paper used in this publication is acid-free and meets the minimum requirements of American National Standard for Information Sciences— Permanence of Paper for Printed Library Materials, ANSI Z39.48–1984.∞

Contents

Preface to the Paperback Edition

In the 1970s and 1980s, I used to allow six hours for the one-way trip from Seoul to San'gongni: an hour to get to the Chŏngnyangni train station, buy the ticket, and board the train; two hours and twenty minutes on the train to Ch'unch'ŏn; a thirty-to-forty-minute wait in the Ch'unch'ŏn bus station; another hour on the slow country bus on bumpy, unpaved roads to Fishplay Shore; and then an hour walking over Tang Kogae Pass to San'gongni itself. I had to leave Seoul no later than 11:00 AM or risk walking over the mountain pass in the dark.

In a return trip in 2012, I checked the Internet for the direct bus to San'gok Mountain. Boarding the bus at the Kangbyŏn terminal at 2:25 in the afternoon, I sped up the Kangwŏn Freeway [*kosok toro*] through tunnel after tunnel, exiting to proceed by smooth, paved highway through the mountains to Broadmart, the local market town. I noticed the huge, new, two-story school there as we headed toward Fishplay Shore, the old jumping-off place for the village of San'gongni. I was surprised when the bus passed the large parking lot with its concession stands serving river and mountain visitors on the Fishplay side of the river and went straight across the bridge to drop me off—less than an hour after departure—at the foot of the mountain at a vaguely Swiss-looking hotel and shop labeled "San'gok Mountain House." I could have ridden all the way into the village and been dropped off in the middle of Big Hamlet, where I had lived in the 1970s and '80s, but for old times' sake, I wanted to disembark at the foot of the mountain and walk into the village over Tang Kogae, something I hadn't done for twenty-plus years.[1]

•

---

1   The original fieldwork upon which this book was based was carried out in 1976–77 and 1983, but I visited the village again in 1988. (I took the bus to the foot of the mountain once in the 1990s, but, being on a day-trip, I didn't have time to walk into the village, which was still not accessible by bus.)

Crossing the pass in 2012 wasn't the same as in 1976, 1977, or 1983, of course. Cars and trucks whizzed by me at forty and fifty miles an hour as I trudged alone up the wide, paved road over the pass. The traditional terraced rice fields were no longer in use, replaced by a succession of restaurants, shops advertising rental skis and boards, and hostels built in a variety of national styles, from French Swiss to ultra-modern to traditional Korean. When I reached the top of the pass, the view of the village took my breath away. To my left, I could view a five- to six-story Italianate "pension," and while to my right Big Hamlet was recognizable, a dozen or so two- and three-story commercial buildings stuck out. Welcome to the ski gateway and river resort village of San'gongni!

My Japanese colleague Itō Abito had joked with me just two weeks earlier, when I mentioned my plans to visit San'gongni, that I would have to rename this book "San nŏmŏ ap'at'ŭ itta"—"Over the mountains are apartments." We had a good laugh; I never dreamed it would be true. Now, however, I had to face up to what Koreans call a "new heaven and earth"—*sinchŏnji*.

Walking into the heart of the village, I oriented myself only with difficulty, but eventually I encountered some villagers, introduced myself, and was able to chat. The local dialect started coming back. One man had been a child when I lived in the village, and he remembered me. I asked about my former host family, since I couldn't find their house. Their old house had burned down. They were now living in a new brick house with hot and cold running water and indoor plumbing, next to the bus stop. When I mentioned the pensions, he volunteered that the "picnic ladies" who visited the pensions were a problem because of the "boom, boom, boom" of their music late into the night. [2]

I had expected to find a village full of aged empty nesters with a few entrepreneurial farmers farming on a larger scale than in the past. The empty nesters and larger-scale farmers were indeed there, but so were an even larger number of new business owners—those running pensions, restaurants, stores, and other businesses. Far from stagnating, the village was thriving—although not necessarily for the old-time residents, since the entrepreneurs were entirely from the outside. San'gongni may now be even more interesting than it was in the past, but because of the numerous different social groups in the village today, studying it would be much more difficult than studying the straightforward agricultural village of some forty years before.

---

2   The word he used was *p'iknik ajumŏnidŭl*. This seems to be an English rendering of the old Korean concept of *sop'ung*, "an outing by a school or other group involving organized activities such as sports and nature observation." Drinking and singing often accompanied these activities.

•

The changes the village has undergone since the time this book was written help one contextualize the historical moment that this study records. San'gongni in the late seventies was a poor and remote mountain village in a conservative part of South Korea just at the time Korea was beginning the change from a predominantly rural to a predominantly urban economy. San'gongni was inevitably affected by Korea's urbanization: most of the villagers between ages fifteen and thirty had already left for urban schooling or factory work when I was there. Yet I chose, I think with justification, to call the villagers "peasants" because for those living in the village, agriculture was still "a livelihood and a way of life."[3] Most households were self-sufficient in food production to a considerable degree and sold on the market only what was left over after their household needs were met. Little money circulated within the village, and hospitality was a cardinal virtue; I could just show up without worrying about whether somebody would put me up overnight. Time was not money. I was able to interview at least one person in every household in the village, and I spent many an hour chatting or drinking with a variety of villagers.

The New Village Movement was in full swing. The first mechanical "tractors"—engines that could be equipped to plow as one walked behind them, or be harnessed as a power source for carts or for threshers—had arrived in the village the same year I did. Most people still plowed and harrowed the fields with cattle throughout the 1970s. The village had all the organizations promoted by the government—a nominal 4-H Club, a women's organization that ran cooperative stores, a village strongbox, and a couple of cooperative credit societies (*kye*) organized by the Agricultural Cooperative to foster purchase of the first mechanical plows, in addition to the traditional "marriage and funeral" societies. I was told the village was going to be electrified soon and maybe furnished with a bridge across the river. There were plans for tourism, too, but with the area's primitive transportation infrastructure, these plans seemed pie-in-the-sky to me.

•

In 1983, when I did the re-study included in this book, both the electricity and the bridge had become a reality. Tractors had largely, though not entirely, replaced cattle for plowing, but otherwise life didn't seem that

---

3   For a discussion of the term, see Robert Redfield, *Peasant Society and Culture: An Anthropological Approach to Civilization* (Chicago: University of Chicago Press, 1956), 27.

much different from what it had been six years earlier. People had heard that the area was slated to be inundated by a reservoir needed for the 1988 Seoul Olympics, and they worried about the level of compensation the government was planning for their land.

Only during my 1988 visit (a period not covered in this book) did I begin to feel that people were becoming more market-oriented. When I arrived on foot that year, for example, my host family exclaimed, "Why didn't you call us? We would have picked you up at the bus stop with the tractor." People had televisions. An old friend I visited casually picked up the phone and invited other friends over for drinks with me. The threat of inundation had passed, and I found a few farmers growing cash crops rather than subsistence crops: ginseng and Oriental medicines for sale on the market. Others had increased the scale of their animal husbandry to ten to twelve head of cattle instead of the one or two cows raised in the 1970s. The villagers fretted that the years of expecting inundation had inhibited investment in the transportation infrastructure, which they badly needed to prosper. And so I thought the village would continue to age without dramatic change as only a few farmers adapted their agriculture to market conditions.

But San'gongni has moved on, as Korea has moved on. When I first studied San'gongni, it was "Korea" to me. Now that I have done research in different parts of Korea over more than thirty-five years, I would not claim that San'gongni—or any village—could be "typical" of rural Korea at any point in time. While there were other villages as remote and poor as San'gongni—particularly in mountain areas—there were also villages that had been fully incorporated into the capitalist money economy since the 1920s, if not before. In some areas by the 1970s, hired field labor had replaced labor exchange and labor teams for a generation or more, or cash cropping had been common for a century or more. Many villages then and for the next decade were prospering through market gardening to the cities, and peasants located in proximity to urban development were selling their land and retiring on the proceeds. Many parts of even rural Korea have never been as socially conservative as were the stolid peasants of the relatively undifferentiated Yŏngsŏ region of Kangwŏn Province that, like all Korean regions, has its own distinct cultural tradition.

Some of the people I knew in the 1970s and 1980s (or their children and grandchildren) were still living in the village in 2012, but the way of life described in the pages of this book has largely disappeared. When the book was first published in 1988, urban Koreans still recognized the lifestyle described here as one familiar from their own youth or that of their parents or grandparents. This is no longer the case for the Korean youth of today, who are removed three generations or more from village life. So, today this study must be read historically. It's about San'gongni—a particular village at a particular historical juncture—isolated, operating as a coherent social unit, and maintaining relatively conservative notions of family and clan organization. What it would later become is a very different story that will have to be told elsewhere.

Clark W. Sorensen
January 2013

Acknowledgments

This work could never have been completed without the help of many others. Stevan Harrell, as chairman of my dissertation committee at the University of Washington, provided me with inspiration, advice, and encouragement without which I would never have reached the field. Dr. Suh Doo Soo, of the University of Washington (retired), provided me with crucial letters of introduction that greatly facilitated my original fieldwork in Korea. Dr. Jun Hyup Kim, Director of the Asiatic Research Center at Korea University, graciously agreed to have the center serve as an institutional sponsor during my 1976–77 fieldwork. Dr. Kwang Kyu Lee of the Department of Anthropology at Seoul National University first suggested I study "Sangongni," wrote a letter of introduction to the head of the village conveying my desire to do fieldwork there and generously provided me with the interview schedules from his 1976 fieldwork in the village. On subsequent trips to the field, he has always been generous in helping me and other anthropologists find assistants and whatever other help we need in Korea.

Support of my 1976–77 field research in Sangongni was provided by a Fulbright-Hays Predoctoral Grant, and a Stout Grant from the University of Washington. My 1983 fieldwork was supported by a travel grant from the International Cultural Society of Korea and by a Faculty Development Grant from Vanderbilt University.

Over the years, a number of graduate students in the Department of Anthropology at Seoul National University have aided me in my field research, explained things I have had difficulty understanding, and expanded my knowledge of Korean life. During 1976, Kim Hong-Jun assisted me, and in 1983, Hwang Ikchu, Cho Kyŏngman, Kang Ŭnju, and Pak Kŭmhwa all were excellent assistants whom I have much to thank.

Numerous people have been generous in supplying me with difficult to find written materials. The head of the county in which Sangongni is situated provided me with statistical yearbooks for the county. Larry Burmeister kindly supplied me with the articles by Kim Dong-hi and Chŏng Yŏngil and Cynthia Brokaw provided me with Kuramochi Kazuo's important article.

I have benefited from the comments and criticisms of this manuscript by a number of people. I would particularly like to single out Judy Gorodetsky who helped me smooth the language of the manuscript; Jim Palais, whose careful comments on both the form and substance of the manuscript have substantially improved the book; Roger Janelli, whose deep knowledge of the ethnographic literature on Korea has helped me view my material in the context of Korea as a whole; Laurel Kendall, whose keen appreciation of women's roles and perspectives in Korea has sharpened my appreciation of the rural division of labor; and Donna Leonetti, who helped me with some of the demographic material. Ron Spores, Arthur Demarest, Dan Cornfield, and Kathy Folk have all read parts of the manuscript and made valuable suggestions that have led to its improvement. In addition, I have benefited from the comments of several anonymous reviewers. Needless to say, remaining deficiencies are all my own.

I would like to thank Reidel Publishers, and John Wiley and Sons for permission to use copyrighted materials.

My largest debt is to the people of Sangongni who have put up with me and my nosy ways on numerous occasions. May they, and all the people of rural Korea, prosper and easily cross over all the mountains they meet.

Over the Mountains Are Mountains

Korean Peasant Households and Their
Adaptations to Rapid Industrialization

Korean words and names cited in the text have been given in McCune-Reischauer romanization according to the standard Korean pronunciation given in Yi Hŭisŭng's *Kugŏ Tae Sajŏn* (1971). Korean names are normally cited in Korean order (surname first, no comma). When the reference is to an English language publication, however, English word order, and the spelling of the name as given in the publication is used. Some authors who have published in Korean and in English are thus cited in two different forms (e.g., Kwang Kyu Lee [Yi Kwang-gyu]), but all such cases are cross-referenced in the bibliography.

CHAPTER 1

Over the Mountains Are Mountains

People had a proverb for life: *san nŏmŏ san itta*; over the mountains are mountains; as soon as you overcome one crisis, another one looms.

Chang Yŏnggŭn was born in 1914 in San'gongni, a collection of small hamlets in the mountains some twenty-five kilometers southwest of Ch'unch'ŏn, the capital of South Korea's Kangwŏn Province. He has lived his whole life as a farmer, eking out a living in the same small ravine overlooking the river where his present house stands. Although most of the sons and daughters of his neighbors and himself have left for town, by traditional standards he is in an enviable position. He owns more than a hectare of irrigated riceland, owns a small amount of rainfall field, and has two sons at home to run the farm and support him in his old age. Today he has electricity and television, access to motortillers and mechanical transport, and his life is comfortable, but, like most Koreans his age, he remembers when things were different. In his youth most farming was done by hard stoop labor, and one family could manage only a small farm. Fields were reaped with a sickle, and every day for weeks afterward farmers like Chang had to spread dried sheaves in their courtyards and thresh them with a flail. Wives had to separate the grain from the the chaff with winnowing baskets, and husk each day's grain laboriously with a mortar and pestle.[1] With so much hand labor necessary for survival, households had to be large, however, so the village was full of young people with high spirits and willing hands. Now, at the age of seventy, Chang's recollections are hazy and the thick dialect he speaks difficult to understand, but he remembers playing gong in the farmer's band that went through the village during peak agricultural periods drumming up enthusiasm for work. There were also drum players and dancers, and like many such bands found in rural Korea during those days they

3

carried a banner with the traditional saying written in Chinese characters: *Nongsa ch'ŏnha taebon.*

"Agriculture is the foundation of the world," it said, and in the sense that most of the production that supported all classes of Korean society was agricultural production, this was literally true in Korea. As late as 1960, agriculture, forestry, and fisheries accounted for almost two-fifths of the gross national product—twice as much as industry (Mason et al. 1980:100)—and Korea was fundamentally a society of peasants. Almost 60 percent of the people of Korea were farmers and more than 70 percent of the population lived outside the major urban areas. Urban traditions and urban life were still tainted by their association with the Japanese who had dominated city life during the recently ended colonial period. The problems of Korea were the problems of the peasant, and to understand Korea one had to understand the rural villages. The words that Yi Kwangsu, Korea's foremost prewar novelist, put in the mouth of Hŏ Sung, the protagonist of his 1933 novel, *Soil,* were still apropos: "If you say Korea, aren't the peasant masses 80 percent of the population? Isn't food, too, the most important of life's materials, with clothing coming next? When you look at it like this, and speak of those peasants over there, aren't they the root of the Korean people? Their trunk?" (Yi Kwangsu 1975:60)

In the decade following the Korean War many of South Korea's rural districts held over one thousand persons per square kilometer. Sangongni, being in a mountain district, was less densely settled than many other Korean districts of the time. In the township in which the village is situated, population densities ran around seventy-five persons per square kilometer. The density per square kilometer of agricultural land, on the other hand, came to around one thousand persons. Informants say Sangongni had some 150 households, which would have included about nine hundred residents. Some 90 percent of the villagers made their living by farming, but holdings were small and productivity much lower than it is today. The average household holding of riceland could not have been much more than one-third of a hectare and of rainfall field only slightly more. Improved seed and commercial fertilizers were once again just becoming available at prices farmers could afford after the disruptions of the first years after liberation and of the Korean War, but production could barely keep up with population growth. At prevailing levels of productivity—about 2.2 metric tons per hectare for unhusked rice and perhaps 700 kilograms per hectare for the major rainfall field crops such as barley, millet, and sorghum (United Nations Korea Reconstruction Agency 1954:88–89)—a farmer with a small holding of perhaps two-thirds of a hectare could count on producing just barely enough food to feed himself and his family. Some 80 percent of his production was consumed at home and money, that scarce commodity, was used only to pay taxes and buy a few tools. Many householders experienced periods of hunger—especially in the spring when their rice was consumed and the barley was not yet ready for harvest. Those who owned little or no land had to make ends meet through day labor, handicrafts, or animal husbandry. Some, driven by hunger, would harvest crops before they were ripe, parch the grain, and eat it.

Chang and his fellow villagers were almost totally self-sufficient. Like most other Korean villagers of his time, Chang would have marketed only about 20 to 30 percent of his crop and consumed the rest (Han'guk ŭnhaeng 1958:I–125). He was only peripherally concerned with affairs outside his village and household. This was probably just as well, however, because agricultural prices were depressed. It was hard to get ahead by any means. Being so close to the subsistence margin meant that even a moderate fall in crop yields due to drought or blight, or a small fall in crop prices assumed major proportions. Most people considered themselves lucky to make it from one crisis to the next. People had a proverb for life: *san kŏnnŏ san itta;* over the mountains are mountains; as soon as you overcome one crisis, the next one looms.

In 1983, Sangongni was still a peasant village, and almost 90 percent of the villagers still made their living primarily by farming, but it was not the Sangongni of a generation ago. Fields were still reaped with sickles, but threshing, winnowing, and husking were all done mechanically. There were only 97 households in the village, and 397 people. Average farm size had risen to 1.36 hectares. High-yield strains of rice were routinely sprouted in plastic greenhouses before being set out in fields with ample inputs of fertilizer and pesticide. Yields for rice and other crops had risen to among the highest in the world. Chang and his fellow villagers could routinely expect yields of 5.4 metric tons or more per hectare of unhusked rice and 1.8 metric tons per hectare of grain crops on rainfall fields. At least three-quarters of what he produced was over and above what he needed for subsistence and entered the circulation system of the Korean economy. Although the villagers were still self-sufficient in food staples such as rice, barley, and major vegetables, other foods such as noodles, liquor, meat, and fruits were regularly purchased at the local periodic markets. Since most of the crop was marketed, crop prices were a vital concern. They all needed money for electricity, phone calls, fertilizer, pesticides, pumps, clothes, and school fees for the education they had to provide their children if they were going to succeed in today's Korea.

The villagers of Sangongni have a higher standard of living than ever before, but they are also more dependent upon outside forces than ever before.[2] They depend upon the local branch of the Agricultural Cooperative Federation to provide them with improved seed, fertilizer, agricultural chemicals, agricultural machinery, and to effectively market their crops. To keep their competitive position in village and national agriculture they must constantly improve their techniques, so they need to be able to read the agricultural pamphlets put out by Agricultural Guidance Office about improved farming practices and new crops. Such a large proportion of their crop is marketed that they now must watch agricultural prices closely and make a guess as to which crops, both those controlled by the government and those allowed to fluctuate with international markets, will be the most profitable. They adjust their cropping patterns now, so that they can maximize their income when they dispose of their crop. They also must make decisions, at the prodding of the government, about how to spend their time and money for village improvements made under the auspices of the New Village Movement.

Today, Korea is predominantly an urban-industrial society. Two-thirds of the population live in cities and agriculture accounts for less than one-fifth of the national GNP. Those who have remained in the countryside have substantially improved their standard of living. Even the poorest households are equipped with televisions and radios that link them to town and provide them with national and international news. With the rural exodus that began in the sixties and continues only slightly abated in the eighties, villagers have brothers, sisters, aunts, uncles, or cousins living in Seoul or Ch'unch'ŏn. No longer can a farmer assume that his children will make a living on the land. Most families have a representative in the city, and constant circulation between town and country of people and goods knits the country together. If he can't make it in the country, perhaps a man can in the city. The opposite is also true, as the occasional returnee from the city will attest. Children can sometimes get factory jobs, and the remittances from these can be used to put a sibling through school or to buy a new parcel of land. The villagers of Sangongni have been ineluctably drawn into Korea's new urban-industrial future.

What has brought about this tremendous change in rural life? How is it that only Korea and Taiwan, of the nonpetroleum-exporting, developing countries, have been able to sustain growth rates of more than 7.0 percent for a generation and aspire to the ranks of the developed countries? The "Korean miracle," of course, has not gone unnoticed in the world press or in academia. Over the past few years, economists and others have diligently searched for its causes and consequences. A recent series of books on Korean development,[3] for example, has included volumes on foreign trade and aid, urbanization, rural development, education, modernization, and entrepreneurship. The outlines of Korean development are now fairly well known. Industrialization was achieved through the creation of export-oriented large industries financed, in large part, with foreign capital. Agriculture provided little of the capital for growth and, rather than leading development, lagged behind until finally stimulated by expanded urban markets, raised government price supports, and increasing supplies of key inputs such as improved seed and fertilizer (Ban, Moon, and Perkins 1980:3–10). But all along, the rural villages were supplying the labor for the growth of industries and of cities.

These facts are well known, but their importance for village social structure has been inadequately dealt with. We know from statistical studies that changes have taken place in rural Korea. We know, for example, that the living standard has risen, that people are better educated, that farms are larger and population smaller. We know that there has been a massive rural to urban migration for the past twenty years, and we can even make a guess as to who the migrants have been, judging from the continuous aging of the rural population. The meaning of these changes for rural social organization is more difficult to fathom, however. Has rural social organization been fundamentally altered? Are the important rural social units—the family, lineage, hamlet, and village—organized on different principles than when Chang was in his prime?

The nature of changes in village organization during a period of rapid development forms the core of this study. The power of urbanization and industrialization to promote social mobilization and transform society from "traditional" to "modern," of course, is one of the classic themes of the social sciences from the time of Marx, Tönnies, and Weber to Parsons and Eisenstadt. Whatever the causes of industrialization, for example, we know that a result is a tremendous increase in the division of labor, a constant and increasing substitution of mechanical for manual or draft labor, an increase in employment for wages in large, bureaucratically run factories, the creation of a need for technically trained managers, and a tremendous expansion of the importance of market relations in all parts of society. All of these innovations in production are seen by most social theorists as potent forces promoting change from traditional social relations based on multistranded ties of kinship and inherited status to more single-purpose social relations based on "rational" or utilitarian considerations such as merit, efficiency, or profit (Potter 1968). Modern means of transportation, moreover, allow the concentration of industrial, commercial, financial, administrative, and communication facilities in central places so that cities become the place of residence of the largest proportion of the population. Urban residence exposes people to large, heterogeneous populations, and an extremely specialized and competitive occupational structure where social mobility is possible, and utility and efficiency at a premium (Wirth 1938). Urbanization, thus, is seen along with industrialization as a potent force breaking down traditional classes and modes of social interaction based on kinship and traditional status, and a force promoting the impersonal, single-purpose, utilitarian, social relations thought to be characteristic of modern societies.

With the rapid industrialization and urbanization of Korea, then, we expect to find radical changes in Korean society, but in a rural village like Sangongni, we run into a contradiction: those social forces that are often thought to be the cause of change in modern industrial societies are, by and large, absent. When we look at the industrialization of South Korea as a whole, of course, we find indeed that the division of labor has increased, wage labor has become predominant, the market has expanded, a need for technicians has increased, and utilitarian relations that give relatively little consideration to traditional status and kinship norms are used. Although this is true of Korea as a whole, it is not true of Sangongni. Unlike what has been reported for more accessible villages in Korea (Janelli and Janelli 1982:19; Kendall 1985:48), and unlike what has been reported for former pure farming and fishing villages in Japan (Dore 1978:93; Norbeck 1978:264; R. J. Smith 1978:114–29) and generally in Taiwan (Harrell 1981; Gallin and Gallin 1982; Hu 1983), Sangongni has not experienced a growth in wage labor or the influx of local small-scale industry. What is true of industrialization, moreover, is also true of urbanization. Sangongni has been profoundly affected by migration out of the village, but those who leave for urban jobs stay permanently in the city. Returnees are too few as yet to profoundly affect local social relations. Although Sangongni and villages like it have provided the population that has streamed into the cities during Korea's industrialization, none of the characteristics of the city that are thought to transform the social relations of traditional villagers—large size, heterogeneous population, impersonality, a complex and competitive division of labor—even remotely apply to a village like Sangongni. If modernization is thought of as social mobilization—raising one's standard of living, using mechanical sources of motive power, using the telephone, responding to the mass media, and acquiring modern education—then indeed Sangongni is modernizing, but insofar as modernization requires as a mechanism of transformation a direct contact with those characteristics of industrialization and urbanization outlined above, it should be absent from rural villages like Sangongni.

Because of the national integration of economy and society, however, the influence of industrialization cannot be confined simply to those persons who participate in wage labor and urban life. Even in the past, Korea's villages were not totally self-sufficient, but were affected by developments in the larger society. Some of the surplus that was generated by peasant farmers was siphoned off to enter the national circulation system. Both before and during the Japanese colonial period (1910–45), some peasant production was marketed directly by producers or used to pay taxes, though the largest amount of produce that entered the circulation system was paid as share rent to landlords and marketed by them. In addition to the small number of urban merchants, professionals, and bureaucrats, there was a large landlord class whose subsistence depended on peasant labor (Gragert 1982; H. K. Lee 1936). Korea, thus, was already a stratified society with a division of labor by class. Not all persons produced what they consumed, and different types of specialists tended to be geographically concentrated. Functionally distinct settlements—religious communities, agricultural villages, market towns, cities—had already emerged and were knitted together economically by the circulation of goods and services. Agricultural villages like Sangongni were specialized subunits of a larger whole. The recent industrialization of Korea has intensified this national division of labor. Now there are more types of settlement and many more specialized interdependent niches in the socioeconomic order, but Sangongni's niche has remained much the same: provision of raw agricultural materials—primarily subsistence materials—for the maintenance of villagers and a portion of the other more specialized classes of society.

The consequences for rural life of the differentiation and integration of society in which villages such as Sangongni are part of a national and international division of labor united through market relations has been an important element of those few works that have attempted a comprehensive analysis of the effect of capitalist industrialization on peasant farmers. Taking their cue from elements of the works of Marx and Engels (Marx and Engels 1955; Marx 1969), such writers as Kautsky (1899) and Lenin (1964) have elaborated an integrated theory of how peasant societies should be transformed during capitalist modernization and development. These theories focus on the changes in rural class structure that should follow the development of commodity production and the integration of peasant farms into national and international markets. Kautsky, for example, thought the destruction of household handicraft production by competition from more efficient industrial enterprises would force peasants to purchase on the market what they formerly produced at home. This, along with increased taxes caused by gentry and landlords who themselves would require more money for the purchase of new manufactures, would force peasants to switch from production for home use to the production of agricultural commodities for sale on the market to earn money. Penetration of the market into peasant societies, however, would make farmers prey to price fluctuations and the manipulation of middlemen. Their greater need for money would force them to increase the scale of their agriculture to survive, but land would often not be available. Instead, sons and daughters, who no longer would have winter employment in handicrafts, would become surplus and would have to migrate from the farm to become wage laborers. Back on the farm this would create seasonal shortages of labor that could only be overcome by hiring temporary wage workers.

The ultimate result of this market participation would be the penetration of capitalist relations of production, based on the contradiction between ownership of the means of production and wage labor, into the countryside where they had not existed before. Only those relatively large landowners who would be able to increase the scale of their agriculture through the use of hired labor would be able to successfully switch to commodity production. The middle and small peasants who relied on their own family labor would not be able to produce on a scale large enough to support themselves, and, faltering more with each successive agricultural crisis, would fall prey to moneylenders and eventually lose their land. No longer controlling means of production, these peasants would become "proletarianized"—would have to live by selling their labor to capitalists in either a rural or urban setting. The industrialization of the cities, then, would lead to increasing differentiation between rural entrepreneurs who cultivate cash crops using hired labor, and peasant proletarians who, having lost their land, would have no choice but to supply the wage labor for these commercial agricultural enterprises.

In place of the old peasant family partnership, which works its own estate exclusively with its own forces, a swarm of hired workers come into the larger peasant establishments to till the fields, herd the cattle and bring in the harvest under the command of the property owner. The class contradiction between the exploiter and the exploited, between the owners and the proletarians, penetrates into the village, yes, even into the peasant household itself, and destroys the old harmony and community of interests. . . . So the development of the capitalist mode of production in the city alone is already capable of completely revolutionizing the basis of peasant existence in the old sense, even without capital making its entrance into agricultural production and creating the contradictions between large and small enterprises. [Kautsky 1899:13]

Certain of these processes first noticed in Europe in the nineteenth century have also been apparent in Sangongni and other Korean villages during Korea's recent rapid industrialization. Handicrafts, which had already been receding in importance during the early years of this century, are now almost totally absent, though most women over fifty can still recall weaving in their youth. There has been greater and greater participation in the market as people develop more income and urban tastes. A massive migration of farmers to the city, where many of them have become wage workers, has led to a fall in rural population and a decrease in family size as surplus sons and daughters have sought employment outside the family farm. Many people have shifted from exclusive reliance on subsistence crops to more remunerative cash crops, and this has been accompanied by a gradual increase in farm size.

In other respects, however, the change in the social organization of Korean villages like Sangongni does not conform to the expectations of Kautsky's model. Although the class structure of Korea as a whole and of Sangongni has changed as a result of Korea's development, these changes cannot be adequately described in terms of the development of capitalist farming and the proletarianization of the small and middle peasants. Even after twenty years of rapid development, land ownership, which was reformed during the Korean War, has not become seriously concentrated by world standards (see chap. 6). Farm size has gradually increased in rural Korea as migrants have left and sold or rented their land, but the integration of urban and rural labor markets that has been made possible by the improvements in communication and the massive migrations these improvements have made possible, have led to rural shortages of labor and a precipitous rise in agricultural wages rather than the immiseration of the peasantry expected by Kautsky (Kuramochi 1985). All of this has been accompanied by the use of less rather than more hired labor (Dong-hi Kim 1979; Chŏng Yŏngil 1984:46), with almost 80 percent of the farm labor continuing to be supplied by family members.

Far from being forced out by an inability to make ends meet, most urban migrants have left behind viable farms where they could continue, if they desired, to provide a subsistence for themselves and their families. What has brought them out of the villages under these conditions is the realistic expectation since the mid-sixties that they will be able to improve their own lots, or those of their children. The middle peasants, whom Lenin and others (Lenin 1899; Banaji 1976) have expected to be one of the main victims of proletarization, have been the main rural beneficiaries of the developments of the past twenty years. Urban migrants have come in large numbers both from the smallest and the largest rural landowners (cf. Brandt and Lee 1981:111). Although a large proportion of these migrants have indeed become wage workers who do not own their means of production, many have used the income from sold land to invest in businesses or education. Koo and Hong (1980), in fact, found that in Seoul the largest proportion of both capitalist and petit bourgeois house heads in a random neighborhood sample were of rural background, and that these small capitalists and businessmen of rural origin make up a very large proportion of the population (15.3 percent and 32.7 percent, respectively).

The reasons the expectations of Marxists such as Kautsky and Lenin have not been fully realized lie not so much with their idea that increasing rural participation in markets will follow the industrialization of cities and change peasant life, but with their faith in the necessary superior efficiency of large-scale organization, their disregard of the possible independent effects of the interaction of population and environment, and their consequent too-rigid ideas of the conditions made both necessary and possible by capitalism.[4] Although the consequences they expected have been approximated in certain times and places—even Korea itself during the Japanese colonial period (Grajdanzev 1944:105–22)—the way prices have been set, capital invested, and productivity improved in Korea since 1960 have led to conditions of employment and wage structure that were not predicted by Marxist theory.

Kautsky and others, both Marxist and non-Marxist (Lenin 1899:38; Scott 1976:9), have often seen participation in market relations as the penetration of new forces into a peasant economy for which such relations are alien, and thus have given insufficient attention to possible opportunities provided to peasants by the market in specific situations (Popkin 1979:69). Kautsky thought, for example, that increases in production brought about by the need for money would glut the market and bring down prices, so that peasants would become worse rather than better off as they intensified production (1899:11–12). In any case, the importation of agricultural commodities from colonies or countries with "oriental despotism," where extreme exploitation of the peasants would be the rule, was expected to drive prices below the subsistence level for small-scale agriculturalists (1899:240–41). Neither Lenin nor Kautsky dreamed, however, that urban demand would be able to drive prices up or that governments would find the will or the way to reform land-tenure relations, artificially support crop prices, and provide means by which small-scale producers could obtain access to modern technology and capital at reasonable rates of interest. In Korea and other East Asian countries, the rapid growth of urban manufacture for export has opened up urban jobs, thus relieving rural underemployment, and has made possible rapid real gains in urban wages, which have rebounded back into the countryside to raise wages there as well (Potter 1968:179). The small-scale peasants of rural Korea simply have had opportunities and choices open to them that could not have been envisioned as recently as a generation ago.

Thus although Sangongni would have to be classified among the poorest and remotest third of villages in Korea, it has been integrated into a complex national polity and economy for some time. Its demographic structure and agricultural base have both been drastically affected by the urbanization and industrialization that have taken place elsewhere in Korea. More than half of all the children born in the village between 1941 and 1970 now live in major cities in all parts of Korea. Because of its integration into the world economy, moreover, the decisions that seem most to affect the villagers are made in Seoul, Tokyo, London, and New York, rather than at home in the village. Price controls on major crops are administered centrally from Seoul. During the fifties and early sixties, when keeping urban grain

prices down was the major concern of the government, low government purchase prices depressed rural living standards and encouraged
rural to urban migration in spite of high urban unemployment. When,
in response to a widening urban-rural gap in the standard of living,
the government reversed this policy in the early seventies, rural living
standards began to improve and capital investment become more feasible for rural dwellers. Prices for other rural products have been affected by international actions. When the Japanese in 1977 decided to
restrict the importation of raw silk cocoons to protect their own farmers from Korean competition, this important village cash crop immediately became relatively less attractive. Villagers, who learned about
the action within a day of its announcement in Japan, assumed that
eventually cocoon prices would fall because of it.

With Kautsky and others, then, we can accept the principle that the
larger social and economic context in which villagers operate conditions their behavior. This truism only states the theme of our inquiry,
however. Which specific conditions have affected the villagers, what
processes have achieved the effects, and what the over-all consequences of these processes have been for village social structure remain to be determined. There is more to social structure than economic organization and class relations, and it would be a mistake to
treat Sangongni and villages like it as a residual category: as simply
what has been created by industrialization elsewhere, urbanization
elsewhere, and integration into markets administered and manipu-
lated elsewhere. Village life had a coherence and integrity before industrialization began, and it continues to do so. If in one sense the
villagers are the object upon which social forces beyond their control
operate, they also have important social resources at their disposal.
The material and political conditions within which they operate may
constrain their moves, but they don't fully determine the goals toward
which the villagers direct their behavior, nor do they fully determine
their lives. It is within the realm of possibility that the changes in
village life we have noted above are mostly superficial and that the
villagers of Sangongni are organizing their lives according to the same
principles they always have—just with a higher standard of living.

CHAPTER 2

Development without Structural Change in Sangongni Households

How is it possible for there to be dramatic change in the circumstances of people's lives without there being change in the social structure of their households, the most crucial institution for their survival? For those anthropologists and sociologists who prefer to define social structure in terms of social relations (Radcliffe-Brown 1965) or in terms of patterns of behavior (Murdock 1949), this would be a contradiction in terms. One could take a village like Sangongni, identify a series of role dyads and define social structure in terms of the reciprocal behavior expected and observed of the incumbents of these role dyads. If the relations between incumbents of role dyads changed, the social structure would be seen as changing. Thus, for example, the central importance of the father-eldest son dyad in rural Korean households might be noted, along with the expectation that eldest sons will live with and support their parents in their old age. As the frequency of patrilocal marriage among eldest sons declined, one could talk about social change—most likely in terms of the breakdown of traditional household structure. Alternatively, one could segment and classify patterns of observed behavior and perhaps statistically summarize the frequency of each pattern, calling the resulting contingency table the social structure. It could be recorded that on the night before the death anniversary of an ancestor up to four or five generations removed, sacrifices are held in the house of the eldest male descendant in the seniormost line. It could also be noted that men exchange labor with each other to transplant rice, and record the frequency of this behavior. Whether the analysis is in terms of frequency of patterns of behavior or in terms of dyadic social relations, however, any substantial changes in social interaction will necessarily require a new description of the social structure and thus could be described as "structural change."

By these criteria, of course, we already know that Sangongni has been in a process of change for some time. Villagers now take rice to the mill to be polished rather than husking it at home. They sometimes watch television rather than go to a friend's house to socialize. They send their children to school rather than have them work on the farm, and eldest sons sometimes move to town rather than live with their father. But while these methods of describing social structure are admirably direct and fairly replicable,[1] they have serious limitations. The number of dyadic relations considered in a society may be extended "almost indefinitely" (Lévi-Strauss 1963:304). One has no method for deciding which patterns are basic and which ones superficial (Leach 1961:31). The idea of social structure, moreover, signifies something "of more than purely momentary significance" (Firth 1951:30). If social structure is defined in terms of patterns of behavior, then, an implicit assumption that these patterns are rather stereotyped and stable is introduced. If contemporary observation of society does not justify this assumption, stability of stereotypic behavior may then be imputed to the past with variation in the present being interpreted as the result of acculturation, the introduction of market relations, or the breakdown of social norms (anomie). Yet historical study of those societies for which good documentation exists gives us little reason to suppose behavior patterns in the past were any less various in complex societies than in the present (*see* Wolf and Huang 1981). In past years many residents of Sangongni participated enthusiastically in folk religious activity, for example, but even then many others looked on such activity as base superstition unworthy of a virtuous man or woman.

When the village is considered in the context of Korea as a whole, moreover, these problems multiply. Not all villages are characterized by the same patterns of behavior. In some villages lineages are well developed and highly ramified, while in others they are not. In some villages ancestor worship is done on the veranda, while in others, such as Sangongni, it is done in the inner room. In some villages, a great deal of hired labor is used, while in others labor exchange is more common. The statistical pattern of concrete activity of each of these villages is somewhat different from other villages, yet all are Korean and they surely must share a common core. How is one to deal with this inconsistency and variation? It is possible to suppose that variations in patterns of observed behavior are the manifestation of different, competing ethical systems such as the hierarchical lineage-based and egalitarian community-based ethics proposed by Brandt for Korea (1971:25–28). Alternatively one might hypothesize that such variation is the expression of differential class adherence to social ideals, as Hsu has done to explain variation in the complexity of Chinese family organization (1943:561; 1959:129). In each of these cases, however, the reasons why some people adhere to one set of norms and some to another, or why many individuals do not consistently follow the same set of norms on all occasions or throughout their life cycle remain to be explained. What, in other words, motivates people to follow or not follow a given set of norms? Do we have to assume that people always unthinkingly follow the norms provided them by circumstances? Or, perhaps, do we assume that whatever people do, it must be the expression of some internalized set of norms?

That Korean villages, like their Chinese and Japanese counterparts, exhibit variation is not particularly surprising but does point to the necessity of developing a more sophisticated framework for dealing with village social life than description and summary of patterns of behavior (Goodenough 1961:525; 1971). We can begin, following Raymond Firth, by distinguishing the patterns of concrete activity observed in the field, the *social organization,* from principles by which activity is organized, or *social structure* (Firth 1951:28–36). It is the social organization, rather than social structure, that is described by statistical models of the observed behavior of individuals (Lévi-Strauss 1963:286). The same sorts of things that motivate individuals also underlie social organization. We can assume that much of this behavior is purposive and rational: that is, given certain assumptions about the world and how it works, much behavior can be seen as a logical means by which a certain end may be achieved (Frank Cancian 1966; Bennett 1976:35; Popkin 1979:31).[2] Even seemingly irrational behavior may often turn out to be rational if the assumptions shared by the actor and other members of his society about the nature of the world, the goals one should seek, the values that are important, and the means most likely to be successful—in other words, the culture of the society—are accepted. A rural Korean who is ill, for example, may request a shaman to perform an exorcism to cure the illness. Although this behavior might be considered irrational in the context of modern medicine, if one accepts traditional Korean operating assumptions about the world and the etiology of sickness—that sickness is caused by restless spirits that will not leave a person alone until properly appeased (Kendall 1985)—the behavior becomes rational. The means chosen should logically (though not necessarily empirically) bring about the desired end.

To the extent that the actions of individuals are dependent upon assumptions about the nature of the world, appropriate goals, and effective techniques learned by them as members of society, the culture of social groups can be seen as one of the sources of the distinctiveness and regularity of a group's social organization. That part of culture consisting of shared principles for the regulation of social behavior may be called *social structure*. Like other parts of culture, social structure is not absolutely determinative. It does not consist of rules telling one how to behave in each situation, but rather is made of the principles one uses to decide what behavior is appropriate to attain a particular end in a particular situation. Until the circumstances under which this seeking must be done are known, however, which rules come into play and how they work to mold social organization remain indeterminate.

The structural rule for succession to the house headship in Korea, for example, is primogeniture: the eldest son should always succeed to the headship of the household upon the death of his father. This rule, of course, depends upon the condition that there be an eldest son. When there is no eldest son, other rules come into play: adoption of an agnate, the acquisition of a concubine, or the arrangement of an uxorilocal marriage for one's daughter. Each of these alternatives is more or less disagreeable, but which one will be chosen will depend upon further circumstances such as how much land is owned by the household, and how vigorous the surviving widow is (if there is one). The fission stage of the family cycle operates in a similar fashion. Today, only eldest sons can marry patrilocally, while younger sons must marry neolocally. This means that younger sons must leave home at or before their marriage. The age at which they leave home, whether they marry at the time of leaving or later, and the age at which they do marry are all not regulated by social structural rules, however. These aspects of behavior do vary with such circumstances as what career the son is preparing for, whether labor is needed on the family farm, and whether his parents can afford to set him up in housekeeping. Or again, the organization of lineages and participation in tombside ancestor worship ceremonies in the autumn (*sije*) was considered very desirable in traditional Korea. Everyone is descended in the male line from someone and thus everyone at least potentially belongs to a lineage, but in fact, lineages were organized only by some rural people. This is not only because one required property that could be deeded to a lineage organization to finance the expensive *sije*, but also because some people who had the requisite wealth were in an unfavorable genealogical position and thus not inclined to invest their resources in an activity that would enhance others' status more than their own.

Examples could be multiplied, but I think the point has been made: behavior and thus social organization are the result of the interaction of social structure—cultural principles for organizing social behavior—with concrete circumstances (Goodenough 1961:525; 1971:30–32). The circumstances that can condition social structure are extremely various and include both environmental factors such as productivity of crops and social factors such as the rate of tenancy. At their simplest, as in the demographic example above, the application of a social structural rule may depend upon whether a particular kinship role is occupied or not. Other cases, however, can be more complex. In the organization of a lineage, for example, whether a structural option is chosen or not depends upon a complex calculus of relative advantage. Is a man better off donating his land to a lineage organization and going for prestige through conspicuous consumption of high-status rituals,[3] or is he better off husbanding his wealth and using it directly for the satisfaction of his needs, but risking being classified as a vulgar know-nothing?

This kind of decision making, of course, is the typical means-end minimax calculation familiar to us from economics. Until the goals toward which this calculation is directed are known, however, which course of action is most rational cannot be determined (Goodenough 1971:30; Godelier 1972:9). In many cases, the goal toward which calculation is directed is the familiar one of maximization of pecuniary profit, but this is not a necessary assumption of the framework outlined here. The solution to the above problem of whether to organize a lineage, for example, really involves a choice between profit goals and social status goals, either of which can be rationally sought within the framework of Korean society.[4] Since such choices can be made, neither the rules of social structure nor the circumstances that condition the operation of these rules (social forces) are sufficient to fully determine social organization. It is clear that each social actor has a decisive role to play as a decision maker (Barth 1967). Rather than follow rules, he formulates a goal-directed strategy for manipulating them to attain desirable goals in light of his personal circumstances.[5]

The explanatory task of the anthropologist, then, cannot be confined to describing the rules of social structure, or even these plus the circumstances in which they are applied. To fully explain people's rational behavior in a particular society,[6] it is necessary to account for observed variation in behavior by specifying the cultural principles upon which all legitimate behavioral variants are based in the society, the various goals toward which they are directed, and the circumstances that make one strategy objectively more rational (more capable of attaining specified goals) than another for particular people in particular circumstances (Barth 1981:15). Although informants are seldom capable of fully specifying their cultural knowledge, goals, or strategies as such (Boas 1911:67; Malinowski 1922:12; Lévi-Strauss 1963:281–82), the demonstration that observed behavior would suffice for people to attain culturally recognized goals in observed circumstances justifies inferences about goals and strategies, and the construction of models of social structure based on them.[7] Once this is done, what at first blush seems like structural change can often be analyzed as a shift in goals or strategies conditioned by new circumstances, but with the same social structure. Most changes in Sangongni household organization in the last twenty years, in fact, are precisely of this sort. It is argued, for example, in chapter 6 that the fall in household size and the migration of successors from rural households does not necessarily mean the demise of the corporate stem family, but rather a new strategy, based on traditional principles, for the allocation of household labor in response to the opportunities of industrialization.

Kautsky, Steward, and Chayanov: Structure, Function, and Adaptation

Changing economic circumstances (production costs, wage structure, conditions of access to means of production, market opportunities), changing environmental circumstances (resource bases, man/land ratios, cropping regimes), changing demographic circumstances (birth rates, death rates, rates of migration), or changing political circumstances may make old strategies untenable, may make different strategies for attaining traditional goals feasible, or may make it possible for the members of a society to attain previously impossible goals. In each case circumstances can be a potent factor encouraging social change. This fact has encouraged many social scientists to think of conditioning circumstances as "social forces" which in some sense "cause" changes in social organization, or even cause specific social relations themselves. In the crudest cases, the physical metaphor of force is taken literally, and various social or economic circumstances are seen as direct and independent causes of social organization (Buckley 1967:8), but even in more subtle analyses the use of the metaphor of physical force still has the insidious effect of discounting the role of individual actors within the social system and obscuring the need to account for the variety of their options, the variousness of their goals, and the precise nature of their motivation. In the more subtle analyses of peasant societies, the efficacy of the forces are seen to reflect a necessity either of internally generated development, as in Kautsky and Chayanov, or of relations to the external environment, as in the cultural ecology of Julian Steward.

The explanation for social change that underlies Kautsky's and Lenin's analyses of the impact of industrialization on peasant farmers is based on what Rader (1979) would call a "fundamentalist" interpretation of Marx. In this interpretation, the wide influence of which is attributed by Llobera (1979:253) to Engels, the impact of industrialization on peasant farms rests on the functional integration between forces and relations of production, and between the base and superstructure of society. The forces of production are seen to require certain corresponding relations of production that individuals enter into "independently of their will" (Marx 1971:8). When the forces of production become developed enough, they necessarily come in conflict with the relations of production and lead to a period of upheaval in which the relations of production again are brought into conformity with the forces of production, forming a new economic foundation, or mode of production. Because of the functional integration between the mode of production, or base of society, and the rest of the social structure and culture, or the superstructure of society, this change in the mode of production will sooner or later lead to the transformation of the whole society. Thus in Kautsky's analysis of agrarian change under capitalism, the main source of change is the development of new forces of production in the cities—machines and mechanical power. These machines and mechanical power were assumed by Kautsky and others to operate most efficiently only with certain relations of production, that is, in large-scale factories with a wage labor force. Most of Kautsky's analysis in *The Agrarian Question*, then, is devoted to showing how the superior efficiency of factories based on wage labor will eventually force peasants, through the processes of immiseration and proletarianization, to enter the relations of production characteristic of capitalist industrial society. All the effects of industrialization, then, are traced back to changes in forces of production.

This explanation of social change, which is most clearly and suc-cinctly stated in Marx's famous sketch of his theory of history in "Preface to *A Contribution to a Critique of Political Economy*" (Marx 1971:8–9),[8] rests on four assumptions: (1) that there is a necessary one-to-one functional correspondence between the forces and rela-tions of production such that at a particular stage of the development of the forces of production there can ultimately be one and only one set of relations of production;[9] (2) there is a less fixed functional cor-respondence between the mode of production (the base) and the rest of the institutions of society (the superstructure); (3) the forces of pro-duction change according to their own inner necessity, and thus are the independent variable in social change; and (4) there are no signif-icant objective choices available to people in their entry into relations of production, so their consciousness and their motivation as individ-uals for engaging in economic and other activity are irrelevant for the long-term development of the system.

These basic assumptions upon which fundamentalist Marxist theory is built all have an element of plausibility, but most of them cannot be accepted in an unmodified form. While it is certainly true, for example, that people do not choose the relations of production (the forms of property ownership, the way surpluses are appropriated and the way labor is compensated) available to them in their society, one cannot assume by that fact that individual decision-making is ir-relevant. In Sangongni, as in most societies, people make economic choices. Each individual has, at any time, a range of options for access to means of production and for engaging in occupations with various types of distribution of the products of their labor. These options, the goals toward which people orient themselves, and the decisions they make are discussed in detail for Sangongni in chapter 7. However, as has been elegantly demonstrated by Heston (1971) in his discussion of the Indian cattle complex, people's goals are culturally specific. A person's most rational strategy of action cannot be deduced from first principles, and the direction of change cannot be determined a priori. One reason the consequences Lenin and Kautsky expected to result from the spread of market relations into peasant society have not been borne out in Sangongni is that villagers have not entered into wage labor and market relations as a matter of necessity, but as a means of improving their material well-being at a time when subsistence agri-culture was still a viable but less remunerative option. As is shown in more detail in chapters 6 and 7, the efficacy of changed circumstances in this case did not come from pepole being forced to engage in new relations of production, but from the motivation to engage in new types of behavior stemming from the possibility that newly available relations of production (new circumstances) could be used in new strategies to attain old, as well as new, culturally specific goals.

However limited they may seem, the existence of choices, as defined by the social and economic structure and the availability of resources in particular cases, makes the one-to-one correspondence between forces and relations of production necessary for Kautsky's analysis unlikely. One need only note, perhaps, the wide variety of economic systems founded upon similar technology and environment among people with similar cultural traditions in East Asia to suspect this is true. Due to the ambiguity of the precise referents of "forces of production" or "relations of production" in the works of Marx and Engels, it is difficult to formulate a rigorous test of the validity of their functional hypothesis (Adams 1981:604). One interpretation would list "labor power, raw materials, tools, techniques and the organization of working personnel" under forces of production, and "the division of labor" and "the economic class structure" (distribution of the means of production) under relations of production (Rader 1979:12; but see Wolpe 1980 for other interpretive possibilities). If this is an accurate appraisal of the intentions of Marx and Engels, then we can rephrase the fundamentalist interpretation of their theory something like this: the level of development of technology as applied under specific conditions of land, labor, and capital availability creates the social division of labor and the distribution of the means of production, which in turn condition social organization and culture. Stated this way, the affinity of Marxist analysis to cultural ecology as defined by Julian Steward is patent.

Steward's explanations, as Kautsky's, are causal: he wants to know the origin of particular cultural features, and operates with the hypothesis that the cultural core ("the constellation of features which are most closely related to subsistence activities and economic arrangements") will be determined by a society's complex technology and productive arrangements accumulated in the course of adaptation to the natural environment (Steward 1955:37–39). Steward proposed to study these causal relations in individual societies in three stages: (1) identify the interrelationship of productive technology and the environment; (2) identify the behavior patterns involved in exploiting a particular area by means of a particular technology; and (3) ascertain the extent to which these behavior patterns involved in exploiting the environment affect other aspects of culture (pp. 40–41). This research program could be restated in Marxist terminology with little distortion: ascertain whether specific forces of production require specific relations of production in specific environments and thus determine the mode of production. Then study the amount of influence the mode of production (the base) has on the superstructure of social, legal, religious, and ideological institutions.[10] Steward differs from fundamentalist Marxism in a number of important respects, however. He considers the assumption of a close functional relationship between forces and relations of production (between the application of technology in the environment and the cultural core) a hypothesis for scientific validation rather than an assumption upon which further analyses would be based. He is thus more flexible in his notions of the direction of cultural change, advocating multilinear evolution rather than the uniform sequence of evolutionary stages posited in most previous theories of social evolution. Equally significant is his emphasis on the explanatory value of the need to adapt to the environment.

By adaptation, one generally means the condition of fitting into the environment, or of acquiring the needs of the members of society without drastic degradation of the environment. In principle, thus, it is a simple requirement, but it is one that has been very hard to utilize in a way that is both cross-culturally valid and noncircular. Of course in the crudest sense, one can consider adaptation to be the provision of those basic goods that are necessary for the maintenance of life: perhaps 3000 kilocalories per day of food energy, 30 grams per day of protein, adequate water, and in cold climates, adequate shelter and clothing. The explanatory power of this fact, however, is limited. After all, if a society exists, or if a person exists, then by definition that society or person has satisfied the minimal requirements for life (Lévi-Strauss 1963:13). Although simple societies of hunters and gatherers may not be much above this level, the residents of complex societies have long since decided that the necessities of life are more various than those listed above, and it is impossible to make a catalogue of these necessities that would hold for all societies.

Nevertheless, Steward and many of those who have been inspired by his work often have been tempted by the fact that minimal adaptive requirements can sometimes be specified to assert that the necessity to satisfy adaptive requirements in a given environment with the technology at hand causes social organization (Ellen 1982:54). Such arguments usually rest upon the assumption that there are certain universal needs that must be met for a society to survive, and that the environment (which may be conceived, depending upon the study, either in the narrow sense of physical environment or in the broad sense of all things external to the society) presents problems that must be solved by the application of energy, technology, organization, and ingenuity for these needs to be met (Ember and Ember 1983:1–4). By solving such problems, societies achieve adaptation (sometimes, but not always, conceived of as homeostasis, the maintenance of things in a physiological equilibrium). In the vocabulary adopted here, this is equivalent to saying that technology and circumstances together determine behavior whose goal is always adaptation, or the solution of problems posed by the environment. In the strictest sense, however, a causal proposition can only be accepted after four conditions have been demonstrated for all cases for which causality is supposed to apply:[11] (1) the cause and the effect are spatially contiguous; (2) they are temporally contiguous (usually with the cause preceding the event in time); (3) the relationship is invariant (i.e., whenever the cause and enabling circumstances are present, the effect will take place); and (4) the relationship is asymmetrical (i.e., the flow of influence is always from cause to effect and never vice versa) (Nagel 1961:74–75). In a causal argument based on adaptation, the needs are usually conceived as the cause, the technology and environment as conditioning factors, and the social institution one is trying to explain as the effect. To show the needs to be the cause of an institution in such cases, the needs must be contiguous to the institution, and temporarily prior to it. The institution must be present at all times when the needs and the conditioning circumstances are present, and the existence of the needs must not depend upon the presence of the institution.

In the case of nutrition, the priority of the needs can easily be accepted without an historical demonstration. In other cases, however, the demonstration of temporal priority of the needs requires an historical perspective and a kind of documentation that has been almost impossible to achieve in anthropology. Apart from the minimal requirements for survival mentioned above, the only proof we often have of a hypothesized need is that there is an institution to satisfy it, and in such cases, the invariance and asymmetry of the hypothesized cause and effect relationship is clearly suspect (J. Friedman 1974:457). However, there are certain propositions that, if true, would allow us to accept adaptive necessity as causal even in the absence of historical documentation.

If, for example, it can be shown that survival is impossible unless a particular environmental problem is solved and if it is true that with a particular technology in a particular environment there is only one strategy that will solve the problem, then a causal role for adaptive requirements may be accepted even based on synchronic, or cross-sectional, analysis. Usually, as has already been mentioned above, however, alternatives to any particular strategy exist, and adaptive requirements cannot be shown to be the cause of institutions in this way (see also Freilich 1963). We can accept, for example, that the provision of food between December and May in mountain Korea is an environmental problem, since no crops can be harvested during this period and home-grown crops provide 90 percent of the village diet. As shown in chapter 4, moreover, there is some evidence of an elevation in death rates during this period that is correlated with marginal caloric intake. The village solution to this problem is to store staple crops in granaries for winter use, to preserve vegetables by pickling them in salt, red pepper, and garlic, and to consume special nutritious holiday and sacrificial foods. This is not the only possible solution to the problem, however. Domestic animals could be kept to provide milk and milk products over the winter, or summer crops could be exchanged for food items available from other parts of the country or from the ocean during the winter months. Thus, although pickling vegetables and storing grain are the solution to the problem of Korea's seasonality, Korea's seasonality cannot be considered the cause of this behavior, but rather a conditioning (or selective) factor. A fortiori, the social behavior associated with pickling vegetables, storing crops, and celebrating holidays and ancestor worship rites cannot be caused by the need to adapt to Korea's seasonality.

Even if the above proposition is not true, if the goal of all societies can be shown to be adaptation, and a cross-culturally valid operationalization of the concept of adaptation can be made, then a causal role for adaptive requirements may be accepted even without historical demonstration. The cultural materialism of Marvin Harris (1966; 1979) is based on this kind of argument (J. Friedman 1974:457). This differs from the above case in that the goal is assumed to be a general characteristic of all societies, rather than ones specific to particular times and places. By limiting societies to one goal, the direction of rationalization may be specified beforehand by the anthropologist and the number of "best" strategies often reduced, once a society's level of development is known, to one. This would be true, for example, if a process of social selection based on the "efficiency of adaptation" (however defined) were in operation. Those societies most efficiently adapted to the environment would tend to be selected and thus, over the long run, only those strategies that have been rationalized toward the goal of adaptation would survive. To utilize the concept of adaptation so that it can serve as the goal toward which all societies are rationalized, one must define it in such a way that a society's or institution's success of adaptation can be objectively measured in a cross-culturally valid way. Leslie White (1949), for example, proposed per capita energy use and the efficiency of that use as a measure of cultural development.[12] Alexander Alland (1970) has proposed that the effectiveness of adaptive traits be measured in terms of carrying capacity or increase in the population that are made possible by them. Richard Adams (1975:126) has proposed Lotka's Principle (Lotka 1922) that "those life forms that channel and degrade more energy will have a selective advantage over others." Others have proposed various input-output measures of which perhaps the best known is Marvin Harris's (1971) "technoenvironmental efficiency" formula.[13]

These operationalizations of the concept of adaptation, however, raise problems of the most formidable sort. Most of those that are easy to measure are in some respect counterintuitive. Population, for example, is easy to measure, but if population is a measure of adaptive success, then China would have to be considered the best adapted country in the world with India not far behind. Although energy consumption measures are intuitively more satisfying, it is difficult to define which energy flows are most important in specific cases, and unless relevant flows can be accurately measured, which strategy will lead to "evolutionary advance" is impossible to predict. Most sophisticated operationalizations of the concept of adaptation are based on assumptions of questionable validity and present almost insoluble technical problems of measurement. Formulae for carrying capacity, for example, are based on an assumption that technology and patterns of production and consumption will remain fixed as the carrying capacity is approached (Street 1969). Boserup (1965) and Hanks (1972), however, have shown that in many cases an increase in population can make a little-used but known intensification technique more attractive because increased population alters the value of variables in the production function. Even if we accept the assumption of unchanging technology, moreover, our techniques of measurement are often too crude to be useful (Street 1969). Finally, no one has been able to satisfactorily demonstrate the empirical reality of the assumption that society's goals can be reduced to one. It seems most useful, then, to regard the requirement for adaptation as a *constraint* or *se-*

lective factor on strategies, but not their cause. In chapter 7, for example, we will show how the village subsistence needs, population density, and productivity conditions household land-tenure and farming patterns, yet leaves room for a variety of strategies of household formation and migration and thus does not determine household or village social structure.

In spite of the difficulties of using adaptation for causal purposes the requirement for adaptation plays a crucial role in Steward's thought: it supplies the necessity (cf. Dore 1961:846). Both Kautsky's and Steward's theories of society are functionalist in the sense that their explanation of the reason for certain kinds of social organization in certain situations depends upon a necessary functional relationship between two parts of society; that is, it is assumed that the need for specific conditions in one part of society forces an institution in another part of society to assume a form in which it will be able to supply these conditions. For Kautsky the fit is between the forces and relations of production, and secondarily between the mode of production and superstructural institutions. For Steward the fit is between the application of a certain level of technology in a specific environment and the cultural core, and secondarily between the cultural core and the rest of the institutions of society. Both were aware, however, that a functional fit between two institutions is a symmetrical, noncausal relationship. One might show, for example, that loosely defined social groups in a hunting and gathering society facilitate the use of simple hunting technology in a particular environment, but unless one can show that the application of this technology is a prior requirement of social life, one's explanation lacks causal necessity. The need for adaptation, being one of the few needs that can be assumed to exist even without historical demonstration, thus plays a crucial role in the attempt to show causality in Steward's early synchronic studies. As the discussion above shows, however, the need for adaptation is almost impossible to use this way in a rigorous fashion. Steward seems to have realized this, and in his later work began to focus on historical change, where the establishment of causal priority of explanatory elements is more likely.

Marx, even in a fundamentalist interpretation, was ahead of Steward on this point, since he was from the beginning interested primarily in social change, and never seriously attempted systematic synchronic analysis. Nevertheless, his theory of social change was logically very similar to Steward's and had some of the same problems. His assumption of the necessary functional correspondence between forces and relations of production could not in and of itself explain social change, since a functional relation in and of itself does not establish the causal priority of one or the other of the two parts of the dyad. Marx's solution to this problem was not recourse to adaptation but rather a deductive demonstration that purported to prove that the forces of production have an internal developmental dynamic that makes them change as an independent variable. Marx only attempted to work this out in detail for the development of capitalism with his laws of the appropriation of surplus value and of the diminishing returns of capital, which he thought would eventually lead to the overthrow of the system. The logical structure of this argument is very similar in broad outlines to Harris's cultural materialism (though the use of dialectic gives it greater flexibility to adequately deal with complex phenomena, as will be discussed below). The significant goals toward which social behavior is rationalized are reduced to one—the maximum development of the forces of production—so that the single most rational course of behavior can be ascertained objectively without taking into account the consciousness of individual actors (which is usually thought to be a false consciousness, anyway). This explanation, like the adaptive one, requires a precise operationalization of the goal toward which behavior is seen to be rationalized, if it is to be more than dogma. If one is confined to a simple Marxist framework, however, this is difficult, since the precise nature of forces or relations of production was never clearly outlined in the works of Marx or Engels (Adams 1981:604). The idea of the causal priority of economic forces in peasant production, moreover, was challenged in the early years of this century in A. V. Chayanov's analysis of the organization of Russian peasant households.

Chayanov noted in his major work of 1925, *The Theory of Peasant Economy* (Chayanov 1966), that a number of characteristics of peasant economic behavior in Russia, as studied by agricultural officers from the 1880s on, did not conform to the expectations of conventional economic analysis. Farmers often would not use labor-saving equipment because it would displace household labor; sown crops were not confined to those with the highest market price and lowest production costs as the logic of the maximization of profit would dictate; wages tended to be inversely proportional to the price of bread in Russia (the opposite of the relationship found in England). Chayanov related these characteristics to the organization of the peasant farm, where the capitalist concepts of rent, wages, and profit would have no meaning. In contrast to the capitalist farm, where the entrepreneur hires labor and tries to make a profit from the difference between the market price of his produce and his costs of production (rent, materials, and wages), Chayanov analyzed the peasant farm as a family labor farm in which food, clothing, and other necessities are produced for family use with family labor. Wages are not paid as such, but are only determinable at the end of the year by dividing the total crop by the number of hours worked (if known), so that calculation of profit in the capitalist sense is virtually impossible. The head of the family, moreover, plays two roles at once: on the one hand he is a producer who has to use his family labor to work his farm as best he can, but on the other hand he is also a consumer with needs to be met.

Because the unit of production is also a unit of consumption, the amount that must be produced is influenced by the number of consumers in the family. Because the unit of consumption is also a unit of production, the amount of work necessary to meet the consumption needs of the household is affected by the amount of labor available in the family. So, though in the capitalist farm the scale of production is limited only by the availability of capital, the family labor farm is limited by the size of the family labor force. In the capitalist farm, the intensity of labor is proportional to wages, and of production is proportional to crop prices; in the family labor farm it is proportional to the number of mouths to feed in the household. For each family, the marginal utility of one more unit of consumption will gradually fall as needs are met more and more adequately. Each additional unit of labor, on the other hand, will become more and more arduous. The size of the farm and the intensity of labor on the farm, then, is the point where the marginal utility of consumption curve and the marginal drudgery of labor curve meet. These curves would not be the same for each family. The amount of consumption necessary and thus the marginal utility of consumption curve rises with the size of the family. The amount of labor available, and thus the marginal drudgery of labor curve, falls with the number of adults in the family. Each family will have a different point of equilibrium of the two margins and a different level of intensity of labor and consumption that would depend upon its size and composition.

The dynamic interaction between consumption needs and family labor supply, thought Chayanov, helps explain peasant behavior that at first seems anomalous. The resistance to labor-saving machinery seems irrational until one realizes that unless the family labor displaced by the machine can be used elsewhere, there is no net gain from mechanization but simply the replacement of cheap family labor by expensive machine labor. The production of many crops on a single farm seems irrational until one realizes that in the absence of well-developed markets and transportation, peasant farmers produce for use rather than exchange and thus must grow enough of each crop to meet their needs for that crop regardless of market prices. The inverse relation of wages to the price of bread is a result of the subsistence nature of farming: when harvests are poor, prices rise, but peasants with poor harvests throw themselves on the labor market to make ends meet and wages fall.

Chayanov saw peasant farming as being stimulated primarily by the consumer demand of the family. This helped him make sense of the statistical material available that showed that the size of the family farm in Russia was proportional to the number of consumers, that the income per worker rose but per capita fell with the rise in the ratio of consumers to workers. Pressure of consumer needs compelled the Russian peasants to work until these needs were fulfilled. Because of this, they might work at lower and lower returns, until consumer need was satisfied. It often followed that the return to labor of certain kinds of peasant income-producing activity was below the local prevailing wage rate, and that the rents peasants were willing to pay in some situations were higher than capitalist analysis would justify. Because of this tendency for self-exploitation, Chayanov thought peasant farmers in certain situations might actually drive out more efficient capitalist producers.

A natural consequence of the motivation provided by consumption needs and labor availability in this analysis is that the size of the family farm will be proportional to the size of the family.[14] The family, for Chayanov, was basically a biological unit, so he reasoned that "this biological nature of the family determined to a great extent the limits of its size and, chiefly, the laws of its composition" (Chayanov 1966:54). Because of the correlation between farm size and family size, and because of the independent biological nature of the family, then, variation in the size of farms and the intensity of farm labor ought to be largely a function of the family cycle. Chayanov introduced statistical evidence, the validity of which is still controversial (Shanin 1972; Harrison 1975, 1977a, 1977b), which purported to show that the size of Russian peasant farms between 1882 and 1911 changed in response to demographic variation in families over time (Chayanov 1966:67). For Chayanov, then, differences in farm size among peasants was not evidence of growing class differentiation brought about by the spread of capitalist relations of production, but evidence of cyclical demographic differentiation, a phenomenon that predates the introduction of capitalism to the Russian countryside.

Many of the phenomena first noted by Chayanov and his coworkers in the early years of this century have also been characteristic of Sangongni. As late as 1976, most food and about half of total family requirements were produced on the farm. Some four-fifths of the labor on peasant farms in Korea continues to be provided by family members (Chŏng Yŏngil 1984:46). There is a statistically significant correlation between the number of consumers in the household and the size of the farm. As in early twentieth-century Russia, the amount of land cultivated per worker rises with rising family consumption needs,[15] while the land cultivated per consumer falls.[16] Chayanov's model of the equilibrium of the marginal utility of consumption and the marginal drudgery of labor on the family farm is an elegant demonstration of how these phenomena are related to motivations conditioned by consumer needs and family labor supply.

The explanatory power of Chayanov's theory is limited, however, by his inability to consider the organization of peasant farms within alternative economic contexts and his inability to convincingly deal with capital investment. His explanation of the disinclination of peasants to mechanize production when this mechanization would displace family labor, for example, rests on an assumption that there are no alternative uses for family labor that would have as high a return for the family as work on the family farm. In other words, it assumes that the size of the farm cannot be increased to absorb the more efficient labor of the family members that mechanization would bring about, and that there are no wage labor opportunities sufficiently remunerative to justify the replacement of family labor. This was true of Sangongni in the early sixties when urban wage labor was not available and rural competition for land extremely intense. At that time, on-farm investment was extremely low and peasant farming seemed static, but this situation changed when rapid industrialization began. The existence of urban wage-labor opportunities for surplus family members encouraged investment in labor-saving devices on the farm. As a result of these investments, the same farm could be run with fewer people (allowing the rest to take urban jobs without reducing the farm's viability), or the farm could be expanded in size as rural-urban migration reduced competition for land. These phenomena in Sangongni point to the importance for household organization of land-tenure relations and capital investment incentives, things upon which Chayanov is either silent or incoherent (Skalweit 1924; Harrison 1977a). Though his theory of the peasant farm rests on motivational assumptions, to explain self-exploitation Chayanov must assume that peasants are incapable of rational calculation of their return to labor, when a more convincing explanation would certainly involve exploring the lack of real alternatives available for the use of household labor off the farm (Scott 1976:14).

As in Steward and Kautsky, the gravest shortcomings in Chayanov's model come from the difficulty of combining structural insights with causal explanations. Chayanov's argument, like the arguments of Kautsky and Steward, rests on a hypothesized functional correspondence between two parts of society—family and farm. Like Kautsky and Steward, he was not satisfied to simply note the relationship, but wished to use the relationship as part of a causal explanation of larger social phenomena. Just as the independent development of the forces of production was seen as the impulse for change in Kautsky, the development cycle of the family was seen as the independent variable in Chayanov's explanation. His notion of the family as a biological unit which "naturally" develops in a certain way little influenced by external circumstances is clearly inadequate, however. Not only is there no discussion of the cultural features that structure the Russian peasant family (is it patrilineal? joint? stem?), but, as was pointed out by Marxists at the time of Chayanov's publication of his theories, there is little consideration of the possibility that family structure is a function of differentiating land-tenure relations rather than the reverse (Solomon 1977:131). This catches Chayanov's theory on the horns of the familiar dilemma that also caused trouble for the theories of Kautsky and Steward. What *does* cause social change? Forces of production seem a plausible candidate, yet the possibility that demographic and structural features of the family may cause change relatively independently of other institutions of society points to the futility of trying to find one grand cause for the main features of social organization. Chayanov's model of the family labor farm, however, has the virtue not shared by the models of Kautsky or Steward of being amenable to quantitative analysis. This raises the possibility that his theory can be operationalized in such a way that models based on it may be precisely tested for the degree to which they account for data collected in real societies (cf. Greenhalgh 1985). It is a tantalizing frustration that the quantitative techniques available to Chayanov at the time of his writing were not able to do full justice to the huge amount of very detailed information available to him from zemstvo farm budget surveys.

Causality in Structural Theories

I have dealt with these questions of strategy, adaptation, and structural consistency at length not only because an understanding of these concepts is necessary for our understanding of the change that has been taking place in Sangongni, but also because there has been a tendency in recent anthropology to confuse strategy with necessity, and culture with social organization. I have used the concept of strategy because I am convinced that we cannot assume a priori that all actions are rationalized toward the same goal or that there is one and only one "best" solution to an environmental or other problem. If we remove cultural assumptions about the world and individual motivation from our analysis of societies, we come up with a notion of social process in which conscious rationality is considered nothing more than false consciousness that masks the true moving forces of society, while somehow behavior that promotes some a priori goal (adaptation, maximum development of the forces of production, etc.) is institutionalized by apparently mystical means. By confusing the requirement of adaptation and the functional interdependence of institutions with causality, what *is* is confused with what *has to be*. Sangongni is a functioning village in which people work hard to meet their needs and produce enough surplus to participate in a complex economy. Their present adaptation is not the only one they could have, nor is it necessarily optimal. Their present social structure is admirably adapted to peasant agriculture, but this same social structure is well adapted for an industrial society, too. Villagers do their best to reconcile their desire to attain cultural ideals of proper behavior, meet their adaptive requirements, and cope with the challenges of making it in a highly competitive industrial society. Each villager finds himself in a different situation, however, and the most rational course of action for him may not be the most rational course of action for his neighbor.

Kautsky, Steward, and Chayanov all wanted to find the causal key that unlocks the secrets of the structural development of society, but each of them had a different candidate for the *primum mobile* of social change: forces of production, technology in environment, family cycle. Each of them recognized that the amount of variation possible among the social institutions of a society is limited by the functional integration of its institutions. The difficulty for all these theorists lay in trying to combine these two elements. The integration of the elements of the social system does not conform to the requirement of asymmetry for strict causality as outlined above, and each of the independent variables hypothesized by the various theorists could not, in the end, be isolated from significant influence by other elements of the social system. That this is the case was recognized to an extent by Marx and Engels, who, in criticizing "vulgar materialism," cited what they called the "dialectic" relationship between the base and superstructure of society. In Engels, dialectic refers to a diachronic process of mutual interaction in which "an historical impulse, so long as it is first set in the world through ultimately economic causes, now can turn on its environment and become its own cause itself" (Engels 1968:98). This seems like an early description of the feedback found in integrated systems (Buckley 1967:52–58; Bertalanffy 1969:46; Godelier 1972:159). Had this insight been developed more fully in conjunction with a precise operationalization of the concepts of forces and relations of production, a satisfactory explanation of how societies could be functionally integrated and yet develop new structures might have emerged.

The conceptualization of multiple dependent variables that mutually influence each other can be attempted through the use of systems theory (Francesca Cancian 1960; Bennett 1976:164–67; Ellen 1982:177). Systems theory is specifically designed to deal with change in structured wholes. In a systems analysis, one divides a society into elements all of which are related to each other in terms of functional consistency. Unlike the causal analyses discussed above, the elements in the system are not divided into dependent and independent variables, and unlike the tendency in dialectical analyses, the mutual interaction does not have to be limited to dyads such as the forces and relations of production, or base and superstructure. Rather, all elements are united in a single system in which each element may have multiple feedback relations with several other elements. Change in one element will tend to lead to changes in all others, but it is not necessary to decide a priori that a certain element, whether forces of production, technology in environment, or demography, is the most important source of change: all can be recognized as dependent on each other. Accounting for change does not depend upon identifying an independent variable (although such variables are not disallowed). The amount and direction of change is controlled by feedback loops that themselves may be regulated by flows of information (Buckley 1967; Bertalanffy 1969).

The structural form of Sangongni can be seen as made up of a number of interacting systems. These systems are formed by the assumptions about the nature of the world, the knowledge, skills, and techniques available to the villagers, their goals and their values—in other words, their culture. As a result of culture, people use certain techniques of organization and of subsistence to attain valued goals. The relationship between elements is a consequence of this. A system of relations, however, has no content until it is organized under concrete circumstances not inherent to it. These circumstances—abundance of resources, man/land ratios, demographic parameters, market conditions—are historically derived, and do not assume their precise form as a matter of structural necessity or some principle of development immanent to the social system. These circumstances condition the operation of the system, while the internal relations of the elements limit the range of variation possible and the direction of social change. The need for adaptation, rather than causing the system, is a limiting variable. The nature of these limiting adaptive variables will be specified in later chapters, as well as the idea that household size, land tenure, farm size, and migration strategies on family labor farms are elements of a single system in which no variable can be taken as independent. This analysis will make it possible to illustrate how the mutual interdependence of the elements of the family system limits the range of variation of any one of them, and prevents one from advancing a conventional causal explanation for social change in these institutions. Again the central importance of changes in strategy in response to changing circumstances will be affirmed.

Sangongni: Changing Organization, Stable Structure

I first visited Sangongni in December 1976. It was one of a number of villages suggested to me by Dr. Kwang Kyu Lee of Seoul National University, who had recently surveyed them for the National Investigation of Folk Culture (Munhwa kongbobu 1979). Of the villages I visited, Sangongni seemed the most suitable for my study because it was a stable agricultural village with mixed surnames, with no marked aristocrat/commoner cleavages,[17] and one in which irrigated riceland formed only about half of the agricultural land. It also had a beautiful mountain setting. At that time, the village was extremely isolated and could be reached only by foot after fording or ferrying across a swift river. It had no electricity at a time when rural Korea was 90 percent electrified, and at least half of the houses still were roofed with straw in spite of a ten-year campaign by the government to get people to convert to tile or corrugated iron.

I wanted to study a village like Sangongni because I thought that in an isolated, long-settled, undisturbed village the consequences of the interaction of the rules of social structure with the requirements of ecological adaptation would be clear, and a Stewardian analysis would allow me to understand these elements in functional terms. As I collected genealogical, demographic, and agricultural data my expectations seemed to be confirmed. Of course, agricultural technology was clearly rapidly advancing. Vinyl greenhouses were used to sprout rice seedlings. Composite fertilizer was used in the fields. There were even a few motor tillers and power sprayers that had been introduced into the village around 1975. But in other respects, the village seemed traditional. There were a number of well-organized lineages. Household organization basically conformed to the rules of the 1958 New Civil Code, and those villagers that were wealthy in 1977 seemed to have been wealthy in the past.

It was only toward the end of my first year of fieldwork that I began to realize that many of the assumptions of village stability I had made were mistaken. As I analyzed my data, I began to understand the tremendous scale and importance of off-farm migration. When talk began of farm prices and the Japanese quota on Korean silk cocoons, I began to realize that the village was integrated into the world economy. I listened to the villagers discuss the impending electrification of their village and excitedly talk about watching television. I began asking about the past and found that whole lineages had disappeared from the village in the past fifteen years. I found other lineages had become disorganized as the pivotal households upon which their organization depended had moved to town, and I found that many villagers had lived in joint families in the past, although there was none in the whole district in 1977.

Although I had collected the rules of social structure, these did not seem sufficient to explain the behavior that I was observing. The attraction of life in the cities was very strong, but I found that some people were more likely to succumb to this attraction than others. As is typical of migration of this sort, the migrants were mostly young and in their prime years. But age was not the only selective factor. The economic circumstances of the household were also conditioning factors. In general, the richest and the poorest households seemed to have been the likeliest to leave (cf. Brandt and Lee 1981:111). This made sense. The poor householders had little to keep them in the village and the rich ones could afford to give their children the education that would help them succeed in urban occupations. Only the middle peasant households would be better off in the village than in town. I found also that there was a relationship similar to what Chayanov found for Russia between farm size, household labor force, and complexity of the family. Unlike what Hsu had hypothesized for China I could discern no class differences in adherence to the rules of social structure in Sangongi. Rather, just as Cohen had found for Yen-liao in southern Taiwan (1976:230–31) and Sang-bok Han had found in Kagŏdo Island off the south coast of Korea (1977:54–55), the frequency and timing of events possible in all classes of society varied with the productive needs of the household (Sorensen 1981a:618–29).

It was clear to me that there were a number of social changes going on in the village. As people were moving out of the village, land was changing hands. If land-tenure relationships were related to the size and complexity of the family, however, it followed that the size and the complexity of the family should be affected, too. I came away from my 1977 study of Sangongni with as many questions as answers. I knew what the social and ecological organization of the village was at one time, and could make some statements about the ecological adaptation of the villagers, but I found myself in the same situation that Steward had been after doing his ground-breaking synchronic studies (Steward 1938). Adaptive and other functional needs are limiting and molding factors, but not causal factors. The social organization of the village was obviously the result of processes that had not been stable—at least not for the fifteen years before 1977. With data from only one time, however, I could do little more than conjecture about the diachronic processes going on in the village. Thus in 1983, I came back for five weeks of additional fieldwork. With the aid of four student assistants and my previous knowledge of the village, I was able to do another complete survey of its social organization, land tenure, and farm size. Farmers were beginning to switch to cash crops on larger farms. I found the village had continued to lose population and those who remained continued to acquire land as others moved out, but that the core of social values and the functional relationships of fundamental institutions had remained the same in spite of dramatic change in population, household size, farm size, and productivity. Migration out of the household was still selective, but while in 1977 I had been struck by the importance of outside economic forces on the households of Sangongni, in 1983 I was struck by the tenacity of the basic structure of the rural household.

In rural central Korea, the corporate[18] agricultural family is the basic socioeconomic unit. It forms the core of the productive household, which is the unit of residence and nurturance for children, adults, and aged, the unit of agricultural production, the unit for the primary processing of raw foodstuffs, and the unit for the distribution of the necessities of life. There are certain functional requirements that must be met for each of the roles of the household to be efficiently taken care of. In agriculture, there are requirements for land, labor, tools, and stock; in the processing of food for labor, tools, and raw material; in the care and nurturance of family members for labor, food, clothing, and money. The members of the household play multiple roles. Production and consumption, residence and nurturance all are dependent upon one another—they are structurally integrated into a system. Many of the characteristics that are conventionally associated with such households in anthropology were not present, however. Production was done in the context of a market economy with private property in land, and the peasants were not target workers like the shifting cultivators that Sahlins studied in his famous essays on the domestic mode of production (Sahlins 1972; Donham 1981). The surpluses the villagers were producing were so substantial that only a few old people living outside stem families had to rely on nonkin for subsistence, and when this was necessary they were given state relief by local authorities rather than having to rely on an informal redistributional network (Sorensen 1986:147–48).

The structure and composition of the household, moreover, is not determined solely by functional requirements. Rural Koreans use certain structural rules to determine who is and who is not eligible for household membership. These rules are an historical legacy of all Koreans. Kinship is reckoned patrilineally. Succession is reckoned by primogeniture. Marriage should ideally be patrilocal for eldest sons and neolocal for other sons. The eldest son and his wife, as successor to the house head and house mistress, have the responsibility for taking care of the house head and mistress in their old age and worshiping them after their death. In general, the result of these rules of social structure is a social organization in which some families are nuclear families of parents and children, while others are stem families of aged parents, the eldest son and his wife and children, and perhaps a couple of unmarried siblings. But although we can tell from the rules of social structure what the possible permutations of family type are, we cannot tell what the social organization will be in any particular instance without taking other factors into account. We don't know how many stem families we will find in a village until we know at what age people marry, how long they live, and what proportion will succeed in producing eldest sons. We don't know how many nuclear families to expect until we know how many younger sons are being produced. We don't know what family size to expect until we know birth and death rates. All of these factors, moreover, can be modified by migration. This means that a proper understanding of the influence of the demographic development of the family on farming in the village must include not simply an analysis of the "natural" development of the family as was done by Chayanov, but also a consideration of the interaction of the culturally specific family structure of Korea with demographic variables that themselves are influenced by the circumstances in which goals are applied.

Since the household is a functionally integrated unit of residence, production, and consumption, the size and composition of the household membership affect the size and composition of the productive labor force and the scale of its needs (T. C. Smith 1977:108–11). Thus, on the one hand, the size and composition of the household are dependent upon the interaction of social structural rules and demographic variables, but on the other hand, the requirements of the household as an integrated unit of residence, production, and consumption put practical constraints on the permissible variation in household age and sex composition. To give a simple example, it is possible for the rules of social organization interacting with demographic factors to generate a household consisting of too many consumers with not enough producers. The most familiar example is a widow with a large number of children. Although these households might be produced, they will not survive if they do not form viable units of production and reproduction. Thus either the demographic parameters or the social structural rules that create such households must be modified in such a way that the adaptive requirements of the household can be met. Because of the functional integration of the various aspects of household organization, however, this is no simple matter. Change in the number of producers also changes the number of consumers. If an unmarried son leaves the household to reduce household consumption needs, for example, he also reduces household productive labor and thus may not improve the position of the household at all. Strategies to cope with one adaptive requirement of the household must be structurally consistent with other household institutions. Thus variation in household size and composition is limited and constrained not only by demographic variables and functional requirements, but also by the requirement of structural consistency.

All householders of Sangongni use the same social structural rules to make decisions about their life. All of the agricultural households must meet the same adaptive requirements for family members, and all are subject to the same constraints of structural consistency. Nevertheless, the social organization of all households is not alike, because in rural Korea access to farmland is not equal. If the amount of labor available to a household depends upon the size and composition of the family, the amount of labor that can be used, and the rate of return on that labor, depends upon how much land the household owns. This means that a strategy that is rational for one household will not necessarily be rational for another. A household with small amounts of land may need large amounts of labor because the return to labor is lower on tenancies than on land owned by one's own household. A household with slightly more land, paradoxically, may find it needs to retain less labor in the household because the return to labor is higher on one's own land and is thus sufficient to provide for household needs. The necessity for this modification of Chayanov's insights was recognized by Skalweit long ago (Skalweit 1924), and has recently been reemphasized by McGough (1984) in his interpretation of variation in Chinese domestic group formation. Neither of these scholars, however, has tried to account for land-tenure patterns, quantify labor requirements, include demographic and ecological factors in their analysis, or account for social change.

The process of social change, which in Sangongni was already well under way by 1977, thus had a number of dimensions having to do with changing opportunities, changing circumstances, and a changing balance in the structural interrelationship of institutions within the family. With the development of new opportunities for social mobility in the urban centers, the household began to take on new burdens, such as providing secondary and higher education for children who have academic ability, or trying to provide opportunities for urban marriages and employment for the children of the household. With the industrialization and modernization of the rest of the Korean economy, the circumstances to which people adjust themselves have changed. Death rates have fallen and life expectancy has increased, so that the consequences for household composition of high fertility have changed. The increasing efficiency of the National Agricultural Cooperative Federation in providing improved factors of agricultural production and of the Agricultural Guidance Office in providing technical advice has helped farmers to increase their yields. Mechanization, begun first in food processing and apparel, and then later in field agriculture, has altered the amount of labor necessary for the efficient operation of a farm household. All of these things have changed the relationship of the adaptive requirements to the factors of production available to the household, and have altered the balance of the structural integration of the Sangongni household.

Even though the industrialization and urbanization of Korea since the mid-sixties has not directly touched Sangongni, by altering the circumstances that condition household strategies of adaptation, and by providing new opportunities for household members, these forces have had a profound effect on village adaptation. If the requirements of adaptation have changed and the details of the structural integration of the household have been modified, however, the way that the household has to meet adaptive requirements, and the way that the requirements of residence, production, and consumption are combined in a single unit has not changed. Just as the changing circumstances of the larger economy of Korea affected which household strategies were most rational, the functional requirements and condition of structural integration of the household affected how people responded to these new circumstances. Thus social change was not a one-way street but a process of interaction between rules of social structure and changing circumstances that led to the generation of new strategies, the discarding of a number of old strategies, and the retention of other strategies. Did this process also require modifications of the rules of household social structure? On the whole I would say no.

It is the thesis of this study that radical as the changes in the household organization of Sangongni villagers have been, these changes have been largely ones of strategy rather than of social structure. In spite of changes in village circumstances caused by the rapid urbanization and industrialization of Korea, the structural integration of the household as a unit of production and consumption has remained. Massive outmigration and changes in agricultural technology have taken place, but I believe the adaptive requirements of the household and its structural integration have acted as a force that has molded the villagers' adaptations to modern life every bit as much as the changes in their circumstances. Patterns of behavior common in the past were always just a few of a wide range of possible permutations of cultural rules contingent on socioeconomic conditions. With a change in conditions, one finds a change in the frequency of permutations without a fundamental change of the system. Contrary to the expectations of some modernization theorists (Goode 1963), the growth of market relations has not led to the convergence of rural Korean family organization to a Euro-American pattern. Recent work on the family systems of rural areas in Taiwan (Gallin and Gallin 1982) and, to a lesser extent, Japan (R. J. Smith 1978), has shown complex family organization being retained, even thriving, during rapid industrialization. The rural stem family system in Sangongni has also remained a vital force.

The heavy outmigration and consequent modification of village family organization found in Sangongni has been typical of the changes in outlying villages of South Korea—that half of the villages that are neither periurban nor closely linked by major transportation arteries to urban centers—for the past twenty years (Sloboda 1980:354). Between 1975 and 1980, the mean household size of all South Korean counties (which include all areas not within the administrative boundaries of cities) fell from 5.36 to 4.81 in a manner similar to Sangongni, and the available evidence suggests that outlying villages in other parts of Korea share social characteristics with Sangongni. On-jook Lee (1980:121), for example, found extended families to comprise 31.5 percent of a 1977 sample of rural natives in Posŏng County, an outlying area in the extreme southwest of the Korean peninsula. This is almost precisely the proportion (32.2 percent) of stem families in Sangongni in the same year. Other villages studied in the seventies in Korea that are close to cities or ecologically distinct look somewhat different. Janelli and Janelli (1982:28), for example, found in 1973 that 45 percent of the families in a lineage village near Seoul were stem in form, a phenomenon they attribute to the ease with which villagers could commute to nonfarm jobs. Chun (1984:19), on the other hand, found in 1976 only 17.5 percent of the families in a mixed farming and fishing village on Chindo Island to be stem in form. In a sense, however, the typicality of the statistics for Sangongni or other villages is beside the point. These statistics of social organization are the result of the interaction of the principles of social structure with local circumstances. Where local circumstances have been similar, as in many outlying villages, we would expect similar social organization, but even in those villages for which circumstances are different, if the functional relationships established in this study are indeed characteristic of Korean social structure, the inner dynamic of the social structure as exhibited in Sangongni should still apply.

CHAPTER 3

Development and the Influence of a Mountain Environment

Subsistence agriculture with hand tools and draft animals has been the dominant mode of life in Sangongni as long as people can remember. Even as late as 1983, the income of four-fifths of the households was acquired exclusively through agriculture, with more than half of the remaining households gaining a major part of their income from farming as well. The traditional technology of Sangongni's farmers, which included knowledge of several crop rotations, seed selection, sprouting of seedlings in special seedbeds for transplantation in the fields, and the on-farm manufacture of compost, was in many ways quite sophisticated, and allowed the peasants of the village a certain latitude in how they chose to crop their land. To this traditional repertory of techniques has been added, in recent years, commercial fertilizer, pesticides, and machinery, as well as the scientific knowledge that the consultants of the Agricultural Guidance Office and the Agricultural Cooperative Federation provide. Market relations have become more important, but the characteristics of the Korean mountain environment continue, as they have in the past, to condition the possibilities for the operation of villager's farms. As will be shown in detail in following chapters, the management of farms and the organization of families are closely related. Because of this the geographical characteristics of the mountain environment, even though they do not determine village social structure, condition the social organization of the village.

These geographical characteristics of Sangongni are of two types: those related to the location of the village in an area remote from major urban centers, and those related to the climate and topography of mountain districts in central Korea. The location of the village conditions the effectiveness of administrative links with the national polity and the way the village articulates to the national economy through the marketing system. Kautsky, of course, already recognized that increasing participation of peasants in market relations would have a profound effect on their social organization, but he never explored how the articulation of regional market systems structures these new relations (cf. Skinner 1964, 1965a, 1965b; C. A. Smith 1976). Not only does the articulation of the village into the market system affect household cropping patterns and labor requirements, however, but it also affects the opportunities villagers have to diversify their household economy, and the degree to which villagers can accumulate capital. In addition, the climate and topography of Sangongni's environment limits the length of the growing season, the seasonal distribution of water, and the availability of fields of different types. By conditioning the cropping regimes available, the climate and topography thus also affect the labor requirements of households and village social organization.

Each of the geographical characteristics of the mountains is not simply a given of the environment, but is related to the level of development of the technology available to villagers. The economic significance of the remoteness of the village from major urban centers, for example, obviously varies with the availability of mechanical means of transport and paved roads—something that has not been constant over the past generation (Keidel 1980:147–58). Other aspects of village technology have also changed. In the following pages, as we explore the geographical and agricultural characteristics of the village, we will see how the significance of climate and topography for the management of farms and the organization of households has changed with changing circumstances so that by the mid-seventies, the peasants of Sangongni had the incentives they needed to make substantial investments in agricultural improvements.

Locational Factors

Sangongni is located in the Yŏngsŏ region of Kangwŏn Province directly east of Seoul. From the Kyŏnggi Province boundary near the center of the Korean peninsula, Kangwŏn Province extends all the way to the Sea of Japan, and before the division of the Korean peninsula stretched over 200 kilometers from thirty-seven to thirty-nine degrees north latitude (or from about the latitude of Norfork, Virginia, to that of Washington, D. C.). Kangwŏn Province and Kyŏnggi Province together cover the central part of the Korean peninsula, consisting of the Han River Basin and the mountains that surround it (see fig. 3.1). Economically and culturally, the two provinces are closely tied to one another, but ecologically they are quite distinct. Kyŏnggi Province has extensive rich lowlands broken up by occasional upland areas. Kangwŏn Province, on the other hand, is mostly upland and can be divided into three narrow strips running north to south. The westernmost strip along the Kyŏnggi Province boundary is a rugged landscape of mountains punctuated by good-sized valleys where a string of regional cities has developed. Starting with Ch'unch'ŏn, the provincial capital located just south of the thirty-eighth parallel, Hongch'ŏn, Hoengsŏng, and Wŏnju line up in a north to south direction. Each of these cities is a county seat and good roads link them all to each other and Seoul. The major population of Kangwŏn Province lives in these cities or in the rural areas surrounding them. Geographically, this westernmost strip of Kangwŏn Province is really an extension of the Han River Basin into the foothills of the T'aebaek Range.

To the east of this strip rise the high mountains of the T'aebaek Range proper. Here the average elevation is above 500 meters. Farming is quite distinct and a mountain economy based on the cultivation of unirrigated field crops, the gathering of herbs, mining, and forestry prevails. The crest of the T'aebaek Range is in the eastern side of the province close to the coast where the mountains plunge precipitously down to a narrow but fertile littoral plain on the Sea of Japan. This plain is the third geographical region of the province. All of the area to the west of the crest of the T'aebaek Range—the Ch'unch'ŏn-Wŏnju foothills, and the high mountains—is known as Yŏngsŏ ("west of the pass"). The area east of the crest is known as Yŏngdong ("east of the pass"). Traditionally, the Yŏngdong region has been isolated from Seoul and the rest of Kangwŏn Province. The residents of this region speak a distinctive dialect that Sangongni villagers have a hard time understanding and have close ties with the coastal areas of the southeast. The Yŏngsŏ region, on the other hand, has always had fairly good communication with the capital.

Although the Yŏngsŏ region is mountainous and thus relatively isolated and poor in comparison to the rest of Korea, the social organization of the villages does not differ in essentials from that of richer villages closer to Seoul. The people speak a variant of the central Korean dialect spoken around Seoul and build the typical central Korean L-shaped farmhouse. As in other parts of central Korea the villages of the Yŏngsŏ region are settled primarily by peasant agriculturalists who harvest a single annual crop of rice from irrigated fields, and a

Fig. 3.1. Korea since 1953

number of other grain and vegetable crops from rainfall fields (many of which are steeply sloped). Apart from the two major cities of the region—Ch'unch'ŏn, which because of nearby hydroelectric power has become a provincial center of industry, and Wŏnju, which has major military facilities—the region is not industrialized. Urban areas are devoted primarily to providing administrative services, education, marketing, and health care to the surrounding villages.

Sangongi lies at an elevation of approximately one hundred fifty meters. The village consists of six named hamlets ranging in size from two to thirty-two houses (see fig. 3.2). Four of these hamlets are large enough to form the nucleus of a *pan,* or village administrative section. The main hamlet of the village, often known simply as Big Hamlet, is a mixed surname settlement set amidst dry fields in a small mountain basin. Its thirty-odd houses are so scattered that there is hardly anything in the village that one could call a street, though paths suitable for wheeled vehicles connect all the houses with one another. In the past when the hamlet was larger, the settlement pattern was more nucleated, but as people have left the village, their houses have been pulled down and crowding has been reduced. Since in this part of the village there is plenty of land, all of it unirrigated and thus of moderate value, there is no reason why people have to live close together.

Big Hamlet is the first part of the village encountered after walking in from the bus stop at Fishplay Shore some three kilometers away. The center of town is not well defined: on the right is a modern, concrete government warehouse, on the left a half-timbered building with the rice-milling machinery, a large ginkgo tree, and a house, conspicuous with its sliding glass doors, which serves as the village pharmacy. A modern, concrete village hall with a cooperative store was erected a few years ago next to the rice mill. Since it doubles as a drinking establishment it now forms the focus of the settlement.

South from the center of town a dry creekbed ascends the valley. This skirts the Presbyterian church, established some fifteen years ago, and runs past the last house to 300-meter Alder Pass that leads, by a trail impassable to vehicles, to the next valley and the township office. Another branch of the creek runs to a higher hamlet in the next administrative village, and then even higher into the mountains to hamlets with no irrigated fields at all, but only dry ones that used to be cultivated by fire-field farming (*hwajŏn*), a form of shifting cultivation fomerly common in mountain areas. Today these higher villages are practically deserted with only a few farmers and charcoal burners re-

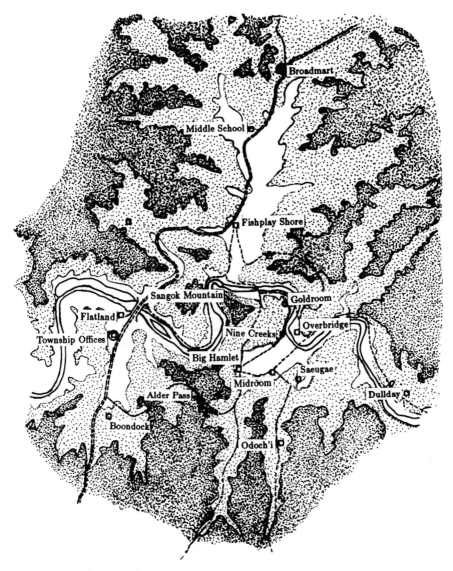

Fig. 3.2. Sangongni

maining. Twenty years ago, however, even the steepest slopes were farmed, and large villages could be found in the highest mountains.

Midroom, another of the hamlets of the village, lies to the east of Big Hamlet and is connected to it by a concrete bridge over the creek built as a New Village Movement project. This hamlet is the site of a modern concrete one-story school complete with concrete houses for the teachers and their families and a grove of very large chestnut and cherry trees. About fifteen of the twenty or so houses of this hamlet are within a stone's throw of one another. Conspicuous, too, are several tall tobacco-drying houses. In contrast to Big Hamlet, which is a mixed surname hamlet, the residents of Midroom are predominantly of a single lineage, which explains some of the differences in the settlement pattern of the two hamlets. In traditional times, younger sons would build their houses close to the house of their parents, and over time a clustered settlement of agnates known in Korea as a "one-clan hamlet" (*tongjok purak*) would develop. A mixed surname settlement like Big Hamlet, being made up of several such clusters, shows less geographic and social unity than a single surname hamlet such as Midroom. The irrigated fields stretching off toward the river from the hamlet are the richest in the area, and are owned mostly by members of this lineage, which dominates the village politically. Over a small pass to the south lie a few scattered houses in another named hamlet, Saeugae, and farther up yet another one-clan hamlet dominated by a less powerful lineage that is part of another administrative village.

East of Midroom is one of the major tributaries of the North Han River. Although the river has been bridged downstream, it is not bridged here and the hamlet on the other side of the river, known as Overbridge, can be reached from the rest of the village only by ferry or by a stick bridge erected during the winter when the water is low. This hamlet is dominated by the same lineage that inhabits Midroom. Situated in a bend of the river, it is the most concentrated of the settlements of the village and the only one in which the houses are arranged so that there are streets. The river bank is lined with tall poplar trees, and in the summer when there is not a breath of air anywhere else in the village, a slight cooling breeze keeps this hamlet livable. Although most of the inhabitants of Overbridge are not wealthy by village standards, because this hamlet is the traditional center of the same village lineage that dominates Midroom, and because many of the genealogically senior (and thus relatively wealthy) members of this lineage who have since left the village used to live there, many of the houses here are well built and comfortable.

Facing Overbridge from the same side of the river as Big Hamlet and Midroom are a number of ravines with small clusters of houses known collectively as Nine Creeks, due to the large number of small creeks that empty into the river here. This area, like Big Hamlet, is inhabited by several surname groups of mixed background. Chang Yŏnggŭn, the peasant who used to play gong in the farmer's band, lives here. Further down, set in a small riverside valley, is a settlement with only two houses, which because of their small number and isolation are the only ones in the village without electricity, known as Goldroom.

The four main hamlets of Sangongni—Big Hamlet, Midroom, Overbridge, and Nine Creeks—are each separated by a ten- to twenty-minute walk. Some of the more isolated houses are forty minutes, or more, by foot, from Big Hamlet. Nevertheless, they form a geographical and sociological entity. They are situated in two narrow and parallel valleys separated by a ridge. Both valleys are surrounded by even higher ridges so that taken together, they form a natural unit that is connected at Midroom by the flat area occupied by the school. This area makes a basin of the two valleys before they separate again and run in parallel to the river a kilometer away. Although each of the four main hamlets of the administrative village is distinct in name and social personality, they are neither closed nor corporate. Anyone may buy and sell for money or kind the lands around any of the hamlets. People can and do move from one hamlet or village to another depending upon the availability of houses and the location of cultivable land. Because many hamlets are one-clan settlements, marriage tends to be village exogamous, but there is no rule that prohibits village endogamy and a small proportion of the marriages in each hamlet are village endogamous. The hamlets own little property in common and worship collectively no gods not also worshiped by other villagers.[1] They are simply units of convenience brought about by proximity, kinship ties, mutual help, and visiting.

The area around Sangongni is said to have been first settled about three hundred years ago by members of the Sunhŭng An clan. Although the last household of this clan left the village in the early sixties, the present villagers say the Sunhŭng An lived in the village for seventeen consecutive generations. There are still a number of women of this clan in the village married to members of other clans. The Sunhŭng An are said to have been followed by the P'yŏngch'ang Yi, the Haeju Ch'oe, the Wŏnju Yi, the Namyang Hong and the Sŏngju Yi (Yi Kwanggyu, personal communication). Excepting the Sunhŭng

An, there are households of each of these clans still residing in the village, though only the last three can be said to have a functioning lineage organization in the village any more. Genealogically prominent members of these clans, all of whom are well off due to the inheritance system that favors the senior line (see chap. 6), have kept contact with the national clan organization at least to the extent of ensuring the inclusion of themselves and their close kin in the clan genealogies. Elders of the dominant clan of Midroom and Overbridge, which includes among its members two of the three largest village landowners, claim to send representatives to the autumnal rites for the apical ancestor of their clan held in their clan seat. All members of the lineages that maintain autumnal tombside ancestor worship ceremonies are locally recognized as being of yangban background. This is a source of pride to many villagers. Those of yangban background may be more inclined than others to emphasize higher education and orthodox behavior (Brandt 1971:45–49; Janelli and Janelli 1982:47), but in today's Korea one's former estate[2] origin has few practical consequences outside the marriage market. Genealogically important families in the village nevertheless try to keep up respectable ancestor worship traditions and to maintain copies of the most recent genealogies of their clan on hand.

Administration

Local administration in Korea is very centralized. All of the country is divided into a series of nested administrative units whose ultimate source of control is the president of the country. Each province is administered by a governor appointed by the president. The provinces are divided into counties (*kun*), townships (*myŏn*), villages (*li*), and village sections (*pan*). The heads of counties are appointed by the president on the recommendation of the governor, while the heads of townships are appointed by the governor. Village heads are appointed by the township head, and precinct heads are elected.[3]

The township office, located in a village about five kilometers away over Alder Pass, is where the township head (*myŏnjang*) and Agricultural Guidance Officer keep their offices, and where local family registration records are kept. Each family has a register on which births, deaths, marriages, divorces, adoptions, recognition of illegitimate children, and so on, are recorded. The legal efficacy of all acts of family organization, which in turn affect rights to family support, succession, and inheritance, depend upon the content of these registers.

Though the house head is allowed a certain amount of discretion, who can and cannot be recorded on these registers is very explicitly regulated by the Civil Code (Sorensen 1986:141–43). The family registration records, thus, are one of the major means by which the patrilineal, corporate family system of Korea is maintained.

At the township office the township head oversees the collection of statistical information for the government, transmits and implements government directives, and reports upon compliance to the central government. The township head works intensively with the village heads, who are the liaison between the villagers and the bureaucracy of the central government. Village or township heads seldom initiate policy: their role is to transmit information to the higher levels of the administration about village realities and to transmit and implement in the village the numerous directives of the government, which can range from organizing a Four H Club (Sa Eich'i Kurakpu) to making sure grass roofs are replaced by corrugated iron or tile.

In the past the office of village head was usually held by a member of the lineage that dominates Midroom and Overbridge. Today, however, since the duties of the village head take much time and are unpaid, the office is not particularly coveted. Since the mid-seventies, the office has tended to be rotated among prominent villagers whatever the formal method of selection. A separate office, often combined with that of village head, but often also in the hands of a younger man ambitious to lead the village in the adoption of modern ways, is that of head of the New Village Movement (Sae Maŭl Undong). This person, who usually receives training at special government workshops, is responsible for village improvement projects. These projects are decided upon and implemented by the villagers themselves, with the government helping with the provision of materials. Often, however, the authorities have pet projects that they persuade villagers to adopt as their own. Officially, there is a single person for the whole village, but since the hamlet is the natural unit of spontaneous cooperation in labor exchange networks, all the projects I saw in Sangongni were actually organized on the hamlet level.

Four other governmental organizations are in evidence in the township, but in offices separate from the township office: the National Post Office, the National Police, the National Reserve Army, and the Agricultural Cooperative Federation. Of these, the one that has the greatest impact on village life is the Agricultural Cooperative Federation (Nongŏp Hyŏptong Chohap). Although it is a membership organization (72.2 percent of the households in Sangongni's township were reported in the county statistical yearbook as members), the agricultural cooperative is centrally administered by the national government. Branch offices of this organization are maintained in each rural township. Their explicit purpose is to make agricultural factors of production widely available in rural areas ("the right product, at the right time, in the right quantity at the right price," is their motto), to stabilize the market in major agricultural products by administering the collection of the grain that must be sold to the government, and to provide rural credit at reasonable rates of interest. It is partly through control over grains marketed through this program that the government is able to successfully administer price controls.[4] The agricultural cooperative is the major outlet for many important cash crops such as raw silk cocoons, and it controls completely the selling of fertilizer and the marketing of such important government monopoly crops as tobacco and ginseng.

The Marketing System

Although much of the circulation of the major crops and factors of agriculture is accomplished through the agricultural cooperative, and a certain amount of circulation of goods and services takes place under the auspices of itinerant peddlers or brokers, most of the ordinary buying and selling of consumer goods take place through a "natural" system of periodic rural markets and urban central places. Since rural Korean households tend to be largely self-sufficient, nobody has to market every day or even every week. Nevertheless, there are a number of items that every household needs but cannot make at home: shoes and clothing, simple agricultural tools, books and magazines, exotic medicines, manufactured food items (such as noodles, dried seaweed, dried or canned fish, distilled liquor, meat or fruits such as persimmons, tangerines, or pears). Although all rural households occasionally purchase these items, demand is too low in most villages for permanent stores stocking all these items to exist. In 1977, Sangongni had one good-sized private store that sold mostly candy and school supplies. Each of the four larger hamlets also had a cooperative store run by the hamlet women's association known locally as the *ŏmŏni kage* (mothers' store). By 1983, the one private store had gone out of business, and the three mothers' stores for the hamlets on the same side of the river had consolidated into a single store in a newly built concrete building in the center of Big Hamlet. This new store boasted a freezer case for ice cream treats. The mothers' store of

Overbridge across the river was still rotated from house to house. The stock of these stores was similar: ramen, distilled liquor (*soju*), notebooks, pens, and a wide variety of candies for women to treat their children with.

Except for the few food items kept in the cooperative mothers' stores, most purchased items have to be bought in one of the periodic rural markets. In the Yŏngsŏ region virtually every settlement is within an hour or so walk of a market town. Often the site of only a few modest, permanent shops, such towns get their importance from the periodic markets held there when as much as 20 percent of the population of the surrounding villages may spend at least some time in town for the purpose of selling agricultural products, buying ordinary household supplies, perhaps visiting a local fortuneteller, and socializing. Markets are held every five days, so most villagers put off shopping until market day, and use the other days of the week for agricultural work. Because of this, the whole rhythm of rural life revolves around the market schedule, and the location of markets determines to a large extent where and who people meet. The system of periodic markets thus organizes rural society above the level of the hamlet and village both temporally and spatially.

Residents of Sangongni had the choice of two markets within five or six kilometers: Broadmart or Flatland. The schedules of these two markets did not overlap,[5] so that villagers who so desired could have gone to one or the other of the markets every two or three days, though nobody had reason to market so frequently. In fact, because the path to Flatland led over a very steep pass, most villagers regularly marketed only at Broadmart. Because villagers who lived within perhaps ten kilometers of Broadmart regularly converge on the market town, Broadmart and its surrounding villages tend to form a unified social system. However, social activity in market towns is not so intense or exclusive that the marketing area can be considered a closed social system as has been hypothesized for traditional China (Skinner 1964:35–36). Several of the institutions that seem to have integrated market towns and their surrounding villages in China, such as temple organizations, seem to be absent in Korea. Commercialization of the rural economy was much less developed in Korea in traditional times. Much of the marketing is done through the bureaucratic channels of the agricultural cooperative. In addition, most people who have to shop for major items, will, in fact, wait until they have to go to Ch'unch'ŏn, the regional city.

Because of the legacy of the colonial period, when most of the commercial sector was in Japanese hands, and because industrialization in Korea has been concentrated in large cities where export-oriented industries financed in large part by foreign capital have been created, commercial activities are heavily concentrated in the cities. Outside of the cities, good roads are rare—especially in this mountain area—and access to capital, wholesaling, and motorized transport is difficult. Thus, in rural areas there is virtually no industrial activity outside of periurban villages, and commercial development is less vigorous than one would expect, given the amount of purchasing power the peasants have. Markets tend to be articulated in a dendritic pattern (Johnson 1970:83–92) with the most vigorous commercial activity closest to the major cities, and the size of markets regularly falling as distance from major cities increases (Sorensen 1981b:104–7). Lower level markets are dependent on a single very much higher level market (in this case Ch'unch'ŏn), and villagers go straight to the city for things they don't find locally. Because there is no competition among higher-level markets to provide services to the lower-level marketing areas, while several lower-level markets compete to provide primary agricultural goods for the higher-level markets, remote districts such as the one in which Sangongni is situated find themselves at a disadvantage compared to those near large cities where transportation costs are lower (C. A. Smith 1976:34–36).

These disadvantageous terms of trade with the city have had an important influence on the way markets have affected village social structure. The high cost of transportation makes the marketing of crops less profitable in Sangongni than in periurban villages, and the purchase of manufactured products more expensive. Because of this, strategies of subsistence farming are encouraged, while commodity production is discouraged. Accumulation of capital is difficult, and the rate of return to on-farm investment is lower than in other areas of rural Korea. In addition, diversification of the household economy is difficult without the migration of household members, since most nonfarm occupational opportunities are located too far from the village to allow commuting. The village remains primarily a supplier of raw agricultural products to better situated areas, and a consumer of education, technical services (such as medicine), and manufactured goods produced in urban areas. Unlike households in other areas of Korea, such as in the periurban villages of Twisŏngdwi studied by the Janellis (1982) or Enduring Pine studied by Kendall (1985), then, the households of Sangongni are adapted almost exclusively to the labor requirements of peasant agriculture.

Climatic, Topographic, and Agricultural Factors

Central Korea has four well-defined seasons. These have been characterized as a long, cold winter, a short spring, a hot humid summer, and a crisp clear autumn (Bartz 1972:30). Although the latitude of Seoul or Ch'unch'ŏn is comparable to that of Washington, D. C., the weather resembles that of Connecticut more than Virginia. The January mean temperature in Ch'unch'ŏn runs around minus seven degrees Celsius. The August mean temperature around twenty-five degrees. This compares with mean temperatures for the same months of zero degrees and twenty-four degrees Celsius for Washington, D.C. (which is slightly farther north). Most of the precipitation falls in the summer, with July being the wettest month. Since adequate precipitation is concentrated during the growing season, the Korean climate is quite suitable for agriculture. The climate tends toward extremes, however, so farmers can take little for granted.

Korea, being a peninsula surrounded on three sides by water, is subject to a certain amount of moderating maritime influence, yet the main features of the climate can be directly or indirectly attributed to the influence of the Asian mainland. In the winter, cold air masses pile up over Mongolia and Siberia. From the Siberian high pressure zone thus created, winds blow down over Korea and North China, creating the cold, dry winters so characteristic of this part of the world. In the summer, this process occurs in reverse. As the plains of North China and Manchuria heat up, a low pressure zone is created that eventually sucks warm moist air from the South China Sea up into Korea and North China. This southwest monsoon brings the torrential rains of July—the *changma*.

The precipitation that Korea receives is extremely concentrated, with almost 30 percent falling during the monsoon season in the single month of July. Floods are common and the rivers have huge beds that are dry most of the year only to fill to overflowing during the July rains. The flow of the Han River at Seoul in July, for example, is twenty times that of January or February (Bartz 1972:19). Precipitation also is subject to extreme variability. Variations from the mean of as much as 40 percent are not uncommon in a year, and over the forty years between 1932 and 1972, three successive dry years occurred five times. Summer typhoons do not hit Korea as commonly as they hit South China or Japan, and their force has often been somewhat dissipated by the time the peninsula is reached, but the torrential rains they bring in their wake are often extremely destructive. Thus, although precipitation is in general adequate in Korea, and although Koreans are fortunate that most of it falls during the summer growing season, the distribution of rainfall over the growing season is often a problem that must be dealt with to achieve maximum productivity.

Because of the generally adequate spring and summer rainfall, rice cultivation is possible at a higher latitude than in China. Rice is the chief crop in Korea up to about thirty-nine degrees north in all but the highest mountain areas, whereas in Shāndōng and other areas of China at equivalent latitudes, wheat, millet, and barley have been the most important crops. In Japan, where the moderating influence of the ocean is more strongly felt than in Korea, rice is grown as far north as forty-five degrees latitude in Hokkaido. In the most northerly parts of Korea (as in North Korea), however, rice gives way to barley and other field crops. The frost-free growing season in central Korea ranges from about 190 days in the lowland areas of Kyŏnggi Province to less than 165 days in the upland areas. This is adequate time for the maturation of major grain crops, but double cropping is not possible. South of the thirty-seventh parallel (which is located at approximately the southern boundary of Kyŏnggi and Kangwŏn Provinces) irrigated rice paddies are commonly planted in the winter with an unirrigated crop of barley, and in the very southern coastal areas, where the growing season reaches up to 300 days a year, two crops of rice may be harvested.

Neither of the double-cropping regimes, however, are possible even in lowland central Korea, much less the mountain areas with their cooler temperatures and even shorter growing season. The exact mix of land and types of crops grown in rural Korea depend upon the topography and the weather. Korea is a mountainous country where only 23.5 percent of the surface may be cultivated (Bartz 1972:63). Kangwŏn Province is the most mountainous of all the provinces in South Korea with 7.7 percent of the land at an elevation over 1000 meters. Only 9.3 percent of the surface of the province may be cultivated (p. 144). Because of the elevation, irrigation is more difficult than in other areas of Korea and dry fields count for a greater percentage of the total cropland. Whereas 55.7 percent of Korea's total cropland is devoted to irrigated riceland, only 34.3 percent of the cropland of Kangwŏn Province is devoted to irrigated riceland (almost 60 percent of the cropland in neighboring Kyŏnggi Province is irrigated riceland). The slack is made up with a variety of crops cultivated on rainfall field.

Agriculture in the lowlands and the highlands of central Korea can be contrasted in the proportion of different kinds of fields, the size of the farm, and the variety of crops sown. Most of these differences follow from differences in topography in the different regions. Thus, in the lowlands, where much flat land is available and rivers and streams may be easily tapped for irrigation, irrigated rice fields, and thus the cultivation of rice, take up most of the land. If access to a city is not difficult, orchard crops may also be common. As one reaches into the highlands, the proportion of irrigated rice field to the total amount of cultivated land falls. In the highlands, population densities fall below fifty persons per square kilometer. The valley floors, such as they are, are used for paddy, but the main crops of potatoes, beans, corn, millet, and barley are cultivated on sloping fields dependent upon natural rainfall. Due to the shortage of rice straw, houses in traditional times were often roofed with stone slabs rather than straw thatch. Marginal fire field farmers used to be commonly found, and forestry was an important source of income.

In the transitional Ch'unch'ŏn-Wŏnju foothills where Sangongni is situated, the full-blown mountain economy described above is not typical. The topography is broken up, but the valleys are wider than in the high mountain districts, and rice grown in irrigated paddies remains the dominant crop in typical Korean fashion. Although the area of rainfall fields still overshadows rice here (one expects less than one-half of the cropland to be irrigated riceland), rice with its high productivity and prices is still the major source of income. Table 3.1, based on the 1966 agricultural census, gives one an idea of the ecological contrasts one finds as one progresses from the relatively rich counties of the Kyŏnggi Basin (Hwasŏng County) to the edge of this basin (Yangju County), to the transitional Ch'unch'ŏn-Wŏnju foothills (Hongch'ŏn County), to the high mountains (Inje County). Both the percentage of households cultivating irrigated riceland and the

TABLE 3.1
Land and Household in Four Korean Counties

County	Hwasŏng	Yangju	Hongch'ŏn	Inje
Land per household (ares)	124.8	106.0	84.0	108.0
Paddy (%)	60.0	51.0	29.0	30.0
Rainfall field (%)	35.0	40.0	66.0	67.0
Orchard (%)	5.0	8.0	5.0	3.0

SOURCE: Nongnimbu 1966

amount of paddy these households cultivate fall as the land becomes more mountainous. This fall in the amount of paddy is made up, for the most part, by an increase in the amount of dry fields, so there is little difference in the total acreage cultivated by the households of each area. Since dry fields are less productive than irrigated fields, however, incomes tend to fall as districts become more mountainous. As rainfall field makes a poor investment for nonfarmers in these districts, however, land prices and tenancy rates tend to be low. Limits on productivity and the acreage one can cultivate also probably limit the spread in income between the richer and poorer farmers. Sociologically, then, one expects mountain districts to differ from lowland districts in the following ways: (1) economic differentiation is less severe because the opportunity cost of becoming a landowner is lower; (2) social stratification is less severe because the differentiation between rich and poor is limited by the environment; (3) those social phenomena that require a substantial amount of wealth will be poorly developed or absent; (4) cultural phenomena associated with poverty will be more common than elsewhere.

The Agricultural System

Agriculture in Sangongni, as in the rest of Korea, has been in constant change over the past generation. Changes have taken place in all the factors that affect social behavior: techniques of cultivation have been improved, conditioning factors have changed, and the importance of meeting adaptive requirements as a motivation for cropping patterns has receded, allowing goals of income maximization with flexible cropping patterns to emerge. Agriculture has become more productive both in yield per unit of area and yield per unit of labor. Thus, the peasants who have remained in the village have, since the 1970s, been able to raise their standard of living to levels almost as high as in the cities.

One of the most fashionable explanations for the rise in agricultural productivity is "improvements in technology." Rural Koreans are certainly aware of the importance of technical improvements in agriculture, and constant government propaganda on the importance of technology has also left an impression on the village. If asked why they are so poor, the stock response is always, *"kisul sujuni najŭnikka"* (because technical standards are low). Those villagers that believe in progress (and there are skeptics) invariably believe that the key to such progress is technological improvement. The proximate cause of most of the improvements in rural agricultural production have, indeed, been technological improvements. Villagers, for example, cite the use of fertilizer, pesticides, and high yield varieties of crops as the cause of their greater well being.[6]

Equally important to technological changes but harder to conceptualize, have been the changes in conditioning factors that have facilitated the adoption of the new technology. Even during traditional times, the farmers of Sangongni could choose among a variety of crops, tools, and techniques available to them and suitable for application in their environment. Which ones they chose depended upon very detailed and specific considerations of availability of capital, land, and labor, and their proximity to markets. The growing season was limited to about 165 days from May to October, and the adequate but erratic rainfall was concentrated during a single month, which meant that streams were likely to dry out in late summer. Permanent sources of water (such as major rivers) were located well below the level of most of the fields. As important as these considerations were, several cropping strategies with different requirements for capital and labor were possible, and even within one cropping regime, several different means for meeting labor and other requirements could be used.[7] Which cropping strategy was most useful, moreover, also depended upon the organization of the marketing system and the position of the village within it. Given the difficult transportation conditions in remote mountain villages and the unfavorable terms of trade that the dendritic marketing system imposed on remote villages, the most rational strategy for Sangongni peasants was to be as self-sufficient as possible. When transportation costs are high, the profit from marketing crops is reduced, and the cost of purchasing subsistence items rather than producing them oneself is raised. What is saved in transportation cost by producing for one's own use very often offsets the gain made by concentrating on those crops that can be grown most efficiently. Add to this the security that self-production provides from the fluctuations of prices on the market, and a subsistence cropping strategy seems even more attractive. Although many technological changes had been introduced into Sangongni, in 1977 this was the strategy still followed by the majority of farmers. Each farmer had to rationalize his production to produce the most calories on the smallest amount of land possible.

To the villagers of Sangongni, agricultural land is basically of two types: *non,* or irrigated riceland, and *pat,* or nonirrigated rainfall field.

In fact, the ordinary Korean language contains no word that means "field" in the sense of all deliberately plowed and cultivated land.[8] One surmises that the reason is that the cultivation techniques, the mix of crops, the value of the land, and productivity of the different types of fields are so distinct that their differences are psychologically more salient than their similarities. Apart from the two most important categories of irrigated riceland and rainfall field, there are several residual categories of land. Rural Koreans, when asked about their landholdings, will spontaneously reply that they have so much *non* and so much *pat*,[9] but they will seldom volunteer how much forest land (*sallim*) or house-site land (*chipt'ŏ*) they possess. Access to both of these types of land is important for survival. One obviously needs a house site on which to live. Forest is also necessary to provide wood for construction, but even more important, to serve as the source of firewood during the bitter winter months. Ancestral tombs, moreover, are usually placed on such land, though there is usually a place in a village where those without such land may be buried.

Associated with forest and other marginal land are the fire fields (*hwajŏn*). A kind of slash and burn agriculture used to be done on these fields. Formerly they were quite common in mountain areas where public or private forests would be burned and typical field crops such as barley and soybeans planted. Since these fields were often on steep slopes, and since the soil would simply be cropped until it was exhausted, serious erosion and deforestation are associated with it. Because of these problems, in 1966 the Korean government began seriously trying to eliminate it. It was made illegal to cultivate land in public or private forest with a slope steeper than twenty degrees, and fire fields on less steep slopes were required to be turned into plowed land or reforested.[10] There were provisions in the law for compensation for farmers displaced by the elimination of fire fields. By 1977, fire-field farming, which had formerly been quite common around Sangongni, had been eliminated. In other areas of Korea fire-field farmers were fast disappearing. Today, fire-field farming as a way of life is a thing of the past, though there may still be a few fire fields tucked here and there in out-of-the-way places.

To produce most of the crops needed for subsistence, one requires at least modest amounts of all the three kinds of land: irrigated riceland to provide the bulk of the calories consumed; rainfall field to produce other subsistence crops such as barley, soybeans, potatoes (in mountain areas), and vegetables for household consumption; and forest land to provide fuel.[11] Almost all householders, thus, cultivate a variety of types of land so that all the crops necessary for subsistence may be produced. This strategy also has the advantage of offering protection from starvation in cases of crop failure, as well as spreading labor requirements over a greater part of the year.

According to the county statistical yearbook, some 96 percent of the total seeded acreage of paddy and field in Sangongni in the mid-seventies was devoted to the traditional repertory of subsistence crops such as rice, barley, soybeans, kidney beans, maize, daikon radish, Chinese cabbage, red pepper, and potatoes, which would be consumed at home and the surplus marketed.[12] With the exception of a few farmers (who were often self-made men) who had a more entrepreneurial approach to agriculture, householders made no particular effort to focus their production on high value crops, but on the contrary cultivated a mixed variety in small quantities. Most farmers in planning their yearly crop asked first, "What items will I need this year?" often consulting with their wives on their cooking needs. If a farmer expected a wedding, sixtieth-birthday celebration, or some other ritual occasion to come up during the year, he planted cotton fields (for stuffing the quilts that are part of each bride's trousseau) and extra wheat and glutinous rice to brew the unrefined beer (*makkŏlli*)[13] necessary in large quantities for such celebrations. Next he asked, "How much *non* and how much *pat* do I have available?" and finally, "How much male and female labor is there available in my household?" On the basis of this, a peasant householder decided how much land he would cultivate, and what mix of crops he would sow so as to best provide for his needs and make best use of his land and labor. Especially on rainfall fields a great variety of crops was grown, allowing the farmer a good deal of latitude in making his cropping decisions. In Chayanovian fashion, moreover, none of these decisions was independent of one another. The way a farmer met his consumption needs depended on the size and type of land at his disposal, what crops did well on that land, and on the amount of labor available in the household. As will be shown in later chapters, the amount of labor available in the household was related to consumption needs *and* the amount of land owned by the household. The size of the farm was both a cause and consequence of family size; family size was both a cause and consequence of farm size; all decisions were mutually interdependent in an interacting system that included environmental and technological factors but was not determined by them.

Paddy Agriculture

Irrigated riceland, since it is the most productive kind of land, is most highly valued by the villagers. Rice grown in irrigated fields is more than twice as productive as other major field crops grown in rural Korea. This is true whether productivity is calculated in terms of calories or money (Sorensen 1981a:533) and whether it is calculated per unit of labor or per unit of land. Thus in 1960, the gross return per man-hour of labor on irrigated rice was some 129 hwan per hour ($0.20) while for barley and wheat it was only about 33 hwan per hour ($0.05).[14] In 1977, the gross productivity of irrigated rice in Sangongni was around 11,300 wŏn ($22.60) per are while that for wheat was about 2,600 wŏn ($5.20) per are. In periurban villages, where high-value fruit and vegetable crops may be grown for sale in urban markets, rainfall field can be more valuable than irrigated rice field, but in Sangongni any land that is capable of being converted to paddy will be so converted, even at great expense of capital or labor.

In mountainous Kangwŏn Province, only 35 percent of plowed land is paddy, but in this respect Sangongni is relatively fortunate. Of the 103 hectares of paddy and field in Sangongni, 48 hectares (46.6 percent) was paddy in 1977. Much of this land is made up of terraces carved in the slopes of any ravine with running water. In the early seventies, a reclamation project added some new paddy to the village by providing the already leveled and diked land with a secure supply of water from the main stream that runs through the village. Again in 1977, the villagers hired a contractor with heavy equipment to level and dike some rainfall fields in the village that were then provided with water from the river by an old one-cylinder gasoline pump. Between 1977 and 1983 villagers continued to build bits of paddy where water was available, though the area involved was small.

Steepness of slopes seems to have been less of a limiting factor in this mountainous area than the provision of a secure source of irrigation water. In the absence of mechanical devices for lifting water, of course, the capabilities of the villagers have been limited. There were many large fields in the village suitable for paddy if water were available, while, on the other hand, even the steepest and remotest slopes of the mountains have been terraced if only the smallest spring is available to provide water for irrigation. In the mountains surrounding the village I discovered five or six inaccessible springs a hundred meters and more above the village where small *non* had been constructed. Many of these postage-stamp *non* in the middle of the mountain were still in use in 1977, though some had already been abandoned because of inconvenience and poor productivity. In 1977 one could observe farmers leading their draft animals up the steepest mountain tracks, after their main fields had been planted, to these remote irrigated fields. The ability of the farmers to maneuver a cow and plow in one of these small, steep fields was amazing. I saw one farmer plowing with his cow a paddy that might (by a generous estimate) have been two meters square, with a steep drop off on one side and a dike of a higher terrace on the other. By 1983 most of these small terraces had been abandoned, and even some of the larger ones as well. One villager who owned about twenty-five ares of irrigated riceland on one of these terraces had abandoned these fields in favor of rented irrigated riceland in the village because, as he said, productivity was so low that the expected return did not justify the time and trouble of cultivating them.

Sangongni, being close to the top of a watershed, could count only on the runoff from the total area of the village itself. The river, being much lower than the level of the village, was not a source of irrigation water until the introduction of the gasoline pump in 1977. The villagers relied primarily on the small rivulets and streams coming out of the mountain gorges for irrigation. Because of the sharply seasonal rains of Korea, these dried up in the early spring and late summer, so that the amount of land that could be irrigated for rice remained limited.

Lack of paddy may be one of the causes of poverty in Sangongni, but agricultural life revolves around the very seasonal and labor-intensive cultivation of irrigated rice nevertheless. Even as late as 1977, virtually all of the labor was done by hand or with animal power. Mechanization had just begun with the introduction of power tillers around 1975 and there were between four and six of them in Sangongni in 1977. Although by 1983 the number of motor tillers had increased substantially, the mechanization of agriculture had not proceeded fast enough to prevent a reduction in productivity due to labor shortages.

The rice season begins in April with the repair of dikes and the beginning of soil preparation. This is well before the growing season proper begins. Before the introduction of chemical fertilizers, the fertility of the soil was maintained by the use of compost (*t'oebi*), and "guest soil" (*kaekt'o*), soil brought from other areas. If straw compost is used, it must be worked into the soil well before planting time. Thus farmers could be seen plowing leftover rice straw or grass cut from the surrounding hills into the soil well before anything could grow in it. A compost made in the farmhouse can also be used. Generally farmsteads have a separate ash house where the ashes from the fire are stored. These ash houses are also used for other kinds of garbage and refuse and often, too, for urination and defecation. All of these ingredients are allowed to cure over the winter and then may be added to fields in the spring. These "cured" ashes, as well as urine collected in pots for the purpose, was commonly used on rainfall field but not on paddy. *Kaekt'o* traditionally was brought to irrigated fields in baskets set on an A-frame backpack, but nowadays it is not unusual to see a dump truck bringing new soil to an irrigated field. This was done in Sangongni in 1977 when the charge was 2,000 wŏn per load.

While the dikes are being repaired and various kinds of soil improvement projects are under way, the rice seed is also being prepared. Shortly before planting time, the seed is soaked in a mildly saline solution for about a week in a warm place (often on the heated floor inside the house). In 1977, farmers were preparing about one kilogram of seed per are of land. The seedbeds are laid out beginning in about mid-April. Since the early seventies in Sangongni, vinyl greenhousing has been used on the seedbeds. A fertile field with a secure source of water and conveniently located near the majority of the farmer's fields is chosen, and prepared by being plowed, flooded, harrowed, and drained. The seedbeds are marked out on the field with stakes and string, and fertilized with a composite commercial fertilizer of potash and urea allocated to them by the government.[15] Fertilizer is spread at the rate of about one bag (costing 2,300 wŏn) for about 180 liters of seed. When the bed is prepared, the rice seed is broadcast on it, and then clear vinyl supported by bamboo arches erected over them. By this method, the seeds can be sprouted almost a month before the last frost of the season.

All the rice grown in Korea is one of a number of strains of *Oryza sativa japonica*,[16] the only race of rice grain north of 30 degrees latitude. Colloquially, Koreans distinguish the two basic kinds of rice as *mebyŏ* (regular rice) and *ch'albyŏ* (glutinous rice). *Pyŏ* (the *byŏ* of the compounds above) refers to unhusked rice or plants growing in the field, but not to rice seedlings (*mo*), husked rice (*ssal*), nor steamed rice (*pap*). The Korean government has put a great deal of effort into developing improved seed stocks and promoting their use. Numerous strains of improved rice have been introduced, and these new strains were already in general use by 1977 in Sangongni. Progressive farmers could talk about the relative merits of each of the strains, and even each of the substrains. The major strains of rice the villagers told me they were planting in 1977 were T'ongil, Miryang (both numbers 22 and 23), T'aegŭgi, ilban pyŏ (ordinary rice), Yusin, Ponggwang, and glutinous rice. The poorest tenant farmers could plant nothing but ordinary rice, since they lacked the capital to buy the new strains. The more prosperous farmers, however, all tried to choose that strain of rice best suited to the microclimate of each of their fields. One farmer whose seeding I investigated in depth planted five different strains of rice in his seedbeds. Except for the glutinous rice, whose amount was determined by the amount of glutinous rice cake his wife was planning to make and the amount of rice beer she was planning to brew, each of the kinds of rice was selected for the microclimate of the fields he was planting. T'ongil was for his well-watered fields up the canyon, T'aegŭgi, a short-stemmed variety, was for those fields he thought were subject to wind damage, and Yusin was for those fields subject to dessication, and so forth. All of the varieties were those recommended by the Agricultural Guidance Office of the township for villages of Sangongni's elevation and latitude.

After the planting of the seed, the seedbeds are flooded again. The seedlings sprout in about ten days, after which they are gradually "weaned" from the greenhouses in preparation for transplantation (*monaegi*). The preparation of the rest of the irrigated ricefields now begins in earnest. Each of the fields must be plowed, flooded, and harrowed. This can be done by hand, but the most general traditional method is with a cow-drawn plow. The Korean plow (*chaenggi*) resembles the Mediterranean scratch-plow, or ard (E. R. Wolf 1966:32). It is shaped roughly like an A turned on its side with the farmer controlling it from the tip. One foot is attached to the yoke of the draft animals, and the other foot is furnished with a metal plowshare. It may be pulled by one or two animals, though in Sangongni, as in Kangwŏn Province generally, two animals are usually used for plowing. The metal plowshare is spade-shaped and mounted so it scrapes a furrow in the soil of rainfall fields. When irrigated rice fields are being plowed, however, a metal moldboard or *pyŏt* is attached to one side of the blade so that the soil is actually turned over.

In irrigated fields, of course, the object of plowing is not to create a furrow, but to mix the soil. The work of the *pyŏt* in turning over the soil is aided by the plowman, for he must set the whole plow at an angle and lean into it to accomplish his objective. Since the *pyŏt* only works on one side of the plow, the successive passes of the plow must be quite close to one another. Depending upon the condition of the soil, this can be a slow and arduous task (as when the field cannot be properly drained so that the cows become mired in the mud) or it can be done with some dispatch. Under favorable conditions, good farmers could plow five ares an hour or more. With a motor tiller, however, plowing is somewhat faster. One informant in 1983 said a motor tiller could be hired for a day for 20,000 wŏn ($26.67) (or for an hour for 2000 wŏn) and plow forty to fifty ares. Although one could hire a *chaenggi* and team for only 15,000 wŏn ($20.00) per day, it could only plow half as much. Thus, plowing with a motor tiller is at least twice as fast as with a team of cows.

Following the plowing, the irrigated field must be flooded and harrowed. This is usually done a day or so after the plowing, though I have seen fields plowed and harrowed in the same day, with the harrower only one step in front of the transplanting teams. The harrow (*ssŏre*), a long board with wooden teeth fastened to a frame yoked to a cow, can be pulled by a single animal. The harrow is used to break up the last clods of soil into a smooth mud, and to level the field so that the water will be the same height over the whole field when it is flooded. With the motor tillers, harrowing is done with a perforated circular band about a foot wide that rolls over the soil as the machine moves over the field. As with plowing it is quicker than using animals, but the total amount of time spent plowing or harrowing is not great whatever method is used.

Transplantation of the rice seedlings begins in mid-May when the danger of frost is over. This is the most crucial and difficult of the steps involved in the cultivation of irrigated rice. If the seedlings are planted too early, they will not develop properly—the roots and leaves will not grow quickly. If they are transplanted too late the season will be too short for them to mature properly. In Sangongni, some rice every year does not ripen before the end of the growing season. This is most common in the higher ravines, but even rice that is grown down in the village will lose some of its yield if not transplanted in time. Rice that has been transplanted in time should be well established by the time the southwest monsoon brings the rain in July.

Within the village itself, there are other factors besides the length of the growing season that must be taken into consideration in timing rice transplantation. The supply of water is limited. Rains usually come in the early spring, but some of the creeks may dry up again until the coming of the monsoon. If a man's rice fields are *ch'ŏnsudap*, diked fields fed only by rain, two weeks difference in the timing of transplantation may make the difference between having a field with a water supply, or not. It is absolutely necessary for the fields to be flooded during the transplantation itself and for at least one to three days afterward. Because of the potential for the shortage of water during this critical period, each field must be completed in a single day, so that the water can be diverted to other fields after the seedlings have been established. Some irrigation systems with a less secure water supply may have to be done first, and in irrigation systems where the water is insufficient to flood all the fields at once, owners of fields must cooperate so that an order of flooding and transplantation can be agreed upon.

Because each field must be transplanted quickly and because "many hands make work light," the backbreaking task of transplanting rice is accomplished by teams of men in Sangongni. There are various ways these teams can be organized: workers may be hired as individuals for wages or *p'umsak* (the going rate for transplantation work was 2000 wŏn per *majigi* in 1977 and 10,000 wŏn per *majigi* in 1983; a *majigi* is about 6.6 ares here), whole teams may be hired to plant a section of the village fields (a traditional method known as *ture* that has been revived in some areas where there is a labor shortage), but the most common method of organizing such teams for transplantation is through labor exchange or *p'umasi*. In labor exchange, each farmer makes it known when he is going to transplant his fields. Whichever villagers wish to show up on the appointed day join in the transplantation. Plenty of villagers show up without being asked specifically because the recipient's household owes an equivalent day for each day that one works. Each man knows approximately how many man-hours it will take to do his fields, so he will make sure that he puts in enough work for others so that he will get enough work back to transplant his fields. Rich farmers that have more land to plant than they care to work on hire workers in addition to exchanging labor. Often a particular work team is made up both of men doing labor exchange and men working for wages.

The traditional elite pattern was for women not to participate in agricultural activities (Ko et al. 1963:48; Kim Chusuk 1985:215), but the women of Sangongni do much agricultural work, mostly in the rainfall fields, if their household duties do not take up all their time. Nevertheless, it is unusual in Sangongni for women to transplant rice seedlings. During transplantation, not only does the woman have her ordinary housework but also increased cooking responsibilities. On the days in which the paddies of a household are being transplanted, the females must provide the men of the household and all the men working as exchange laborers (but not wage workers) with a meal approximately every two hours. This in itself is a full-time job, and if many laborers have to be taken care of, a woman may have to exchange labor through the women's exchange labor network to get enough help. Naturally this labor acquired by exchange has to be paid back, so that even on days when other households are transplanting, a woman may be fully occupied helping labor exchange partners. If a member of the household has hired himself out for money, moreover, the household women still have to take his meals to the field for him. The spring silk-raising season—primarily a female responsibility—also conflicts with this time.[17]

More labor is necessary for transplanting rice than for any other task of the year, and it must be done within a very short period. Mobilizing enough labor at the right time is critical, and the value of having fields scattered around the village rather than in one place now becomes apparent. That there may be a week or so difference between fields in different locations in the optimal timing of seedbed making, transplantation, and harvest means that the tasks for each field can be staggered so as to make a more efficient use of the household's labor resources. In a mountain area, where the microclimates associated with paddies at different altitudes can be quite diverse, the whole village benefits from the workload for the cultivation of rice being less concentrated in time than it would be if all fields were in the same ecological zone. Thus, the subdivision and scattering of plots characteristic of Korean agriculture does not necessarily lead to inefficiency in the absence of mechanization.[18]

When all the seedlings have been transplanted, the farmers can turn from rice to other crops. As long as the rainy season arrives on schedule, there is little to worry about. Periodic flooding and drying of the fields helps keep the weeds down, so only desultory weeding and spraying for pests and disease is usually necessary. In former times, if there was a drought, there was little the farmers could do for those fields without secure all-season irrigation, and a formal *kiuje,* or rain ceremony, was as effective as anything in protecting the crops. In recent years, however, the introduction of pumps has put the villagers in a much stronger position. During droughts, the problem has seldom been the absolute lack of water, but rather the lack of the ability to raise water into fields that needed it. During 1977, the rainy season was late and several farmers used the village motor tillers to pump water into fields (the pumps had been supplied by the government to the villagers to try to minimize drought damage). Although the rains came before the crop in the village was damaged, the ability to pump water may have improved the yield in some of the fields where the pumps were used.

The rice harvest begins in mid-September. The amount of labor necessary is comparable to the amount necessary to transplant the rice seedlings. Nevertheless, the sense of urgency felt during the transplantation period is absent. The rice has stopped growing because of the cold, so one or two days one way or the other make little difference.[19] The rice must be reaped, dried, tied into sheaves, and brought to the threshing floor before being threshed, bagged, dried, and rebagged. The completion of these tasks requires a large amount of labor, but labor exchange, labor teams, and other devices are not used. By and large, the harvest is completed with household labor.

In reaping, the rule of thumb is the same as for transplanting—one person is supposed to be able to do one *majigi* per day. However, only the youngest and most vigorous workers can manage this much in transplanting rice, while even an old grandmother can manage to reap a *majigi* in two hours or so. Reaping is done with the traditional Korean sickle, or *nat*. A handful of rice stalks is grabbed in the left hand and then cut with the sickle held in the right. As the bunches are cut, they are laid in neat rows for drying, so that they will be easy to collect and tie in sheaves. The rice stalks are said to dry adequately in three days, after which they are gathered and tied in sheaves for threshing. Threshing can be done in a variety of ways and in a number of places. The most traditional way is to take the sheaves home, flail them by hand in the courtyard, and winnow them with a winnowing basket, but no one does rice this way anymore. Some have foot-powered threshers used either in the fields or at home, but the majority use power threshers. These are large machines powered by the motor tillers to which they are connected by a belt. Villagers claimed three persons working hard could thresh about fifty bags (55 kg each) of paddy a day with a foot-powered thresher, but that five workers could do more than two hundred with the power one. The fee for power threshing was 3 percent of what was threshed. Few villagers harvest even as much as one hundred bags of rice a year. As Chayanov noted for some of the peasants of Russia (1966:39), rather than pay a threshing fee, the villagers of Sangongni often continued to spend the week or so after the harvest threshing with household labor, which otherwise would not be put to use.

As the threshing progresses, the pace of work quickens. Many people are anxious to sell some early rice on the market because they are short of money. Taxes have to be paid in kind in November, too, and the grain must be properly dried by that time. The villagers often work late into the night to get the whole crop threshed and stored as quickly as possible. Prices on the free market are somewhat higher than selling to the government, but a certain proportion of the crop must go to the government. The price one receives also depends upon the variety of rice. Of the high-yield varieties, T'ongil and Yusin were not considered top quality, while Miryang and T'aegŭgi were considered better. Villages expected T'ongil to get only about 75 percent of what Miryang would get, and Yusin perhaps 85 percent or 90 percent of Miryang. Many people still considered the traditional ordinary rice known as *iban pyŏ* as the best tasting. The top government price for rice in 1977 was 24,000 wŏn ($48.00) per husked bag (60 kg), and in 1983 the top price had reached 70,000 wŏn ($93.33) per husked bag. The standard answer on productivity questions was always "three *kama* per *majigi*," which works out to 2.4 metric tons per hectare, but this figure is an obvious anachronism that has not been accurate for fifteen years. 1977 had been an especially good year, and people got yields in Sangongni of 6 metric tons per hectare in some cases. Since then the weather has not always been as favorable, and villagers reported lower yields for subsequent years.

Field Agriculture

In contrast to rice agriculture, which, though very intensive, is also very straightforward, field agriculture is extremely diverse and complex. In paddy agriculture everyone simply tries to get the best yield of rice each year from his paddies. Choices revolve around which variety of rice to use, how much capital input such as fertilizer to use, how much glutinous rice the household will need in the year, and so forth. For field agriculture, all of the above decisions are made, but many more additional factors have to be taken into account, such as the current market prices for different crops, what and how many domestic animals have to be fed, and what rotation of the crop will be most suitable for each field. Current cash needs may affect planting as well as such considerations as whether there is to be a marriage or betrothal in the family. Nevertheless, most field crops grown traditionally were, like rice, both subsistence and cash crops. With the recent growing farm size new cash crops are becoming more common, but they have not as yet come to dominate field agriculture. The most important of these rainfall field subsistence/cash crops are common barley (*kŏt pori*), wheat (*ch'ammil*), maize (*oksusu*), sorghum (*susu*), red bean (*p'at* = *Phaseolus angularis*), blackeyed pea (*p'anmitk'ong*), kidney bean (*kang-namk'ong, tangk'ong* = *Phaseolus vulgaris*), buckwheat (*memil*), sesame (*ch'amkke*), and the oil crop, perilla (*tŭlkke*). It would be a large farmer, indeed, to sell more than ten bags of any of these crops, which were commonly grown in plots of around ten ares, or so, in 1977, though by 1983 such fields had become larger.

Wheat and soybeans can be taken as typical rainfall field crops. Wheat can be planted either in the autumn or in the spring. The crop will not grow in the winter in Sangongni, but by planting in the fall, some people feel that they get their wheat or barley crop earlier than if it is planted in the spring. I did not notice in 1977 more than a couple of weeks difference in the timing of the harvest, however, between autumn and spring plantings. For the spring crop, plowing begins in March. The plow is the same one used for irrigated rice fields, but the *pyŏt* that turns over the soil is not used on rainfall field. As with paddy plowing, two cows are normally yoked to a plow and controlled by the single plowman who follows behind. The plowing of rainfall fields takes more work from the team than the plowing of irrigated fields. The soil is harder, and very often the field is not level. Rainfall fields are plowed twice, but since harrowing is not necessary the field preparation takes about the same time as for paddy. Experienced farmers sing to their cows while plowing to keep them going straight and from stopping every few minutes to munch on some succulent morsel of grass or leaves. Plowing takes experience and steady nerves. I have seen novices utterly fail to keep teams under control. In my experience, plowing is invariably done by men (though women I have talked to claim women plow, too, on occasion).

The seeding of barley or wheat is done at the time of plowing, often with a small labor-exchange group of four or five people. The plowman is followed by one or two men or women carrying a hemispherical bamboo basket called a *sok'uri* filled with seeds well mixed with ashes and compost. This mixture is dropped—often along with commercial fertilizer—in the furrows, which are filled by someone following behind with a hoe. Unlike rice, which doesn't have serious weed problems which can't be controlled by herbicides (except for the pesky barnyard millet, *Echinochloa frumentacea*, which mimics rice in looks and habitat), barley and wheat fields need to be carefully and laboriously weeded with a hand trowel. Depending upon when the wheat or barley sprouts, it must be done in late April or early May just before the rice transplantation season. This kind of weeding is done by both men and women—but more often by women. During April one often comes across groups of women formed by labor exchange engaged in weeding major field crops. If the crop has been timed right, it will be ready for harvest at the end of June just before the rainy season. Later crops are also harvested in July or even August.

The season for soybeans is more flexible than that for wheat and barley. Planting ranges from early spring to midsummer, depending upon when the harvest is desired, when household labor is available, and what kind of crop rotation one is using on one's fields. Plowing and seeding are, in the main, like those processes for barley, with one weeding necessary shortly after the plants have sprouted. Some soybeans are harvested as early as mid-July, while others are harvested in September or even later. Bean crops are typically planted to follow barley or wheat so that three crops can be had in two years. Farmers that plant tobacco usually interplant soybeans between the rows in late spring so that when the tobacco harvest is over in midsummer, the soybeans are ready to take over the field. Soybeans are also planted along irrigation ditches and between fields.

Unlike rice and barley, which are usually threshed by power or foot machine, such crops as soybeans and sesame must be done completely by hand. This is, no doubt, one reason they are grown in smaller quantities than the grain crops. Sesame stalks, after being reaped and dried, are brought into the courtyard of the farmhouse and beaten with a flail until the seeds are dislodged. The straw and grain must then be hand winnowed. This is usually done in winnowing baskets (*k'i*) by the women of the household. A breeze is not required for winnowing. The baskets are constructed in such a way that as the grain and chaff are repeatedly shaken up and down, the lighter chaff works its way to the end of the basket and drops to the ground while the heavier grain remains at the other end.

Vegetable Crops

Although not important in Sangongni as producers of cash, vegetable crops are indispensable for subsistence. Even in the market towns, it is difficult to find vegetables for sale, and in the village virtually all vegetables for home consumption are grown at home. Even those households that do not engage in agriculture have to maintain a vegetable patch for home use.[20] If it is necessary to obtain vegetables that one has not grown, the only recourse is to go from house to house trying to persuade someone to part with some of theirs for cash. This sometimes is not easy, because the quantity people plant is usually based on the amount that they expect to use. The average vegetable garden is several ares in extent and, apart from plowing, is the almost exclusive responsibility of the women. Thus, if the house mistress becomes ill and cannot tend her garden, it will go to seed and weed before it will be tended by the husband.

In 1977, a few families built vinyl greenhouses for growing early vegetables. Since Sangongni is too far from the city for market gardening, however, these are not common. Most families are content with their winter store of pickled cabbage (*kimch'i*) and the herbs that can be gathered by the streams and hills in the early spring. The main crops grown by the women in their kitchen gardens are potatoes, sweet potatoes, hot pepper, garlic, two kinds of daikon radish (one hot and one mild), zucchini, cucumber, leaf lettuce, kidney beans, squash, bellflower (*Platycodon grandiflorum*), and Chinese cabbage (*Brassica pekinensis*).

Two kitchen gardens are usually planted: one in the spring and one in the fall. The spring vegetable garden includes leaf lettuce, garlic, radish, kidney beans, bellflower, zucchini, and other vegetables, which start producing by the end of May or beginning of June, and provide fresh vegetables throughout the summer. The fall vegetable garden, planted in midsummer, provides the vegetables for *kimjang,* the manufacture of various pickled vegetables that will be used over the winter. These gardens, thus, are devoted primarily to garlic, Chinese cabbage, radishes of various sorts, and cucumbers. Squash and cucumber are usually trained to grow over the fences of the homestead, or the ash house, and the autumn sight of grass-roofed ash houses covered with vines with their gourds hanging down is typical in country districts.

Other vegetables are grown in separate gardens. These include potatoes, which are an important subsistence crop in mountain areas, sweet potatoes, which because of their association with poverty, are not grown in large quantities, and red peppers. Red peppers are one of the chief ingredients in winter *kimch'i,* but because they are thought to be hard on the soil they are grown in separate gardens. They are a valuable crop, but in 1977 they were grown only for home consumption. By 1983, however, they had become an important cash as well as subsistence crop.

Cash Crops

In 1977, the most important cash crops were tobacco (*tambae*) and silk cocoons (*koch'i*). To these were added by 1983 two traditional crops that had not been raised primarily for cash before: red pepper (*koch'u* = *Capsicum longum*), and true sesame (*ch'amkkae*). The area planted in these crops had expanded considerably. Three crops used in Chinese herbal medicine had also been introduced by 1983: black sesame (*kŏmŭnkkae*), ginseng (*insam*), and foxglove (*saengjih-wang*). Several of these require a large initial investment in land and planting, but then require less care over the years. Ginseng, for example, needs to be planted in the shade provided by small thatched roofs erected over the field. Although the price of ginseng is high, the roots do not reach proper size for seven years. These crops are considered quite speculative by the peasants, and, since they have no experience with them and the payoff for them is, at least in the case of ginseng, far in the future, they make peasant farmers a little nervous. In fact, the owner of the largest ginseng field in the village was not a peasant farmer at all, but the owner of the rice mill and village pharmacy. The true (or "white") sesame crop, for example, was wiped out by a heavy rain in late summer and was almost a total loss. Ginseng and tobacco are government monopolies and those villagers that grow them get the seedlings through the agricultural cooperative and must sell the entire crop back to them. Although this may limit the potential profits of the crop, since the price is guaranteed beforehand, it also reduces the risk for the peasant.

Those who grow tobacco are required to grow no more and no less than four *tan*, or about 40 ares. In 1977, five houses planted tobacco, though by 1983 only two houses were still doing so. The seedlings are sprouted in vinyl greenhouses, and then must be transplanted into fields plowed and hoed in a special way to create raised rows where the seedlings are set (Sorensen 1981a:465). These rows are covered with plastic to raise the soil temperature and help control weeds. A great deal of labor—something like 120 manhours—is required to transplant four *tan* of tobacco. The labor requirement is so great that even the largest households must hire some of the labor used to transplant tobacco. As with other field crops, the tobacco has to be weeded several times as well as being picked several times. If everything is done efficiently, one task succeeds another with no interference. First the tobacco greenhouses are made, then the tobacco is transplanted, then the rice seedbeds must be made, then the tobacco must be weeded, then the rice must be transplanted, then the tobacco must be weeded again, and then picked and dried in the drying houses with fires underneath. Thus the combination of tobacco and rice will keep even the largest household busy from April through June. Few other field crops can be managed by such households during this period.

The production of raw silk cocoons was probably the major source of ready cash for villagers in 1977, and it continued to be important in 1983. The raising of silk is almost as labor intensive as tobacco, but the number of households involved is much greater. Though silk can be raised twice a year—in the spring and in the fall—the trees must be severely pruned right after the spring silk season to get a second crop of mulberry leaves to feed the worms, and many villagers did not bother with the second crop.

The silkworm eggs are bought from the agricultural cooperative. They hatch in mid-May, and an intensive month is spent feeding them the only thing they will eat: newly sprouted mulberry leaves. After twenty-nine days, they stop eating and spin their cocoons, after which they are gathered up to be sold back to the agricultural cooperative. Unlike tobacco, where the area one must plant is fixed, silkworm raising can be varied by the amount of eggs one buys and thus the amount of silk one raises. Although the majority of households raise some silk, only those households with enough rainfall field to spare from subsistence crops and a large female work force raised enough silk to require a separate mulberry orchard. Other households plant their trees between fields, along irrigation ditches, or around their houses. Mulberry trees even grow wild in the mountains, and one enterprising widow with no land used to gather wild leaves in the mountain for sale during the mulberry season. Silkworms are voracious eaters and it is a full-time task for one or two people to pick the fresh leaves needed every day for the worms.

When the silkworms are about to spin their cocoons, they stop eating. At this point, a wooden frame is set up in the room of the house (usually the *anbang,* the inner room of the house mistress) where the worms are being raised and a plastic mesh is put in the frame so that the worms will have a place to attach for spinning. If they are too crowded, they will get in each other's way and produce inferior cocoons. In a couple of days, after the spinning is done, the cocoons are gathered, cleaned, and graded. In 1977, top quality cocoons were going for 1900 wŏn ($3.80) per kilo. A good harvest was 50 kilos, with about 3000 wŏn ($6.00) for the eggs, so a net profit of 92,000 wŏn ($184) could be had for a month's work.

Tree Crops

Orchard crops other than mulberry are not important in this mountain area. The only tree crops that can survive the rigorous climate, according to villagers, are chestnuts and jujube (*taech'u*), a chewy red fruit somewhat smaller than a prune with a flavor reminiscent of dates. Two thousand chestnut trees had been given to the village in 1975 by the township government to reforest a mountain area destroyed by fire, but these have not produced. Other fruit trees such as plum are sometimes found in the village, and cherries grow wild in the mountains, but none of these is exploited commercially. This is both because of the rigors of the climate and the difficulty of transportation for something so delicate and perishable as fruit.

Although fruit crops have yet to become an important village income, the sale of lumber rights was a good source of money for those that owned tracts of forest. Forest land was not subject to land reform after World War II, and many villagers—especially those of elite background—own in their own right, or are part owners with their lineagemates, of large tracts of forest. Since most villagers are short of capital, the planting of trees for lumber has not been usual even among the more prosperous villagers. Many deforested slopes that can no longer be cultivated because of their steepness and the erosion control laws have remained covered only by scrub oak. Other slopes in the village have recently been clear cropped because of an infestation of a beetle that is killing the pine forests all over central Korea.

Animal Husbandry

The main domesticated farm animals of South Korea are chickens, cattle, dogs, and pigs. Chicken, the only meat commonly eaten in the village, is raised by women on grain grown by the household. They are also allowed to scratch outside—though if they get into the vegetable patches they will pick at the leaves of the lettuce and make it inedible. They are raised from chicks brought into the village by itinerant salesmen from large commercial hatcheries. Eggs are highly valued, and are eaten raw or cooked. The epitome of the easy life, according to traditional thought, is "eating lots of eggs." Few people, however, eat them more than once or twice a month, and meat traditionally was eaten no oftener.

Dogs are also considered edible (although some people do not approve of eating dog meat). Dogs are fed leftover rice and other food that people also eat, but they are not considered pets; they are raised either for food or cash. The dog soup season is late summer, and during this period some of the village men usually prepare dog soup once or twice for themselves and their friends. The soup, known as *posint'ang* or "health preserving soup," is also prepared in special restaurants in Seoul and other big cities. It is considered a great delicacy in late summer, and during this season dogs fetch good prices. They went for about 15,000 wŏn in 1977 and around 30,000 wŏn in 1983.

Pigs have to be penned and require a good deal of food. Although the agricultural offices have been promoting the raising of pigs for some time, in 1977 there were only two pigs in the village. Their number had raised to around ten by 1983, but the raising of pigs was not popular and was confined to only a few households who did not keep it up in subsequent years. Cattle, on the other hand, had exploded in numbers. In 1977, cattle were kept primarily as draft animals. Although calves could be sold for a good price to both farmers who wanted to raise them as draft animals and at the cattle markets, villagers felt in 1977 that the price one could get did not justify the trouble and expense of raising them and walking them the twenty-five kilometers to the cattle market in Ch'unch'ŏn. All of this had dramatically changed by 1983. Villagers told me that calves were going for a million wŏn (about $1333 at the 1983 exchange rate), two-year-olds for a million and a half ($2000), and cows (which are more valuable because they produce calves) for three million wŏn ($4000). Although cattle are still being raised as draft animals, they are also being raised for sale. While in 1977 few farmers had more than a cow and one calf, in 1983, most villagers had more than one cow, and some were raising as many as six. One farmer in the next village up the canyon had built a large barn where he was raising fifteen head of cattle. Prices for cattle, however, had fallen again by 1985, to the extent that it has become an explosive political issue.

Labor Complementation

The exact mix of crops that a farmer cultivates is an individual strategy. We have already noted in the discussion of rice agriculture that a moderate scattering of fields not only increases a peasant's security from crop failure, but also spreads his peak labor needs a little more evenly. This phenomenon of labor complementation can be seen even more dramatically when we compare the seasonal labor patterns of the different crops. With a given population, a village can cultivate only a certain maximum amount of riceland without mechanization—

that amount the total village labor force can handle at the peak labor period, the transplantation of seedlings. Although population may be increased to meet labor demands for rice during this peak period, this is an inefficient strategy because each worker has to be supported the whole year long, even if his work is only used one month out of the year. Effective choice of cropping patterns so that the peak labor periods of different crops do not coincide can allow the household or village to use its labor more efficiently, however.

In Sangongni, the timing of the peak labor need for the various crops was complementary in most cases. This can easily be seen if the crops are divided into three groups: rice, spring crops other than rice, and summer crops. The agricultural calendar begins in March with the plowing of the first rainfall fields for the vegetable gardens of the women, and for wheat and barley. At this time, the total amount of agricultural work that has to be done does not make full use of household labor resources. Things pick up in mid-April when the rice seedbeds must be prepared. These are mostly completed by the first of May. During the next two weeks, two big tasks have to be done: the first weeding of the wheat and barley fields must be completed, and the main rice fields must be plowed and prepared for transplantation. In those households with extra females that can be spared from domestic labor (such as those with a new daughter-in-law) these females work on the weeding to free the males for the preparation of the rice fields. This is practical labor complementation rather than part of the male-female division of labor. Both males and females weed and who does it depends upon the precise labor situation within the household. This task must be completed by the time the rice transplantation starts. From mid-May to mid-June, the labor resources of all the villages in Korea are strained to the limit during the transplantation of rice. This season corresponds with the spring silkworm season. Thus, only if a house has surplus female labor *or* if it does not have enough riceland at its disposal to occupy its time will the raising of silk take place on a large scale. The wheat and barley harvest follows the transplantation of rice. After the barley harvest the summer crops can be put in. These include various beans, maize, and other grains such as millet and sorghum, which are not commonly planted any more. In rainy July, there is less demand for labor. Things pick up in mid-August when the *kimch'i* gardens have to be put in, and the fall silkworm season gets going. The rice harvest follows the planting of the *kimjang* gardens and the end of the fall silkworm season. These relations are shown in figure 3.3.

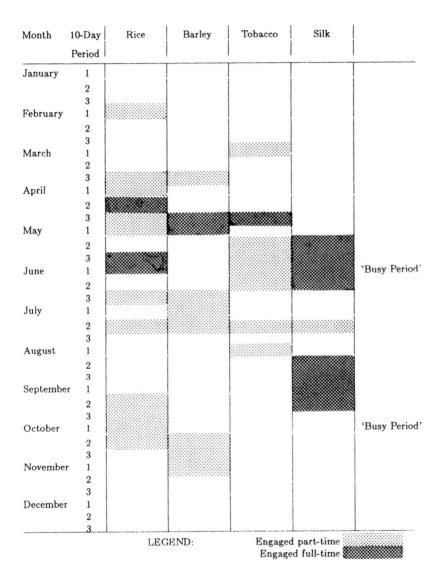

Fig. 3.3. Timing of labor requirements of major crop groups

Each household, then, requires some of each of the kinds of land in the village: irrigated riceland (*non*), rainfall field (*pat*), and forest land. It is a good strategy for householders to have such land for at least three reasons: (1) they can grow each of the crops they need for their own use in the environment where transportation is difficult and the terms of trade favor those villages near the city; (2) it allows householders to spread the risk of crop failure over several crops with different environmental requirements; and (3) it allows for the efficient complementation of farm labor over the growing season so that all the labor demand isn't concentrated into a short period.

Culture, Environment, and Agricultural Growth

Agriculture as practiced in Sangongni is in evolution. Techniques and crops are changing as Korea becomes wealthier and develops a more elaborate economy with a more intricate division of labor. Agricultural villages are more closely tied in with the national and world economy. How has this enabled the farmers of Sangongni to reach a higher standard of living, rather than become proletarianized as Kautsky expected? To improve their standard of living, it has not been enough to simply adopt new techniques and increase production. All of these things could have happened without increasing the standard of living if productivity per capita had not increased. Over the past generation the amount of labor input in Korean farms has declined, while the productivity of the same farms both in gross terms and in per hectare terms has increased. Some of the reasons for this phenomenon are known. Capital inputs into agriculture have steadily increased. Per hectare usage of fertilizer and pesticides have steadily increased as have purchases of animal feeds and farming materials. Production is up, but the amount of cropland has been static and even the farmland per worker has changed little since 1967, the year of peak farm population. Mechanization, on the other hand, only got going in the late seventies, and thus is not responsible for the increase in productivity before that time.

How could Korean villagers reduce the amount of labor on their farms without mechanization, and yet increase their productivity? In answering this question, it may be helpful to think of Korean villages like Sangongni as going through three stages of development since World War II. These stages might be termed the *traditional* from the end of World War II through the late 1960s, the *transitional* during the seventies, and the *mechanization*, which has begun at different times in different villages, but which is going on right now in San-gongni.

The Traditional Stage

For the traditional stage of Korean agriculture, we have emphasized the relationship of Korean agricultural practices to the environment. We have seen, however, that even in traditional times the farming system of Sangongni could not be interpreted simply as the application of a certain technology in a certain environment (Steward 1955:38–39). This is because the significance of technology and environment for production and social organization varies with such sociological circumstances as the way the marketing system is organized and the level of capitalization of society. We have interpreted the subsistence strategies of traditional Korean farmers as an adaptation to at least five environmental and sociological factors: the short growing season, concentrated and erratic rainfall, population density (which created a shortage of land suitable for agriculture), poor transportation, and a dendritic marketing pattern that imposed unfavorable terms of trade on villagers distant from urban centers.

Given these environmental and sociological circumstances, the traditional Korean householder had a single problem: how could he produce, with family labor and simple hand tools on a very small amount of land, enough to feed himself, the landlord, and the tax collector? His strategy was to concentrate on producing the most calories per space of land that he could, with the labor he had available. By converting rainfall field into riceland, he could double his production per unit of land, and double the productivity of his labor. By providing secure irrigation for his riceland, he could not only provide himself with a certain amount of insurance from crop failure, but also could raise his productivity even more. Where land was short, then, even considerable investment of time and money was justified for converting rainfall field to irrigated field. Since labor could be used for few other activities during the off-season, its use in converting land to irrigated paddy, moreover, did not entail taking labor away from other productive activity. Under such circumstances all land that could be converted to paddy using hand labor should be so converted.

In the mountains, however, the environment places limits on the amount of land that can be converted into *non*, so there is considerable agricultural land that must remain rainfall field. Given the goal of the rural householder—to provide subsistence for himself and his family—and given the condition that only small amounts of land of any sort were available, he could maximize his caloric output by planting grain crops consumable by humans on rainfall fields, too. Thus, in spite of low levels of productivity, farmers planted their rainfall fields in foxtail millet (*Setaria italica*), oats, broomcorn millet (*Panicum miliaceum*), sorghum, and other low value crops that are seldom seen any more but which at the time could provide a marginal peasant with enough food to tide him over to the next harvest. Households were large and holdings small (the average farm size in Sangongni during this period could not have been much larger than sixty or seventy ares) and productivity just barely adequate. Most people were happy to be able to produce enough to live on, and many people knew times of hunger where all they had to eat were gruels made of unhusked sorghum and other coarse crops. Agricultural wages were low. The smaller farmers had to supplement their incomes with day labor or handicrafts such as making straw bags, rope, or sandals, or (for women) weaving home-grown cotton, hemp, or silk during the slack season. Since labor was cheap, farmers with substantial holdings did not have to work them themselves. Even though they were poor by international standards, such farmers considered leisure a status attribute of the yangban estate, and since they could get a live-in farmworker virtually for the price of his keep, maintaining a yangban lifestyle did not seem extravagant.[21]

Although the land reform of the 1950s had reduced the contribution of tenancy to rural poverty and thus raised the rural standard of living (Ban, Moon, and Perkins 1980:291), most farmers were still hard pressed to generate a significant surplus (see Mills 1960:62). Cows for plowing, for example, could be kept at almost no extra cost if they were fed on the grass alongside irrigation ditches, leftover rice straw, and rice polish, but few farmers had the capital necessary to acquire even a calf.[22] Most villagers must have had to hire a team to plow their land, or prepare their fields with manual labor. Thus, because of the high population density and the shortage of good land, farmers were plagued by a lack of capital, and by a system where the generation of surpluses that could be invested in modern agricultural inputs was almost impossible.

Although capital-intensive inputs into agriculture such as improved seed and more fertilizer would increase productivity, as was noted by Chayanov (1966:198), there is a trade-off between consumption and investment in peasant households. The requirement of adaptation—that the farmer produce enough food for himself and his family—

limited investment and had kept most Korean farmers from being able to generate the necessary surplus to be able to afford such inputs. The problem was not one of knowledge or culture, it was not one of technology or environment, but rather one of circumstances. Unless the price of agricultural crops were raised substantially, unless the rural crowding could be reduced, unless the unfavorable terms of trade with the city could be altered, or unless some outside agency made substantial investments in agriculture, the traditional system could not generate a substantial enough surplus to foster rapid agricultural growth. Government economic planners, worried about inflation and urban political instability, and aware of the availability of cheap subsidized grain from the United States, did not want to raise the price of subsistence crops. Capital was too short to allow massive investment in agriculture and rural infrastructure. Industrialization, thus, had to take the major share of the burden of the rural transformation by absorbing migrants to reduce rural crowding.

Paradoxically, however, there was no particular surplus of labor in the villages. That is, during the peak agricultural season, there was little unemployment of agricultural workers. Farm household surveys for 1960 and 1961, for example, revealed that during June—the peak month—males over the age of fourteen contributed around 250 hours of work, or approximately 6 hours per working day (if we assume 21.4 working days in a 30-day month). If we exclude those over fifty and younger than twenty, under the assumption that males between twenty and forty-nine did most of the work, the hours per working day go up to 10 or 11. Substantial reductions in the rural labor force under these conditions would have reduced production of crops in the country where the food situation was already critical.[23] Attracting people out of the villages would not have helped Korean farmers raise their standard of living unless at the same time efficiency of labor increased. The efficiency of labor did, in fact, increase—not through mechanization, but through capital investment and effective labor complementation.

Although there were no massive infusions of capital into the countryside, some capital investment was necessary to improve the efficiency of traditional Korean agriculture. The institution that was devised to facilitate this investment was the agricultural cooperative. Since it was reorganized and merged with the Agricultural Bank in 1961, the cooperative has been able to loan farmers money for agricultural inputs. Since the cooperative also markets about 10 percent of farmers' after-consumption production, these loans can take the form of advances on a future crop, and thus don't require the traditional collateral. The cooperative can simply deduct the loan amount from the farmer's account in the fall. This, of course, also gives the agricultural cooperative a good deal of leverage in implementing government policy.[24] Villagers in 1977 reported that the amount of fertilizer they would purchase was simply announced to them by the agricultural cooperative, for example, and was apparently the result of a decision made by higher-ups of how much fertilizer use per hectare would be desirable.

The agricultural cooperative began to be effective in extending credit for modern agricultural inputs in the mid- and late sixties just as the industrialization of Korea was getting under way. At first the capital was provided by the government but more and more of the capital used has come to be self-generated (Ban, Moon, and Perkins 1980:214). As the cooperative became effective in providing credit and modern agricultural inputs, farmers gradually began using more fertilizer, pesticides, and improved seed. Credit could even be provided for such large investments as buying a calf to raise as a draft animal.

All of these things did not change the agricultural system so much as make the same system work more effectively. The farmers no longer had to make compost, because they could use commercial fertilizer. The use of vinyl greenhousing extended the growing season for rice and further improved productivity. What is more, the change in timing of rice transplantation improved the complementation of the labor requirements of rice and wheat or barley. Before the vinyl greenhouses, rice transplantation had had to wait until June when the sprouts were big enough to stand transplanting. This led to the transplantation of rice and the harvest of barley taking place at the same time. The need to harvest barley limited the amount of rice one could transplant, and vice versa. With the vinyl greenhouses, however, the rice seedbeds could be planted several weeks earlier than before so that the seedlings could all be planted by mid-June, before the spring wheat or barley harvest. Because of this improved labor complementation, the same amount of rice and barley could be cultivated with less labor, and this labor could leave the household in search of work in the city. The number of farm households did not change during this period, but the number of people in the households was falling. With modest increased inputs and capital investment from the outside, farmers could increase their output on farms of the same size while still using less labor. Since the farmer had fewer mouths to feed, the amount of his crop he needed to retain as an adaptive requirement fell, and the farmer began to generate better surpluses.

In the early seventies it became apparent that the living standard of the villages was falling seriously behind that of the industrializing cities, however. Urban migration had become so massive that providing housing and other city services for migrants had become impossibly difficult. Concern over rural living standards and too rapid migration led the government to consider methods to improve the rural living standard more quickly and thus slow the rural exodus to the cities. Fear of inflation and urban unrest had kept the cheap grain policy of the government in place, but policymakers now began to link rates of migration with urban/rural differentials in the standard of living, and it was hoped that a slowed migration rate, by reducing urban competition for unskilled labor, would benefit urban residents too. Thus, the government began substantially raising crop prices. This had the effect of raising the return on investments in agriculture, and undoubtedly was an important incentive to rural investment (Brandt 1971:85).

The Transitional Stage

By 1977 in Sangongni and other places in Korea, the results of the investments of the agricultural cooperative in rural Korea had already made a big difference, and the village agricultural system had entered the transitional stage. Agriculture was still based on the cultivation of traditional subsistence crops with simple tools, but increased crop prices and adequate supplies of capital had made the system more productive using less labor. Almost all of the farmers in Sangongni in 1977 and 1983 belonged to the cooperative, and by 1977, virtually every farmer had a cow that he could use for plowing his fields and that he could sell for cash. Much of this improvement could be attributed to the agricultural cooperative. Those few farmers that didn't belong to the cooperative in 1977, for example, had not been able to plant improved varieties of rice, even though their income at the end of the year probably would have been higher even after paying back the loan if they had planted an improved strain of rice. They simply did not have the capital for the seed, fertilizer, and other inputs that farming of "miracle rice" requires. Even in 1983, when living standards were higher than 1977, the importance of the agricultural cooperative as a source of funds was clear. A large number of farmers reported getting their agricultural capital from the cooperative and one who didn't was paying 3 percent a month on loans he had taken out and reported that he was just getting further and further into debt. Another farmer without capital of any sort had a tenancy upon which he paid 50 percent rent (the going rate for irrigated paddy in the village) on top of which he paid an additional 15 percent of the crop for the capital, which had been provided by the landlord.

These transitional conditions have allowed continued changes in village agricultural life. With the increases in crop prices in the early seventies, even more capital became available for villagers, and with continued off-farm migration—a strategy encouraged by Sangongni's remote location—the size of farms has just about reached the limit of what can be managed by traditional techniques. This change in circumstances has changed the strategy that is rational for the peasants of Sangongni: (1) since production is now well above subsistence needs for most families, farmers can devote land to nonsubsistence crops while still providing for their own needs; (2) with increasing shortages of labor, farmers are looking for crops that are labor efficient as well as land efficient; and (3) they have reached the point where farm size cannot be increased without mechanization. Peasants in Sangongni in 1977, with a few notable exceptions, thought of subsistence first, and profit as whatever was left after subsistence had been taken care of. By 1983, they were turning into profit maximizers, thinking as much about how much a crop would make on the market as how well it would provide them with food. This process, although clearly begun, was not complete. Transportation out of the village was still difficult, and farming for market as well as subsistence was relatively new.

As migration out of the village has continued, the number of farm households has continued to drop. Sangongni lost thirteen farm households between 1977 and 1983, and those households remaining in the village continue to lose labor. Land has continued to be abandoned—especially in the high terraced ravines—but average farm size grew during this period from 1.14 to 1.33 hectares. Although agricultural wages have risen more than twofold over the seven-year period between 1977 and 1983,[25] a serious labor shortage that was not present in 1977 was present in 1983. There were no longer enough farmhands to plant even all the good fields of the village in time to get a good crop. Although there were probably at least a dozen motor tillers in the village in 1983, these did not alleviate the problem very much, because the period of critical labor need has always been the transplantation period. Even with *chaenggi* all the fields could be plowed in time, but there are no longer enough hands to transplant all the fields in time. Villagers are aware of this and reported in 1983 that the agricultural cooperative had promised a rice transplanting machine in 1984 to help alleviate the problem. Rice transplanting machines, however, are much more expensive than motor tillers, and acquiring them will put an even bigger strain on village financial resources than before. As Korean farmers move into mechanization, they are at a crossroads. The level of capitalization that a mechanized farm requires is huge. One wonders if the small family farms now found in rural Korea can support this quantum leap into mechanized farming that the labor shortages are pushing them into. Perhaps the process of rural to urban migration, reduction of farm households, and increase in farm size is far from stopping, but only begun.

Mechanization

Although the switch to the production of commodities for market that Kautsky foresaw has not been characteristic of Sangongni's past development, this may occur in the future. In 1977, there were perhaps three or four farmers who thought in terms of profit maximization. By 1983, it seemed many more farmers were thinking in those terms, though there were still some who farmed in the traditional way for the traditional reasons. Farming in Sangongni in 1983 was a recognizable version of farming in Sangongni in 1977, but change was apparent from the first moment I stepped into the village in 1983 and my host of 1977 asked me why I had walked from the bus stop instead of calling him on the phone so his son could pick me up in the motor tiller. The villagers were rational in 1977. They were rational in 1983. What had changed? The circumstances had changed: size of farm, productivity, village population, pricing structure, population density. Technology had changed. These things were peripheral to household structure, however. The family labor farm as an integrated unit of production and consumption in which the well-being of family members depended on the systemic interaction between farm size, crop fertility, and household labor availability remained the same. Change in any one of these elements brought about change in the others, but no element was free of substantial influence from other elements so that no change—whether it be technology, population density, marketing, or environment—could be seen as responsible for agricultural development in any simple causal sense. The changes in circumstances made goals possible for family members in 1983 that could not have been dreamed in 1960 when Chang used to play his gong in the farmer's band, but these goals still were pursued by people living in households with the same social structure as before.

CHAPTER 4

Subsistence, Productivity, and Household Adaptation

In the previous chapter, the cropping strategies of the villagers of San-gongni were characterized as "subsistence oriented." This subsistence orientation was not seen as the inevitable result of the application of traditional technology to the natural environment, as the result of the conservative outlook that some have seen as typical of smallholding peasants (Marx 1969:198–99; F. G. Friedman 1953; Foster 1973:84), or as the result of a particular peasant affinity for risk-adverse strategies (Scott 1976:5). Rather it was interpreted as a rational adaptive response to a number of environmental and sociological circumstances that were seen to condition village cropping strategies, including remoteness from urban markets, location at the end of marketing channels in a dendritic marketing system that imposes unfavorable terms of trade on the residents of outlying villages, and prices for crops during the sixties that led to low rates of capital accumulation and low rates of return on agricultural investment. Under these conditions, each farmer was seen as choosing his cropping patterns based on three criteria: (1) the amount of each crop his family expects to consume in the coming year; (2) the amount of male and female labor he has to use within his household; and (3) the amount of land of various types he has access to. Each of these criteria is linked to the others and ultimately is linked to the social organization of the household. Here we shall focus on the first of them: the consumption needs of the family.

The subsistence requirements of the villagers in their mountain environment are historically derived. Estimates of cropping needs can be made by farmers on the basis of past experience and productivity. If a farmer thinks he needs a certain amount of various kinds of land to grow crops, he does so on the basis of assumptions about the number and variety of dishes normally consumed in rural Korea. These dishes reflect historical Korean culinary traditions that have a symbolic and sensual aspect as well as being nutritious. At prevailing levels of productivity a household of a given size and composition requires, at a minimum, a certain amount of land of each type to enable the production of those crops necessary to provide a traditional diet adequate for work and survival. This minimum amount of land[1] is an adaptive requirement of the subsistence system that limits the decisions peasant farmers of Sangongni can make about cropping patterns and farm size, and thus indirectly influences the size and organization of the peasant household.

Some adaptive requirements, such as necessary caloric intake, we can assume to have been relatively stable over the past generation.[2] Dietary patterns, on the other hand, are partially dependent upon income and thus subject to change as income increases, even though the basic cultural assumptions underlying food behavior may have changed very little. Additional circumstances that affect adaptation, such as levels of productivity, have also changed dramatically over the last twenty-five years. As in other aspects of their life, then, the interaction between dietary preferences and cropping patterns of the peasants of Sangongni is conditioned by circumstances that have been subject to change over the last generation. The adaptive requirements of the 1980s are similar to those of the 1960s, but their socioeconomic ramifications are entirely different.

Despite the many changes in the agricultural system over the past generation, the dependence of peasant households on their own resources for subsistence has been remarkably stable. As illustrated in table 4.1, even as the money income and cash expenditures of Korean peasant householders have increased, the percentage of their income used to purchase food has remained stable. Items such as meat, which, except for poultry, have always had to be purchased, have increased in their importance in the budget, but others, such as rice, have become less likely to be purchased. "Eating bought rice" has always been stigmatized in Sangongni as an indication of abject poverty. As they have developed more advanced and productive agricultural practices, the peasant agriculturalists of South Korea have devoted some of their enhanced productivity to growing this subsistence crop, which circumstances had sometimes kept them from growing before. The increased standard of living of Korean peasants does not, in this respect, seem to have induced them to abandon old goals so much as to

TABLE 4.1
Proportion of Family Needs Obtained with Cash
(*Whole country agricultural households, in percentages*)

	1964	1970	1976
Total family consumption	33.3	48.5	51.0
Food items	14.5	16.1	15.8
Rice	7.7	4.8	1.9
Secondary foods	45.8	45.2	59.2
Vegetables	14.8	10.4	14.8
Meat	79.4	75.4	80.8
Animal husbandry needs	35.4	57.2	53.4

SOURCE: Nongŏp Hyŏptong Chohap 1978

better realize them. At the same time, as we shall see, they are adding new consumption goals to their traditional repertory.

Eating Habits

Throughout most of the year, the villagers of Sangongni are in the habit of eating three meals a day: one upon arising, one at midday, and one in the evening after the work has been completed. During the spring and autumn agricultural busy seasons (*nongbŏn'gi*)—especially during the transplantation of rice in the spring—this pattern is varied so that as many as five meals are served (three in the fields and usually only breakfast and the evening meal at the house). For the most part, whatever the time of the day the meal is taken, the contents of the meal are the same: soup (*kuk*) with rice or vegetables in it, steamed rice (*pap*), and a number of side dishes (*ch'an*), which vary with the richness and elaborateness of the meal. As an alternative to rice, noodles (*kuksu*) made of wheat or buckwheat, or in extremely poor houses, steamed barley,[3] millet, or beans, can be substituted for the steamed rice, but conceptually as well as calorifically, the center of the meal is usually steamed rice. Many Koreans don't feel that they have eaten at all unless they have consumed at least some steamed rice. The names of the meals, literally translated, mean simply morning, noon, and evening steamed rice (*ach'im pap, chŏmsim pap, chŏn-yŏk pap*). Mothers calling their children to a meal usually simply say, "*pap mŏgŏ*" (eat steamed rice)—even if steamed rice isn't a part of the meal.

The ordinary rice (*ipssal, mepssal*) from which steamed rice is usually made is a nonglutinous medium-grained form of *japonica* rice.
The glutinous rice (*ch'apssal*) grown in small quantities in Sangongni
is used primarily in the making of *ch'apssal ttŏk* (glutinous rice cake)
and in the brewing of *makkŏlli*. Ordinary rice is steamed in the large
iron caldron (*sot*) that is built into the stove. Ideally, it is cooked until
it is tender but not to the point at which the kernels begin to disinte-
grate. Since large quantities of steamed rice are made at one time, at
any particular meal one is likely to eat reheated rice. Freshly made
rice, of course, is considered better and would be made up if a guest
arrived, whether or not the rest of the family were eating reheated rice.
The best steamed rice, *haepssal pap,* is made from the newly harvested
crop (*haepssal*) which has lost none of its flavor through long storage.
Even though Koreans tend to be particular about their rice, they don't
strenuously object to the presence of a few miscellaneous grains or
pulses. (Japanese tourists, on the other hand, were said by the news-
papers to find miscellaneous food items in their rice so unappetizing
as to be unable to eat). Of course pure rice is a more prestigious dish
than rice mixed with other ingredients, but I was surprised to find an
informant in Sangongni agreeing with my statement that "pure rice is
too bland." Even in the richer families in Sangongni rice is commonly
mixed with other grains and pulses so that one usually finds a few
peas, soybeans, chestnuts, or bits of potato lurking in one's rice. For
the poorer households such means of stretching the rice supply are
absolutely necessary.

The content of the soups varies somewhat with the economic level
of the household and the skill of the cook. Typical soups are made
with a fermented bean paste stock, known as *toenjang* or *t'ojang,*
which resembles Japanese *miso*. The soup may be consumed in relatively unadorned form with added cabbage and garlic, in which case
it is known as *toenjang kuk,* or it may be spruced up with soy or mung
bean sprouts, *kimch'i,* fresh vegetables, or potatoes. Other soups can
be made from ingredients such as seaweed purchased in the market,
and flavored with soy sauce (*kanjang*) and sesame salt.

The indispensable side dishes to the ordinary Sangongni meal are
the various vegetables pickled in salt and hot pepper, such as *kimch'i,*
kkaktugi (daikon radish cubes pickled in salt and red pepper), and *oi
kimch'i* (sliced cucumbers pickled in salt and red pepper). In addition,
red pepper paste (*koch'ujang*), or garlic and green onion chopped up
and mixed in soy sauce may be used as condiments. Fresh vegetables
in season are an important side dish, and many of them are made from

crops such as red pepper, zucchini, maize, and white potatoes that were only introduced to Korea via China and Japan from the New World and elsewhere in the seventeenth and eighteenth centuries (Yi Tuhyŏn et al. 1974:106).

On special occasions, side dishes other than these ordinary ones may be provided, including dried laver or *kim* (green seaweed, *Porphyra tenera*, pressed and dried into thin sheets), bean curd (*tubu*), and rice beer. Meat and eggs, the latter often eaten raw, are consumed by those who can afford them, but even the richest villagers don't eat meat every day. Meat is usually cut up into bite-size bits that can be roasted, dried, or prepared with various sauces. Except at regular banquets, it is rare for someone to eat even as much as one hundred grams of meat at one meal. Fish is also enjoyed even in upland villages. In the summer, edible species of frogs can be caught as well as fish, though any longer than a few inches are rarely found. Fresh fish from the ocean is not available in remote mountain villages, but even in traditional times dried fish, or *p'o*, were brought into the villages by itinerant peddlers. These are often an important offering in religious rites and can still be bought at the periodic markets along with a brown seaweed called *miyŏk* (*Undaria pinnatifida*), which is used to make a soup thought to be especially nutritious and suitable for postpartum mothers.[4]

Seasonal Differences in Diet

Because most of the food consumed in Sangongni is produced within the household, the food on the table closely follows the seasons. This is true not only of fresh vegetable crops, such as leaf lettuce and bellflower root that are only available in season, but in traditional times it was also true of staple crops that can be stored for long periods with only minimal deterioration. Throughout the year, 70 to 80 percent of the calories consumed by rural Koreans have been provided by grains (K. Y. Lee 1962; Yi Kiryŏl 1976:26): chiefly rice, barley, wheat, buckwheat, foxtail millet (*Setaria italica*), and sorghum.[5] Although the richer farmers harvested substantial surpluses of these crops, the smaller farmers were hampered in the production of surpluses by shortages of land and capital inputs. Many farmers up until the seventies did not produce enough of any one crop to provide them with a whole year's supply of food. Rather than harvesting their crop once in the fall and subsisting off that crop for a whole year, many peasant farmers harvested only enough of each crop to tide them over to the harvest of the next crop.

Because of this there used to be a seasonal diet in rural Korea as households switched between the crops harvested in autumn and those harvested in the early summer. The main harvest had to last for eight months from October to May when fresh fruit and vegetables were not available. The early summer harvest of barley, potatoes, wheat, and vegetables had to last the four months from June to September. The relationship of the seasonality of the various harvests and the seasonality of the consumption of major crops for thirty months from January 1960 until June 1962 can be seen in figures 4.1 and 4.2.[6] The main harvest, the harvest of rice, miscellaneous grains (such as millet and buckwheat), pulses, and potatoes is in October and November. Since rice is preferred, villagers consumed it in large quantities at this time.[7] Over the winter, rice, potatoes, and miscellaneous grains such as millet and buckwheat, which are harvested in the autumn, were the main foods eaten. As winter gave way to spring, barley was progressively substituted for rice as it became short for many

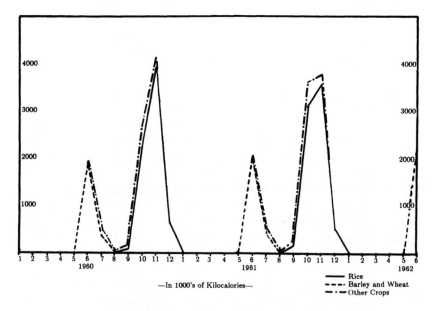

Fig. 4.1. Household harvest of crops by month in South Korea, 1960–62
SOURCE: Han'guk ŭnhaeng chosabu, 1963

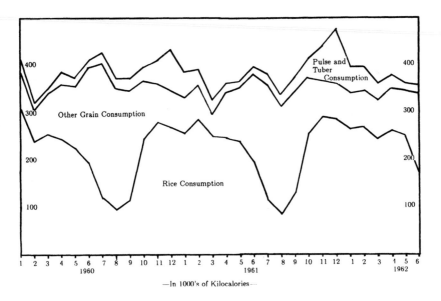

Fig. 4.2. Household consumption of crops by month in South Korea, 1960–62
SOURCE: Han'guk ŭnhaeng chosabu, 1963

farmers (both through consumption and the need to sell substantial amounts of it throughout the winter for money). Thus the late spring, when farmers had used most of their winter stocks but had not yet harvested the June crops, which would tide them over the four months of summer until the main harvest in October, was a hungry period colloquially called "barley pass" (*porit kogae*). Sometimes farmers would be so short of food during this period that they would harvest unripe grain (*p'uppasimhada*), parch it, and process it as if it were ripe.

The spring hungry season seems to be a thing of the past, but other details of the rural Korean diet can still be observed to vary with the seasons. After the vegetable and barley harvests, when people have safely "crossed barley pass" (*porit kogae rŭl nŏmgyŏtta*), everybody eats well. The vegetable gardens that were planted in April yield fresh produce daily. Various *kimch'i*s are made fresh every few days from Chinese cabbage (*Brassica pekinensis*), radishes, or cucumbers, and are eaten along with such seasonal dishes as *ssam* (rice wrapped in leaf lettuce, or *sangch'i*), raw daikon radish, fresh onions, and garlic.

Until August the diet remains abundant. Fish are caught in the rivers and eaten raw, garnished with hot sauce or cooked in stews. Fresh vegetables are harvested throughout the period and in July harvests of beans (soy, mung, broad), spring barley, and bellflower (*Platycodon grandiflorum*) are added to the already abundant food stocks. From the surrounding mountains come wild grapes (*mŏru*) used to flavor *soju* (a distilled liquor) and wild cherries (*pŏt*), while fruits such as plum (*aengdu*) are sometimes found in homestead gardens.

For periods when caloric intake is high, the general adequacy of the diet of inland villages in central Korea can be illustrated by a nutritional analysis of the most important foods of a typical August day's diet—two meals of soup, *kimch'i,* and rice and one of wheat noodles, *kimch'i,* and rice. This is presented in table 4.2. The figures upon which this table is based are adapted from a study done by a team of nutritionists for one week during each of the four seasons in a village in Koyang County northeast of Seoul in 1959 (K. Y. Lee et al. 1962), with modifications based on observations of food consumption patterns in Sangongni. The research of Lee et al. was conducted on a sample of 20 households with 118 persons of all ages and both sexes using the precise weighing method recommended by the FAO (Nornis 1949), in which foods are accurately measured immediately prior to consumption. Participants in the survey were questioned about foods consumed outside of the house or outside normal mealtimes and were given medical examinations to assess their nutritional status. Figures for Sangongni, while adapted from Lee et al.'s study, are estimates based on an assumption of a 3,000-kilocalorie intake per adult male equivalent and are intended to be illustrative rather than definitive. The implications of these estimates, however, differ in no significant way from the conclusions of K. Y. Lee and her coworkers.

Altogether about 84 percent of the total kilocalories assumed to be consumed by villagers in Sangongni are included in this analysis. In typical meals the staples analyzed here are supplemented by a great variety of fruits and by vegetables such as bellflower root, radishes, zucchini, and lettuce. Because the variety of these supplementary foods is so great and because their level of consumption was impossible for me to reliably estimate, this 16.4 percent of the diet has been excluded from detailed analysis. Even excluding these miscellaneous vegetables, however, with few exceptions all the recommended daily allowances of the FAO[8] for vitamins, minerals, and amino acids seem to be met (exceptions are for the B vitamins,[9] vitamin C, and calcium,

TABLE 4.2
Analysis of the August Diet
Estimated Daily Nutritional Intake per Adult Male Equivalent

	Calories	Protein grams	Calcium mg	Iron mg	Vitamin A IU	Thiamine mg	Riboflavin mg	Niacin mg	Vitamin C mg
Rice	1557	28.7	102	3.4	—	0.30	0.13	6.9	—
Noodles	777	26.4	57	2.7	—	0.19	0.13	3.6	—
Soybeans	66	5.5	36	1.3	13	0.18	0.05	0.4	—
Red Beans	66	4.3	21	1.3	4	0.10	0.04	0.4	—
Kimch'i	42	4.4	62	1.1	1087	0.07	0.13	4.6	12
Total	2508	69.3	278	9.8	1104	0.84	0.48	15.9	12
Percent of RDA	(84)	(188)	(70)	(109)	(147)	(70)	(27)	(80)	(40)

Essential Amino Acids (in milligrams)

	Ile.	Leu.	Lys.	Meth.	Phe.	Thr.	Trp.	Val.	Food Intake grams/day
Rice	1270	2492	1094	644	1467	1004	95	1750	429
Noodles	918	1772	523	367	1226	677	270	1040	211
Soybeans	359	614	504	100	390	304	101	372	16
Red Beans	176	320	289	44	219	196	223	19	19
Kimch'i	119	185	116	31	113	116	25	156	221
Total	2842	5383	2526	1186	3415	2297	714	3337	
Percent of MDR	(267)	(573)	(303)	(516)	(1102)	(446)	(370)	(473)	

NOTE: The figures from which the quantities of different foods were estimated are based on Lee et al. (1962), with an assumption of a caloric intake of 3000 kilocalories per Adult Male Equivalent, and foods observed eaten in Sangongni. Recommended Daily Allowances are based on those issued by the FAO for moderately active males of 170 centimeters stature and 65 kilograms weight (Passmore, Nicol, and Rao: 1974). Minimum Daily Requirements for amino acids are those recommended by Hegsted (1963) to the 95% confidence level above the mean. The requirement for methionine assumes an intake of at least 500 milligrams of cystine per day, a requirement met by the above diet. Composition of foods is estimated from United States Department of Agriculture (1963). Amino acid content was estimated from FAO (1970). In this table, 83.6% of the assumed 3000 kilocalorie intake was subjected to detailed analysis.

but some of these would be made up by the fresh vegetables that have not been included in this analysis).

This analysis, which was calculated assuming no intake of animal food,[10] illustrates some interesting characteristics of rural Korean diet. As was observed in Sangongni and has been confirmed by K. Y. Lee elsewhere in Korea (1962), carbohydrates contribute by far the greatest bulk of the calories. A survey of rural villages done between 1972 and 1974 revealed, for example, that some 80 to 90 percent of the calories consumed in rural Korea were from carbohydrates (Yi Kiryŏl 1976:26). Plants provided 97 percent of the protein consumed, but even so, the rural Korean protein intake of approximately sixty-seven grams per day was well over minimum requirements for a population of their stature and activity patterns. Detailed analysis of typical foods eaten, such as given in table 4.2, gives little indication that at this level of caloric intake any of the essential amino acids should be deficient and limit the usefulness of the protein consumed.

The general adequacy of the rural Korean diet during this time of year seems to be related to effective complementation of rice, wheat, and soybean products for protein and B vitamins, and the richness of *kimch'i* for providing vitamins A and C and for providing calcium (though the form of calcium present in *kimch'i* may not be readily assimilated). Not only is the quantity of protein present in rice adequate, but the distribution of amino acids in the protein is good (i.e., with most of the essential amino acids present in approximately the quantity necessary for them to be efficiently used), and what is more, the digestibility of rice is higher than for any other grain crop (meaning that more of its available nutrients are likely to be assimilated).[11] Tryptophan, an essential amino acid in short supply in rice, is abundant in wheat and red beans. B-complex vitamins, which tend to be short in diets based on polished rice,[12] are provided by wheat, barley, and soybean products. *Kimch'i,* while it has a little of everything, is most important as a source of vitamins.

After the June harvest of barley and vegetables, little is harvested until October when the main harvest of the remaining cereal crops (rice, sesame, and buckwheat), beans, and hot peppers comes in. Fruits such as jujube (*taech'u,* a small chewy red fruit with a flavor reminiscent of dates) and nuts such as chestnut are harvested and consumed both raw and cooked at this time of year. Potatoes and sweet potatoes are put in storage and everything is in abundance. In most respects the autumn diet of Sangongni resembles the summer diet except that there is a high consumption of chestnuts—raw, steamed and added to rice, or roasted. This should lead to improved intake of protein and B-complex vitamins in Sangongni where chicken is the only meat regularly consumed (and that only on special occasions such as ancestor worship rituals) and eggs are too valuable to be anything but an occasional treat.

When the first cold of the year ends the growing season, it is time for putting up pickled vegetables and fermented soybean paste (*meju*) for winter. A special vegetable garden in which the ingredients for the winter *kimch'i* have been planted in June is harvested shortly before the first freezes are expected in late November. Hot peppers have been picked early and have been set out in the sun to dry since September, livening up the landscape with their bright red color. The cabbages, radishes, and radish leaves are washed and soaked in brine in preparation for *kimjang*—the making of the winter *kimch'i*. Koreans eat many different kinds of pickled vegetables all year around. The pickling agent in most cases is salt, hence these dishes are generically known as *tchanji*, or "salty food," in Sangongni.[13] During the summer the fermentation of the vegetables in brine is completed in about three days and this *kimch'i* has to be eaten fairly quickly before it acidifies and goes bad. During this period a variety of *kimch'i*s made out of Chinese cabbage (*paech'u kimch'i*), young radishes (*yŏlmu kimch'i*), cucumber (*oi kimch'i*), leeks (*puch'u kimch'i*), and mature radishes (*kkakttugi*) are all eaten. Those made during the *kimjang* season for winter use, however, last much longer than summer varieties and are especially important because during the winter, fresh fruits and vegetables have not until recently been available. For the week or so of the *kimjang* season (classically thought to begin around the time of the traditional solar period of *iptong* or "entering winter," but actually dependent upon the weather), all the women in the village can be seen engaged in the task of preparing these vegetables.

The most characteristic winter *kimch'i*s are *t'ong kimch'i*, *tongch'imi*, and *kkakttugi*. *T'ong kimch'i* is made from whole heads of Chinese cabbage, which are fermented slightly in brine. On the appointed day the women make a stuffing of grated radish slightly fermented in brine, cucumber, and a sauce of red pepper, garlic and sesame oil, and the leaves of each cabbage head are pried open and stuffed with it. As the cabbages are prepared they are placed in large lidded crocks (which hold at least five gallons in most cases) into which brine is poured. The crocks are sealed and placed half-buried in the ground on a terrace behind the house built especially for their storage, called the *changdoktae*. The half burial of the crocks protects the *kimch'i* from spoilage in case of an unseasonable warm spell.[14] In many urban areas clams and other delicacies are added to *t'ong kimch'i*, but this was not done in Sangongni.

The two other varieties of *kimch'i* are made primarily from radishes. *Tongch'imi* is a variety of *kimch'i* in which whole radishes are soaked in brine without other flavoring. It is rather bland in taste, or as Koreans say about nonspicy food, "it tastes boring" (*simsimhada*). *Kkakttugi*, on the other hand, is definitely *not* boring. To make *kkakttugi*, radishes are diced into cubes about an inch square, and mixed with crushed raw red peppers, or red pepper powder, chopped green onion, garlic, and sesame oil. As with the other winter *kimch'i*s, the mixture is placed in a large sealed crock and allowed to ferment. *Much'ŏng kimch'i* is made in a similar way from radish leaves.

Unlike the summer varieties, which can go bad in a week or even less, these winter *kimch'i*s will keep for three or four months. Not only do they add a little spice to the monotonous winter diet, but they are nutritionally very important. All of the winter *kimch'i*s are a good source of vitamin C, and most of them are good sources of vitamin A, calcium, and the B vitamins. Vitamin C, especially, is in short supply in the winter when fresh fruits and vegetables are not available, and the role of *kimch'i* in supplying it is decisive (see table 4.3).

Along with *kimch'i*, bean products are an important complement to the winter diet of rice and other grains. Beans present a different adaptive problem from vegetables, however, for although they can be preserved as long and as easily as rice or any other grain, their assimilation into the diet is difficult, because beans in general are not as digestible as grains and vegetable foods. The soybean especially, in spite of its excellent protein, cannot be digested well unless it is processed in some way. Rather than use beans as a rice substitute, therefore, Korean housewives prefer to process them into more palatable and digestible forms. The basis of many of these transformations is *meju*, a fermented bean paste similar to the Japanese *nattō*. To make *meju*, a woman grinds her beans on a grinding stone, cooks them until they are soft and adds a little wheat to the mixture, which is then wrapped in cheesecloth and hung up in the open air to dry and ferment. The storehouses of most farmsteads have numbers of these dried clumps of *meju*, which look like so many clods of dirt, hanging from the rafters. These clumps of *meju* form the base of soysauce, red pepper sauce, and *toenjang*, the fermented bean soup stock that is so basic to the winter diet.[15]

Other common ways of transforming beans are to sprout them

TABLE 4.3
The Nutritive Value of 100-Gram Servings of Various Kinds of *Kimch'i*

	Kcal	H$_2$O grams	Protein grams	Fat grams	Sugar grams	Fiber grams	Ca mg	A IU	B$_1$ mg	B$_2$ mg	B$_3$ mg	C mg
T'ong kimch'i	19	88.4	2.0	0.6	1.3	0.5	28	492	0.03	0.06	2.1	12
Kkakttugi	31	87.0	2.7	0.8	3.2	0.7	5	946	0.03	0.06	5.8	10
Tongch'imi	9	93.0	0.7	0.2	1.1	0.2	1	—	0.01	0.03	1.0	7
Much'ŏng kimch'i	27	85.9	2.7	0.7	2.4	0.5	3	1702	0.04	0.07	3.3	19

SOURCE: Yi Kiryŏl (1976:122)

(bean sprouts are eaten all winter) or to grind them and manufacture *tubu* (bean curd). Sprouting the beans increases their B-complex vitamin content, while turning them into *tubu* increases their digestibility. The firm, farm-made *tubu* is delicious and considered by the villagers to be very nutritious (*yangbun i chot'a*). Manufacturing it, however, is very time-consuming. The beans have to be ground on a grindstone with water and then cooked. The lees are strained out and then the solution must be recooked and solidified. These tasks go on over several days. *Tubu* will spoil after several weeks, too, so it cannot be made in large enough quantities to last the whole year. Although *tubu* is eaten on special occasions when the work involved in its manufacture seems justified, it is not a daily item of consumption in rural areas where it cannot be purchased. Because *tubu* was made in Sangongni primarily for banquets, the sound of the grinding stone always had a festive ring to me.

Although people eat well through December from what they have harvested in the fall, as the winter progresses the diet becomes more and more monotonous. From late December until the first of May, the daily fare consists of little else but rice, *kimch'i*, and soup. Potatoes are often added to the soup or rice to make it go a little further. For the poorer families, sweet potatoes (which since liberation have spread, with government encouragement, from coastal to mountain areas as hunger insurance) are an important part of the diet. Although the quantity of food available during this time of year is not a serious problem these days, quality still suffers. In 1977, I was not aware of any family who did not have enough calories to get them comfortably through the winter and spring (save one family whose stores were destroyed by fire and had to be replenished by village charity), but some families had to calculate food stocks closely and conserve food. Caloric consumption is lower during this period than other times of year. Perhaps in a few severe cases in 1977, villagers still sold rice for cheaper grains like barley or millet so that they would be certain to have enough staple food to last at least until the first barley harvest in late June, and enough white and sweet potatoes and enough *kimch'i* to last at least until May when the vegetable gardens start producing well.

April is the season for gathering mountain herbs (*san namul*), whatever the food situation of the household. During the middle weeks of this month, the village women scour the brooksides and mountains looking for the leaves of such succulent herbs as *tŏdŏk* (*Codonopsis lanceolata*) and *minari* (*Cardamine leucantha*). *Tŏdŏk* root is also eaten, but at this time of year the leaves are the main attraction. Today such gathering of plants is considered recreational and adds a welcome variety and freshness to the diet in the period before the vegetable gardens start producing, but in earlier times (before about 1955) people also gathered wild plants to avoid famine, or help themselves "over barley pass." At such times the villagers could search the mountains for edible herbs and roots such as arrowroot (*ch'ilk,* sometimes known as kudzu in English). Many people recall this kind of foraging during the Korean War when they fled south to avoid fighting and when their stores were often confiscated by troops or stolen by refugees. Since that time, however, such drastic measures have not been necessary. Younger villagers know little about these famine foods.

Definition of Subsistence

Rural Koreans in Sangongni, then, sustain themselves primarily on rice, barley, wheat, beans, potatoes, and vegetables grown for household use on their own farms. Although, as we shall see, their dietary intake in traditional times was probably not always adequate (and the study of Lee et al. [1962], since it systematically excluded houses known to be so poor as to have to borrow food, probably underestimated the amount of nutritional deprivation present even in 1959) we cannot state with precision at what level of intake malnutrition would have occurred without doing exacting studies of the physiology of the villagers, their activity patterns, and the efficiency of their food absorption (McArthur 1974). Nevertheless, given what we do know about the size, activity patterns, and food preferences of the villagers of Sangongni, an estimate of the amounts of various crops necessary to maintain an adequate way of life can be made. The FAO, in its food and nutrition studies, uses a "reference male" of 170 centimeters and 65 kilograms and a "reference female" of 160 centimeters and 55 kilograms as the basis for calculating nutritional requirements. A 1934 study of the population of Kangwŏn Province found the stature of men to be 163.32 ± 0.52 centimeters (SD 5.48 ± 0.37 centimeters) and that of women to be 149.68 ± 0.48 centimeters (SD 5.01 ± 0.34) (Na Sejin 1964). Although stature in Korea is thought to have risen since the 1930s by 5 to 6 centimeters I met nobody in Sangongni who exceeded my height of 170 centimeters. (In Seoul, however, there are many younger and even middle-aged Korean males who exceed my height.) Thus, it seems appropriate to use the requirements of the reference male as the basis of estimates of nutritional need in Sangongni. When it becomes necessary to take into account variations in the intake of men, women, and children, we will convert the requirements of the latter two categories into Adult Male Equivalents (AME), using the coefficients recommended by the League of Nations (1932).

A reference male who leads an active life, as most rural Koreans do, requires, according to Passmore, Nicol, and Rao (1974), approximately 3,000 kilocalories of food energy per day. K. Y. Lee et al. in their 1962 study found that the actual caloric intake in August of their sample villagers was 3,016 kilocalories. It thus seems reasonable to take a daily intake of 3,000 kilocalories as an appropriate level on which to base estimates of the consumption needs of AME in Sangongni. Lee et al. included in their study a detailed analysis of the food sources of these calories. Based on this work, and what I observed people to eat in the village (but was not able to weigh and analyze), the following proportions of foods (by percentage of caloric intake) in the diet seem to be a reasonable estimate of central Korean rural food intake (see table 4.4). This assumes two meals of steamed rice and one of noodles a day with modest amounts of barley, beans, and tubers mixed in, depending upon the season of the year.

The estimated quantities an adult male would consume of the major staple crops over the period of a year are given in table 4.5. The estimated consumption figures for 1977 in this table are based on the proportion of a caloric consumption of 3,000 kilocalories per day which would be provided by each crop according to the dietary assumptions outlined above. The estimates for rice and barley given in table 4.5 correspond rather closely to figures for the 1976 actual consumption of rice and barley for agricultural households in Korea compiled by the Ministry of Agriculture and Forestry given in the same table. Separate figures were not available for the different bean crops, though judging from the total national bean consumption, my estimates may overemphasize the importance of beans. However, my estimates include use of beans in processed foods, such as in soy sauce, bean curd, and processed into bean cake, while the Ministry of Agriculture and Forestry figures do not, apparently, include these uses in their figures.

Diet and Work Patterns over the Seasons

Observations of the diet of Sangongni in 1977 revealed that its quality varied greatly from season to season. This was apparently also true of

TABLE 4.4
Assumptions of Contribution of Selected Foods to Daily Caloric Intake

Food	Percentage of Daily Intake (by weight)
Cereals	70
Rice	42.0
Noodles (wheat)	14.0
Barley	14.0
Pulses	10
Soybean (*Glycine max*)	2.5
Red bean (*Phaseolus angularis*)	2.5
Kidney bean (*Phaseolus vulgaris*)	2.5
Mung bean (*Phaseolus radiatus*)	2.5
Tubers	10
White potato	5.0
Sweet potato	5.0
Vegetables	5
Pickled	2.5
Fresh	2.5
Nuts and Fruits	5
Chestnuts	2.5
All others	2.5

TABLE 4.5
Annual Estimated Consumption of Major Staple Crops
per Adult Male Equivalent (*in kilograms*)

	Estimated Consumption Need	Actual Consumption In 1976
Rice	127.75	127.08
Barley	44.05	43.89
Soybeans	20.43	
Red beans	24.40	
Kidney beans	7.78	
Mung beans	8.05	
White potatoes	72.04	
Sweet potatoes	48.03	

SOURCE (1976 data): Nongnimbu 1977.

quantity, at least in traditional times. Lee et al. for example found that for their village near Seoul in 1959 caloric intake ranged close to 3,000 kilocalories per capita per day in August and October, but was 2,565 kilocalories per capita per day in December and fell to 2,083 per capita per day in March. This level was low, but not low enough to threaten the villagers with starvation or even malnutrition unless energy expenditure at this time was extremely high. Because most rural Koreans are smaller than 170 centimeters and because recommended daily allowances are usually on the generous side, 3,000 kilocalories per day is probably 20 to 30 percent above the bare subsistence level. Though K. Y. Lee et al. found no evidence of gross malnutrition (scurvy, rickets, or kwashiorkor) in the clinical assessment of the villagers in their study, more moderate signs of undernutrition such as edema and thickening of the ocular conjunctiva were present. Symptoms associated with low intake of riboflavin were common (K. Y. Lee et al. 1962:210). It is likely that much of the population of rural Korea have not reached their full somantic potential due to nutritional factors (Graham 1975:110; K. Y. Lee et al. 1963:459). Weanling infants and the aged were judged to show the most evidence of undernutrition. Clearly at those times of year when the caloric intake of rural Koreans is lowest and when fresh fruits and vegetables have not traditionally been available, the nutritional adequacy of the diet suffered. This was made clear by Lee et al., whose measurements of intake of C and B vitamins during winter and spring reveal significant shortfalls from recommended daily allowances issued by the Health and Social Ministry of the Republic of Korea in 1960 (Lee et al. 1962:208). It is clear, then, that "barley pass" was still a serious problem even as late as the early sixties and the gathering of mountain herbs may once have served to improve the marginal spring diet.

Though the dietary intake of the villagers in this part of the spring was somewhat marginal the work is not. The agricultural work of this time of the year entails a great deal of heavy labor—plowing the barley fields, repairing irrigation ditches, or clearing stones from fields. Later on in May the transplantation of seedlings has to be done and unless the caloric intake increased, it seems likely that many of the poorer farmers must have lost weight and felt hungry during this period. To talk to old people, certainly, one gets the impression that few of them were strangers to periods of hunger a generation ago.

This conclusion can also be inferred from the monthly consumption figures for staples published in the Farm Household Economic Survey for 1960 and 1961 (Han'guk ŭnhaeng chosabu 1963). If it is assumed that consumption of rice and barley, adjusted for the proportion of calories provided by these grains by month,[16] gives an adequate measure of the monthly caloric intake of the rural Koreans in the Farm Household Economic Survey, if the consumption figures are adjusted so as to take into account the size and composition of the households in the survey, and if consumption is expressed in kilocalories per AME per day, then the caloric intake of the persons in the survey[17] will be seen to vary from month to month with minima in March and August (see fig. 4.3). By making a few assumptions about energy expenditure by rural Koreans one can also make an estimate of the monthly variations in energy expenditure.[18] During the winter months when there is little agricultural work to be done, the energy expenditure needs of the subjects of the household survey were minimal, while they gradually rose in the spring to peak in June and July. If we compare month by month estimated caloric consumption with estimated caloric ex-

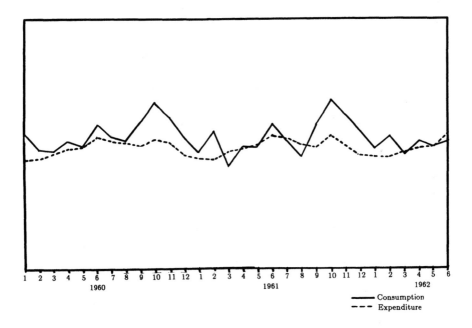

Fig. 4.3. Monthly estimates of caloric intake and expenditure, January 1960–June 1962

penditure, it indeed appears that the energy balance of rural villagers was more favorable in some months than in others. From September through February, dietary intake seems to have been generally adequate, while from March to May—barley pass—and in July and August, the diet seems to have been less adequate given the demand for heavy agricultural work during those months (see fig. 4.3).

Because of the number of assumptions that have been made in the calculation of caloric consumption and caloric expenditure, one cannot say precisely how close any of the figures for caloric consumption or expenditure are to the actual figures for any individuals in the survey. But though the values of these figures are not particularly meaningful in absolute terms, in relative terms, one can have more confidence. Depending upon the absolute value of the figures for caloric consumption and caloric expenditure, the seasonality of diet and labor need could have been a minor annoyance or a serious adaptational problem. If it is assumed, for example, that over a year's time energy consumption and energy expenditure were in balance, then one would find mild seasonal changes in weight. People would put on weight in the fall and winter, and lose weight in the spring and summer. On the other hand, if the fluctuations were more severe, serious health problems may have been the result. One might find, for example, that in vulnerable populations—perhaps weanling infants or the aged of the poorer households—nutritional stress in certain months might lead to higher morbidity or mortality due to the well-known synergism of infection and malnutrition. Adult resistance to typhoid fever and tetanus, as well as juvenile resistance to yellow fever, tetanus, and diphtheria fall with malnutrition (McFarlane 1976) and all of these diseases were found in traditional Korean villages, although most of them are no longer endemic.[19]

In an effort to test the hypothesis that seasonal food shortages may have been serious enough to elevate the seasonal death rate in Sangongni, all the deaths of villagers between 1900 and 1983 for which the year and solar month of death could be established were collated.[20] In all, this could be done for seventy-seven adult deaths. The frequency of deaths by month compared with the monthly energy balance for 1960–61 calculated from the household rice and barley consumption figures as shown in figures 4.1 and 4.2 were then analyzed, using multiple regression techniques. For the whole period from 1900 to 1977, there was no statistically significant correlation. However, when the sample of deaths was divided into two groups: thirty-eight deaths between 1900 and 1961, and thirty-nine deaths between 1963 and 1983, the monthly pattern of deaths in the first group was significantly correlated to the estimated energy balance ($r^2 = 0.44$, $p < 0.02$), but that of the second group was not. It seems likely, then, that nutritional stress contributed to seasonal differences in the death rates in the past, and that coping with seasonal stress due to imbalances between energy consumption and energy expenditure was a significant problem of the adaptation of traditional rural Koreans to their environment.

Customs that Tend to Mitigate the Seasonality of the Diet

If preserving the nutritional adequacy of the diet in the spring was a significant problem for the peasants of Sangongni, two customs would have had the effect of improving the diet and thus peasant adaptations during periods of energy imbalance: household ancestor worship and holiday food practices. The dietary analysis in table 4.2 was made on the assumption that no meat is eaten. Although this is basically true for ordinary meals, most households keep chickens to provide eggs and meat for consumption on important occasions. The most common of these occasions is the *chesa,* the household ancestor worship ceremony. In Sangongni, where the majority of the villagers are organized into patrilineages, the heads of senior households known as *k'ŭn chip*[21] are obliged to sacrifice to up to four generations of ancestors from whom they are descended in the senior male line. Houses of second and subsequent sons are free of this obligation (K. K. Lee 1975:82–84). These sacrifices are done at midnight on the night before the anniversary of the death of the former house heads and house mistresses in each generation. Since each generation includes a house head and a house mistress, such worship is done up to eight times a year.

This kind of household ancestor worship ceremony, known as a *kije,* takes the form of a sacrifice of beer and cooked food offered to the ancestor being commemorated and that ancestor's spouse, followed by a banquet in which the agnatic descendants of the couple and their families share the food (*ŭmbok*) in as elaborate a feast as the house can afford. It is a matter of pride, as well as prudence, for the sacrifice and banquet to be as ample as can possibly be managed: a matter of pride because many of the residents (kin and nonkin) of the hamlet in which one lives will appear on the morning after the ancestor worship ceremony to partake of the leftovers of the banquet, and a matter of prudence because hungry ancestors might, even against their own will, cause trouble for the living (Janelli and Janelli 1982: 97ff.; Kendall 1985: 96ff.). An adequate ancestor worship banquet contains, according to the tradition of one village family, an example of all the good things in culinary life: pork, beef, fish, and fowl; apples, pears, persimmons, jujubes, and chestnuts; liquor, rice cake, soup, and, of course, the indispensable rice. As Sangongni is a relatively poor village, people normally do without the pork and beef, but each sacrifice observed in the village in 1976 and 1977 entailed the cooking of a chicken (eaten as soup with morsels of flesh in it) and the eating of dried fish (*p'o*). In addition a few fruits not produced in the village were usually purchased in the market, and several kinds of *ttŏk* (rice cake, mung bean pancake, etc.) made. All in all, such banquets are hearty and include a number of nutritious foods not normally eaten in Sangongni village.

These banquets can be held any time of year, and thus do not necessarily correspond with periods of energy imbalance. Presumably if they did correspond perfectly with the energy imbalances, those imbalances would no longer exist. The timing of the banquets, rather, follows inevitably from the timing of the deaths of the ancestors. If there is any time of year when deaths are more common than others, then it follows that at that time of year more of these ceremonies, hence banquets, will be celebrated. Investigation of the written genealogy of several lineages in the village revealed that 36.8 percent of the deaths for the last 100 years or so took place in the months of February, March, and April. This means on the average, four of the eight possible ancestral banquets will be celebrated within that twelve-week period—an average of one every three weeks (though even within the twelve weeks the banquets were clustered at the beginning and end of the period rather than evenly spaced within it). If the experience of the lineage for which figures were acquired is mirrored by the village as a whole—and one expects it is, since the deaths used to calculate the regression with energy balance came from a number of different lineages—and since many people in the village share in the ancestral feasts to a certain extent, one expects that the amount of food consumed during these banquets in the spring when food shortages were common is likely to be nutritionally significant.

A similar hypothesis, in fact, has been put forward by Chun Kyung-soo (1983) for the mixed farming and fishing village of Hasami on the island of Chindo off the southwest coast of Korea. Chun's investigation of the diet of villagers there revealed that ordinary meals consisted of four elements: *kimch'i,* steamed rice, soup, and pickled vegetables. Animal protein was consumed in soups perhaps once a week. On ritual occasions, however, animal protein was necessarily consumed not only in soup stock, but also as dried or fried meat. The ancestor worship system in Hasami was significantly less patrilineal and less focused on the senior male line than in Sangongni. Only three, rather than four, generations of patrilineal ascendants were worshiped there, and ceremonies for nonpatrilineal kin (*kidun chesa*) comprised 29 percent of the ceremonies recorded by Chun (1983:273–74). In that part of Korea, moreover, the first-born son is only responsible for worship of the father, with another son taking charge of worship of the mother (Itō 1973:151; Chun 1983:274). Residents of Hasami, then, took part in numerous ceremonies for all sorts of kin throughout the year where they consumed highly valued animal products, leading them to conceive of themselves of being "well nourished by the ancestors." Chun sees the ecological effect of this system as "the distribution of high quality protein throughout the community through a highly valued network of reciprocity" (1983: 275).

Given the more precarious ecological balance in an inland mountain village, the nourishment provided through ancestor worship in Sangongni is much more crucial than in a coastal village. As the structure of ancestor worship is much more hierarchical in Sangongni, moreover, the system results in redistribution of highly valued foods from relatively wealthy high-status households to the households of lineagemates and those neighbors who are able to maintain similar ancestor worship ceremonies and thus similar social status. Rather than reinforcing a generalized egalitarian reciprocity, the Sangongni system (which is more typical of Korean villages as a whole than that of Hasami—see, for example, Janelli and Janelli 1982:99) reinforces the differential status of junior and senior lines in the village and gives the poorest junior households of the village a concrete reason for valuing membership in lineages within which their status is quite low.

Unlike in Hasami, we have seen that there is evidence in Sangongni for seasonal shortfalls of food in both quantity and quality that are correlated with past seasonal patterns of death. These seasonal shortages were not caused solely by inadequate land and technical knowledge, but were also a consequence of the stratification system found in Korea's villages before the completion of the 1950 land reform. Throughout the colonial period, large amounts of rice were exported to Japan, even while consumption standards fell (H. K. Lee 1936: 275). Large landowners extracted most of the surplus from tenant farmers who, along with the landless laborers whose work opportunities varied by season, became most directly subject to seasonal food shortages. Due to the inheritance system, which calls for eldest sons to receive twice what other sons do, senior households of lineages are better off as a whole than junior households. The inheritance system, which villagers explicitly justify by reference to the eldest sons' ancestor worship obligations, thus links stratification patterns to the kinship system so that genealogical and economic prominence tend to go hand in hand.

Total production was probably not stimulated by the ancestor worship system. In fact, by encouraging conspicuous consumption and discouraging capital investment in agriculture, the system may have actually depressed production. The structure of the system did determine who was responsible for financing and preparing ancestor worship banquets, who attended them, and when the banquets would be held, however. If nutritional stress was a significant factor affecting the timing of adult deaths, as the regression of the timing of deaths with the estimated caloric balance of villagers seems to indicate, then the ancestor worship ceremonies would have encouraged the consumption of high value foods at precisely that period when poor lineagemates were most likely to be without adequate food. Since the richer senior households finance the ceremonies attended by descendants of the generally poorer junior descendants of the ancestor, the members of these poorer, junior households would be the most likely beneficiaries. The household ancestor worship ceremonies and their associated banquets, then, would have acted as a negative feedback mechanism that reduced the severity of seasonal nutritional crises among poor lineage members and favored those poor households that maintained lineage ties with their better off senior lineage members.

Of course the timing of the ancestor worship sacrifices is not modified by the causes of death. If death is due to disease, accident, or war—that is, is unrelated to nutrition—the sacrifices still follow and we can assume that in these cases the banqueting is not likely to alter the death rate. The nutritional effect of ancestor worship ceremonies in the years before 1960, in fact, may well have been inadvertent. Ancestor worship is celebrated according to lunar dates (which can vary with the solar calendar as much as six weeks from year to year) while seasonal variations in the diet are presumably more closely correlated with solar dates; the efficacy of the institution of household ancestor worship in counteracting energy imbalances must therefore have been limited.

The other customs that seem more directly related to the spring inadequacies of the Korean peasant diet are the holiday food practices. In table 4.6 is a listing of the major calendrical holidays observed in Sangongni. Of the ten major holidays celebrated in the village, five are celebrated in the first three lunar months of the year—between February 18 and April 24 by the solar calendar. All religious holidays are celebrated with offerings of fruit, beer, and rice cake, but the

TABLE 4.6
Holiday Food Traditions

Holiday	Lunar Date	Solar Date	Associated Food
Lunar New Year	1:1	February 18/ February 13	Chicken soup Dumpling soup Mung bean cakes Rice cakes
Tae Porŭm	1:15	March 4/ February 27	Chestnuts Five grain rice
Hansik	—	April 5/April 6	(same as a *chesa*)
Samjinil	3.3	April 12/ April 15	Rice cake Fruit Rice beer
Village Festival	3:15	April 24/ April 27	Rice cake Fruit Rice beer
Buddha's Birthday	4:8	May 25/ May 20	Rice cake Fruit Rice beer
Tano	5:5	June 2/ June 15	Rice cake Fruit Rice beer
Ch'ilsŏk	7:7	August 2/ August 15	Rice cake Fruit Rice beer
Paekchung	7:15	August 20/ August 23	Rice cake Fruit
Ch'usŏk	8:15	September 8/ September 21	Rice cake Fruit Rice beer
Sihyangje	10 (all)	November/ December	Rice cake Fruit Rice beer

NOTE: First solar date is for 1977, second is for 1983.

spring holidays are also celebrated with certain holiday foods that are supposed to be served at banquets on the holidays themselves and during the holiday period in general. As with the household ancestor worship ceremonies, the senior households of lineages put more money and effort into holiday banquets than others and share their food with lineagemates and neighbors. Unlike the foods associated with the *chesa*, however, the special holiday foods are not made out of expensive ingredients. Five-grain rice, for example, is made out of a combination of grains—including millet and barley—which, except for the rice, are ordinarily eaten only by the poor. Dumpling soup can be made with meat, but it doesn't have to be. (It was generally made without meat in Sangongni). All of these dishes, however, are more work than normal to make and would have the effect of significantly improving the monotonous spring diet (see table 4.7 for a nutritional analysis of these dishes). Dumpling soup (*mandu kuk*), served during the week of the lunar New Year holiday, provides nutritionally significant amounts of calcium, thiamine, riboflavin, niacin, and lysine. Mung bean cake, eaten during the same period, provides good quality protein and calcium. Chestnuts, eaten around Tae Porŭm (the first full moon after lunar New Year), provide thiamine, riboflavin, and good quality protein. Another Tae Porŭm dish, five-grain rice (made up of regular rice, glutinous rice, glutinous millet, sorghum, soybeans, and red beans) provides complete protein (tryptophan and lysine are especially likely to be low among the necessary amino acids) and nutritionally significant amounts of riboflavin and thiamine.

Although the exact solar date of the holidays where special foods are customarily eaten varies from year to year, all of these holidays fall between February and June, the months in which an energy deficit is most likely to appear. The traditional foods that are supposed to be eaten during this period, moreover, provide in good measure those nutrients that are most likely to be absent from the diet. Thus, although the everyday diet from mid-January until the beginning of May when the vegetable gardens begin to produce is monotonous and may be marginal in some respects, the eating practices associated with ancestor worship and calendrical holidays assure that at least five and probably nine or more banquets will be held during this period. When we consider that the leftovers from these banquets are likely to be eaten for several days after the event itself, it is inescapable that these holiday and ancestor food customs provide enough nutritional supplementation to significantly affect the dietary adaptation of the people of the village.

TABLE 4.7
Nutritional Analysis of Holiday Dishes

	Calories	Protein grams	Calcium mg	Iron mg	Vitamin A IU	Thiamine mg	Riboflavin mg	Niacin mg	Vitamin C mg
Dumpling soup	77	4.6	31	1.3	9	0.11	0.04	0.6	0.2
Mung bean cake	176	12.5	61	3.9	140	0.19	0.11	1.3	3.8
Chestnuts (raw)	194	2.9	27	1.7	—	0.22	0.22	0.6	—
Five grain rice	110	3.0	14	1.2	16	0.09	0.04	0.7	0.6
RDA	3000	37.0	400	9.0	750	1.20	1.80	19.8	30.0

Essential Amino Acids (in milligrams)

	Ile.	Leu.	Lys.	Meth.	Phe.	Thr.	Trp.	Val.
Dumpling soup	412	700	603	114	458	359	122	223
Mung bean cake	445	841	972	63	584	398	97	494
Chestnuts (raw)	?	?	?	?	?	?	?	?
Five grain rice	188	385	193	67	209	143	49	213
MDR	1065	940	835	230	310	515	193	705

NOTE: Calculated on the basis of cooked servings of 100 grams each. See note on table 4.2 for remarks on RDA, MDR, and food composition sources.

With the ancestor worship ceremony, any beneficial dietary effects are an inevitable consequence of the ancestor worship system and the timing of ancestral deaths. Thus, one has justification for saying that ancestor worship practices operate as automatic homeostatic devices that counteracted, albeit inefficiently, contributions to seasonal death rates that were related to nutritional stress. For holiday food practices, on the other hand, the exact causal mechanism is less clear. Rural Koreans are aware that some foods are more nutritious than others, and they, like any other people, get tired of a monotonous diet, but whether the holidays cause the consumption of nutritious foods, or whether the reason these foods are consumed on the holidays is that rural Koreans wish to improve their diet remains open. Adaptive effects can be seen, but in neither case can the need for adaptation be the cause of the system. Although it is tempting to try to correlate the stratificational aspects of the redistribution with the need for wealthy families to maintain their labor force, the fact that recipients of the largess of the senior households were primarily kin who, apart from younger brothers not fully separated from their natal household, had no necessary work relation to the senior household, and the fact that nonkin households who did have such a relation were not necessarily included in the redistribution makes such an interpretation difficult.

Land Requirements in Sangongni

This discussion of the dietary patterns of the villagers of Sangongni provides a basis for estimating the amount of various staple crops a householder must plan to harvest to provide for household members. When the productivity of the system is taken into account, the amount of land per AME that must be cultivated for subsistence can be estimated. This parameter will become important in our later interpretation of the interplay of consumption needs, labor supply, and household organization. The productivity of agriculture in Sangongni and other villages in rural Korea has risen dramatically over the past generation (see table 4.8), moreover, and these changes in productivity have motivated important changes in family organization. It is now possible to produce one's subsistence on less land than formerly. On the other hand, Korean farmers now produce (and need to produce) much more than subsistence these days, for they now need cash for manufactured items and for agricultural inputs. The socioeconomic significance of population density or land-tenure relations is much different now than it was a generation ago. Then, subsistence consider-

TABLE 4.8
Productivity of Staple Crops (*in metric tons per hectare*)

	1948–49	1977	1983
Rice (husked)	2.0	4.2	4.5
Barley (unpolished)	0.7	1.9	
Soybeans	0.6	1.2	
Other beans	0.6	0.8	
White potatoes	5.7	9.8	
Sweet potatoes	6.8	23.7	
Summer grains	0.5	*	
Cotton	0.5	*	
Hemp	0.7	*	

*These crops were not grown in large enough quantities in 1977 to justify the calculation of production figures.
SOURCE: 1948–49 figures: United Nations Korean Reconstruction Agency (1954: 88–89)

ations were paramount and almost exclusive, but now other considerations are equally important. Land needs will have to be calculated separately for the traditional and transitional periods. Since the mechanical period is presently being created, we will have to base our understanding of it on projections rather than observations.

Productivity of the major crops used for subsistence in Sangongni and other villages is given in table 4.9. The figures for 1948–49 (which, due to the disruptions of the Korean War did not substantially change until the sixties) are taken from United Nations Korean Reconstruction Agency (1954). Those from 1977 were collected in the field. For 1983, I have field data for rice only, but one may presume gains in productivity of those crops are of approximately the same order as those for rice. In the traditional period, then, it took about 20.8 ares of land to produce enough to support one adult male in comfort. Given the mean family size of around 5.5 that prevailed in rural areas during the sixties, we can estimate that the average family consisted of 4.3 AME. Such a family would need slightly less than a hectare of land, or about one-third hectare of riceland and two-thirds hectare of rainfall field to meet his subsistence needs (this assumes that due to double cropping the size of rainfall fields had to be only about two-thirds of the seeded area necessary for subsistence). On this land he could produce about 530 metric tons of rice (husked), 90 percent of which he would consume at home, and enough of the other crops to provide his subsistence and a 10 percent

TABLE 4.9
Subsistence Land Needs per Adult Male Equivalent (*in ares*)

	1948–49		1977		1983
Irrigated land					
Rice	6.4		3.0		2.8
(Subtotal)		6.4		3.0	2.8
Rainfall Field					
Barley	6.3		2.3		
Soybeans	3.4		1.8		
Other beans	6.7		5.0		
White potatoes	1.3		0.7		
Sweet potatoes	0.7		0.2		
Hemp or cotton	0.3		*		
(Subtotal)		18.7		10.0	
Double-cropping adjustment (× 0.33)**		−6.2		−3.3	
Total subsistence need		18.9		9.7	
Cash needs	(10%)	2.1	(50%)	9.7	
Total including cash need		21.0		19.4	
Family size (in AME)	4.3		3.8		
Land need per family		90.3		73.7	

*Fibers were mostly purchased rather than grown in 1977.
**Because of double cropping on rainfall fields, the rainfall field necessary has been calculated as two-thirds of the necessary seeded area.

surplus to provide cash for taxes and consumer items. The population density that could be supported at that level would be approximately 750 persons per square kilometer of agricultural land, if one-third of the land were irrigated paddy and two-thirds rainfall field.

Luckily for Koreans, in most areas irrigated rice paddy made up more than half the agricultural land. Rural population densities per unit of agricultural land tended to hover around 1,000 persons per square kilometer, and the only way the land could support such densities was through the irrigated rice agriculture, which was twice as productive as rainfall agriculture. Thus, we have estimated the population of Sangongni during this period as approximately eight hundred persons. With forty-eight hectares of paddy and fifty-five hectares of rainfall field, we can guess that villagers were able to produce some 105 metric tons of rice, about 58 metric tons of which they could consume themselves with the rest (some 44.6 percent of their production) being exchanged to provide the other goods needed. On their rainfall field, on the other hand, they would be able to produce only about half of their subsistence needs, with the rest acquired by exchange and taking the major share of the surplus generated by the rice.[22]

Although in Sangongni and other villages like it in Korea, people could produce enough calories for subsistence by concentrating on the more productive rice and cultivating marginal fields that are now no longer in use (such as paddies in remote mountain ravines and fire fields on steep slopes) they were very close to the subsistence margin—especially if they were tenant farmers who turned half of their produce over to their landlords. Close as they were to the subsistence margin, however, it is also clear that the villagers were not economically independent. Rainfall fields being insufficient for the production of necessary side dishes did not lead to a higher consumption of rice.[23] Rather these commodities have been brought in from other parts of the world since the early twentieth century. During the colonial period, for example, levels of productivity were comparable to, and in some cases higher than, those of the immediate postwar period. Due to high tenancy rates and a policy of the colonial administration to encourage rice exports to Japan, however, large amounts of the rice produced in Korea left the rural areas. Cheaper grains, such as wheat, millet, and sorghum, imported from Manchuria made up some, but not all, of the difference (Grajdanzev 1944:117–20). In the postwar period, the grain trade was disrupted and immediate serious food shortages showed up in Korea. During the first fifteen years after the end of World War II, when the food situation was very tight, Korea was the recipient of large quantities of Food for Peace grain shipments (principally of wheat) from America. Later on, as the Korean industrial build-up began, Korea began to purchase these grains on the open market. Today, and for some time in the past, wheat products such as noodles have not been produced in the village, but purchased at the periodic markets. Thus, that part of even the rural Korean diet that is made up of noodles (the primary form in which wheat products are consumed), is purchased, and in most cases is manufactured from foreign grain at ports of entry.

The farmers of Sangongni in 1960, then, produced a substantial surplus of rice, but had a deficit of other products for which the rice was exchanged. Although the per capita land area of approximately 12.8 ares in the village was not sufficient for subsistence if only one-third were irrigated rice, by concentrating on irrigated rice (some 45 percent of their agricultural land), the villagers would have managed to just barely keep their heads above water because of their ability to exchange the rice for cheap imported wheat products. Nevertheless, virtually all of their productive power had to be concentrated in the quest of subsistence, even if exchange was an importance subsistence strategy.

By 1977 things had improved. The productivity per unit of land had more than doubled, and village population had fallen 25 percent from its peak in the mid-sixties. The villagers of Sangongni in 1977 could meet their subsistence needs with only some ten ares of land per AME. Although a population of more than 1,000 persons per square kilometer might have been supported by such a productive agricultural system, population densities per square kilometer of agricultural land had fallen from the 750 person level to 577 persons per square kilometer. The 572 residents of agricultural households, when age and sex is taken into account, were equivalent to approximately 419 adult males, so almost 75 percent of the riceland and 50 percent of the rainfall field could be used for purposes other than the production of subsistence crops.

Because food supplies were secure for all but a few householders in Sangongni in 1977, they could begin to put fields to the production of cash crops. This had already begun on a small scale in 1977 with several houses growing tobacco and several more devoting some of the field to mulberry orchards. In general, however, cropping patterns had not changed a great deal from traditional times. More than a quarter of the farmers were still tenants who were obliged to give half of their production to their landlords. Other farmers simply produced surpluses of the regular subsistence crops that they could easily store as security, take to their children in town, or sell on the market when they needed the money. These farmers, though poor enough by Euro-American standards, had attained the traditional goal of self-sufficiency with enough of a surplus to buy a few things. The need for cash, however, was transforming the system. High productivity made it possible for the farmers of Sangongni to produce bigger surpluses than before, but that productivity was predicated on the ability to earn enough cash to pay for modern agricultural inputs. The farmer of 1977 had to produce substantial surpluses to pay back his debts to the agricultural cooperative and other credit institutions. In

1977, production costs for agriculture that had to be paid in cash (that is, even if we add no costs for noncash outlays like plowing with a *chaenggi*) amounted to at least 10 percent of the crop. Agricultural tools were being purchased rather than being made at home, and the same is true of clothing. There were still a few farmers making a minimal living on extremely small amounts of land with little modern factor input in 1977, but one by one they were moving to the city. Sangongni was in a transitional phase where subsistence already meant something different to the peasants than it had to their fathers.

These changes in the traditional farming system that were already visible in 1977 were even more clear in 1983. Population had fallen to 497 people who were equivalent in consumption needs to 291 adult males. The agricultural system was slightly more productive than in 1977 (judging from rice figures, about 7 percent more productive). Only 17 percent of the riceland in Sangongni was required for the subsistence of the residents of the village in 1983. The rest could be used to produce rice for cash sale. As in 1977, the rainfall fields could produce all of the subsistence crops needed by the villagers and still have more than half left over for such cash crops as tobacco, ginseng, foxglove, and sesame. And for the first time, villagers could consider giving over significant amounts of land to animal husbandry. As far back as 1954, when the United Nations Korean Reconstruction Agency published its report on Korean agriculture, it was recommended that lea farming on marginal slopes (i.e., using marginal land for the seasonal production of pasture) be encouraged to feed livestock. Although dairy farming has been instituted near large cities, this recommendation has not been generally taken up in other contexts. During the fifties and the sixties, the food situation in rural areas was so tight and capital so short, one doubts that there were any unused marginal slopes. In Sangongni, informants reported that at that time steep slopes were plowed and planted in beans and other typical rainfall field crops. During the transitional phase of Korean agriculture, it was most efficient to use scarce capital resources to improve productivity of traditional subsistence crops, rather than promote kinds of animal husbandry with which farmers were unfamiliar.

When the system was still in the traditional stage, when 90 percent of the crops grown by typical households were consumed at home, and when managing to produce enough for one's family to eat well was an accomplishment, farm size was determined partly by the minimum amount of land that a viable farm family could cultivate and still keep itself alive. This seems to have been very close to the actual minimum farm size in remote rural areas where opportunities for wage labor were more restricted than near the cities. In 1977, subsistence considerations, while receding into the background, were still important. A farm big enough to provide one with what is needed for subsistence plus a little bit for some cash needs and for the tax collector, was still a viable, if uninspiring, unit. Villagers, however, were beginning to consider as less and less attractive the return to labor on a farm where modern capital inputs were not used. To afford modern farm inputs, however, it is necessary to farm at a scale larger than mere subsistence. A farm of seventy-five ares was viable and attractive in 1960, because it was large enough to produce the needs for a farmer and his family on household land—thus with the highest return to labor that could be found in a rural area. Such a farm was still viable in 1977 but for slightly different reasons. It was more than twice the size needed to produce one's subsistence needs, true, but subsistence wasn't all that it took in 1977. To get high enough productivity to justify staying in the countryside, it was necessary to use modern technological inputs, and to finance these inputs, one needed to cultivate 10 to 20 percent more land than needed for subsistence. In addition, since many things beginning to be considered necessities in 1977 (such as store-bought clothes, radios, and schooling) had to be paid for with money, a farm had to be large enough to produce a surplus to sell for cash.

Industrialization and Sangongni

When we consider the farming of Sangongni in terms of subsistence, two changes stand out clearly: productivity has risen and population has fallen. Both of these changes have improved the relationship between farming and subsistence. With higher productivity, more crops can be grown on less land with less labor. With a smaller population, fewer people have to be supported on this land. Both of these processes have enabled the farmers of Sangongni to produce better surpluses than they could before. Increasing land productivity has allowed them to generate surpluses by increasing total production, and out-migration has increased the proportion of that production surplus to the subsistence needs of the population.

Each of these two processes is directly or indirectly a result of industrialization. When the village population began to fall in the 1960s, living standards were improving. The peasants who left the villages were not forced out by starvation, but rather lured out by the prospect of improving their (admittedly low in most cases) standard of living more quickly than they could in rural areas. By reducing population pressure, those peasants who left the village freed production that would formerly have had to have been used for subsistence for marketing. At the same time, modest investments in the agricultural sector by the national government helped farmers increase their yield. Most important, however, by draining off excess labor, the out-migration also provided an incentive for improving labor productivity. There was no use keeping all one's sons on the farm if they could be productively employed elsewhere. If more labor were to migrate out of the household, however, the efficiency of the labor that remained had to be increased. As labor productivity improved with more capital inputs, moreover, still more off-farm migration could be considered.

In this fashion, a positive feedback loop generating agricultural growth and an improvement in the rural living standard was instituted. As with any complicated process, isolating the causes for the creation of this loop is difficult, but two factors stand out: (1) changes in farmers' cropping strategy, and (2) changes in the ecological and economic context in which farmers operate. Traditional Korean agriculture was quite productive by world standards. What made Korean farmers poor was not so much the inability to gain high yields from the land, but low productivity per capita. The low per capita productivity in turn was partially due to overpopulation and partly due to social stratification patterns. Rural overpopulation forced farmers to grow their crops on farms too small to generate a substantial surplus above subsistence needs, while stratification patterns led most of the surplus that was produced to be extracted from the local system. On the one hand, no surplus that could be invested in raising per capita productivity was available. On the other hand, an abundance of rural labor with no alternative sources of employment made for low labor costs that provided little incentive for investing capital to raise labor productivity. Without incentive or means for investment in per capita productivity improvements, it is no wonder agricultural living standards were low. Concentrating on producing subsistence by labor-intensive means was the most rational strategy for most peasants, and even large landowners would usually rent out surplus land rather than try to cultivate it themselves with modern inputs.

In the sixties, when agricultural growth began accelerating, two circumstances that had conditioned that system and made a labor intensive strategy rational began to change. Modest amounts of reasonably priced capital became available for rural investment through the re-organized agricultural cooperative, and industrialization offered alternative employment for village labor. With alternative employment opportunities available, it became rational for farmers to use capital to increase their labor productivity. The total income of all family members would be increased if fewer members could run the family farm, letting the others take industrial employment. Thus a new strategy of investment in modern factor inputs that make labor more productive became feasible and attractive.

Economists in discussing modern factor inputs in Korean agriculture often stress most their importance in increasing aggregate agricultural production and in increasing land productivity. Increases in labor productivity are usually discussed as a by-product of mechanization (Hasan 1976:139–50; Ban, Moon, and Perkins 1980:3–111). Peasant motivation for investment in agricultural improvements is not in principle seen as problematic, being simply "rational" behavior for peasant maximizers of pecuniary profit. Since the behavior of many peasants has failed to conform to this expectation of development planners, all too many have concluded they are obtuse. Yet the benefit to a farmer from investment in increased labor productivity is not obvious when labor is abundant and cheap and alternative employment opportunities lacking. Although recent development efforts in Korea have made new capital, technology, and factor inputs available in rural areas, equally important benefits of Korea's industrialization have been the creation of new circumstances where peasants have a clear motivation for capital investment to obtain higher labor productivity. The food preferences of rural Koreans and their desire to produce their subsistence on their own land with family labor have not changed as motivational factors. What has changed are circumstances of population density, farm size, and alternative employment opportunity for labor—even if such employment is outside the village. Industrialization has changed village life by making a different strategy of resource allocation rational, rather than by providing industrial employment directly in the village.

CHAPTER 5

Energy Flow and the Allocation of Household Labor

Whichever factor determining peasant farm organization we were to consider dominant, however much significance we were to attach to the influence of the market, amount of land for use, or availability of means of production and natural fertility, we ought to acknowledge that work hands are the technically organizing element of any production process. And since, on the family farm which has no recourse to hired labor, the labor force pool, its composition and degree of labor activity are entirely determined by family composition and size, we must accept family makeup as one of the chief factors in peasant farm organization. [Chayanov 1966:53]

If the first criterion the villagers of Sangongni take into account in determining their household cropping strategies is the subsistence needs of the household, the second must be the size and composition of the household labor supply. Whatever the mix of crops that is cultivated, of course, these crops must be produced by the application of labor organized in a specific way. In Sangongni, as in rural Korea generally (Han'guk ŭnhaeng chosabu 1963:62; Chŏng Yŏngil 1984:46), most labor is provided by the family itself. This, in fact, is a characteristic of peasant farms world-wide.

Chayanov (1968:53) recognized the prevalence of farms in which most labor is provided by family members, or "family labor farms," as one of the most distinctive aspects of peasant farm organization and the aspect that makes the organization of the family such an important element in the peasant farm economy. Although the absence of wage labor is central to his analysis of peasant farms, Chayanov never directly confronted the question of *why* farms should be run with family labor. In certain passages, it is true, Chayanov seemed to see the characteristics of family labor farms as rational adaptations to the circumstances of peasant life,[1] but his explanation for that rationality revolved primarily around a bookkeeping problem: the difficulty peasants are supposed to have in calculating profit (gross income minus outlays on materials minus wages) when wages paid in money are generally absent (p. 88). This explanation introduced some difficulties into his analysis. Not only did it force him to assume peasants have no real idea of the value of their labor and thus are incapable of choosing those activities that will give them the highest return on that labor, but it also forced him to assume that wage labor is alien to peasant economies, even though wage labor opportunities were present among the Russian peasants that Chayanov himself studied, not to mention in Korea where surveys of agricultural villages in the late fifties and early sixties regularly found that the class of agricultural day laborers who lived solely on their agricultural wages comprised some 5 to 20 percent of the population (Mills 1960:47; Ko et al. 1963:206; Kim T'aekkyu 1964:75).

Patterns of labor allocation are partially derived from cultural ideals of the sexual division of labor, as well as by the needs for labor that follow from the application of a specific technology in a specific environment. In addition, however, the circumstances mentioned earlier that condition cropping strategies also condition strategies of labor allocation. It is not necessary to assume villagers cannot calculate their relative return for different types of labor to understand their predominant use of family labor. On the contrary, one can base one's explanation precisely on that calculation. The subsistence-oriented cropping strategy of villagers leads to the organization of households as closed-loop energy systems.[2] The same factors that encourage the subsistence orientation of village agriculturalists—primarily unfavorable articulation with markets—also limit village opportunities for the employment of family members outside the agricultural household. In such circumstances, the highest returns for village labor can be obtained primarily through the cultivation of household land. Those planning the cropping strategies of the household, then, do well to take into account the amount of male and female labor available in the family and how it can most productively be put to use on the family farm. It is this that puts into motion the systematic interplay between family organization and farm characteristics so striking among the peasants of the village.

The Organization of the Rural Household

Korean pundits and those older Koreans who remember the household organization of their youth cannot help but marvel at the many changes that have taken place in Korean urban and rural households. Until after the Korean War, many peasants lived in large, complex households ruled with an iron hand by the seniormost male. Male and female interaction was strictly circumscribed: high-status women remained as much as possible within their own courtyards, and unrelated males and females interacted as little as possible. Men and women were married early to a spouse of their parents' choosing, whom they met for the first time only during the wedding itself, and the new bride worked like a slave under the strict control of her mother-in-law.

Of course even a generation ago there was a great deal of variation in the organization of Korean households. Most people were prevented from living in large households by poverty and high death rates, and the necessity to help with agricultural labor forced many of the women out of their households much of the time (sometimes to their relief). Still, the differences between the households of today and those of a generation ago seem undeniable. Today rural periodic markets are teeming with women who do most of the day-to-day marketing for rural households, while a generation ago, a respectable woman would not dream of going to market—at least not until she had daughters-in-law to look after the household in her absence. The large, joint family households that used to be found in at least small numbers in every village (cf. Osgood 1951:40–41; Han 1977:91) have totally disappeared from rural areas. Meetings are now arranged between prospective spouses before an engagement is made, and love matches flourish in urban settings. Although in the past it could be assumed that all children would set up households and subsist by farming, today children from Sangongni are going on to middle school, high school, and college, and taking up jobs all over the country as auto mechanics, factory workers, teachers, civil servants, and "salary men" (that is, white collar employees of large companies).

In spite of all these changes, however, the features of the central Korean peasant household that make it the fundamental unit of rural social and economic life have remained. Households must be organized to provide a constant flow of food energy to family members.

No single person can accomplish this alone, but by cooperating in a division of labor, the members of a household can ensure that all tasks necessary for survival are performed within the household. Because of the many functions the household must perform, the household organization observed in Sangongni in 1983, 1977, or earlier was always the result of the interaction of the labor requirements of agriculture, principles for the allocation of labor, demographic parameters, and the economic circumstances in which households found themselves. One would expect, then, that the introduction of new social forces that have changed agricultural technology, birth and death rates, and the general economic climate within which villagers operate would lead to important changes in household organization. The interdependence of family members that is a consequence of the division of labor, however, makes the household a structured system of energy flows, which tends to mold and dampen the effect of fluctuations in outside forces on the internal organization of the farm household. Although new and sometimes unexpected strategies for the allocation of household labor have appeared in the past twenty years, the basic structure of energy flows, and the household division of labor that underlies these flows have changed very little.

In Korean, the word *chip*, which I have translated as household, means "house" in the physical sense of four walls and a roof, in the residential sense of a group of people living under one roof, in the economic sense of a group of relatives who maintain a more or less common economy, and in the cultural sense of a socially defined group of kin. The *chip* is thus similar in concept to the traditional Chinese *jīa* or prewar Japanese *ie* (K. K. Lee 1975:47–50). One's place in the village social system is determined largely by the status of one's *chip*— by the amount of land at its disposal, the genealogical position of its house head, and the level of education of household members—and one's position within that *chip*.

That rural Koreans have a tendency to see an individual primarily as the incumbent of a certain role within a particular household can be seen not only in household registration system (*hojŏk chedo*), in which the position of each legal household member is defined in relation to the house head (Kim Chusu 1984:58), but also in the way ordinary villagers talk about and address each other. A villager may address a close friend of the same sex whose age is within ten years of his own, or a person of the same sex who is more than ten years younger, by his given name, but villagers most commonly address and refer to contemporaries and social seniors indirectly: by teknonymy— referring to a person by the name of their child—or by mentioning their household and household role. A woman with a daughter named Sunjŏng thus becomes "Sunjŏng Ŏmma" (Sunjŏng's Mama), and a man with a son named Yongsik might be known as "Yongsik Abŏji" (Yongsik's Father). These teknonymous names are used both by those who know the children and those who don't.[3] Within the household, of course, social seniors are addressed by their kinship category such as *hyŏng* (older brother), *ŏmma* (mama), or *ajubŏni* (brother-in-law, female ego). Rather than referring to them by name, mothers-in-law commonly refer to their daughters-in-law as *uri myŏnŭri* (our daughter-in-law), and a fifty-year-old woman who has given birth to seven children might still be generally known as such-and-such a house's daughter-in-law by those who are not intimate friends.[4]

Due to the renovated registration system introduced by the Japanese in 1915 (Chŏng Kwanghyŏn 1967:129) and the revisions of the Decree on Korean Civil Affairs introduced in 1923 which made most changes of family status legally dependent upon registration (p. 22), the legal members of a household have been easy to unambiguously determine: they are those persons entered on the family register in the township office. This "legal household" (known as *ka* in legalese[5]) is defined by reference to a legal house head and does not depend on coresidence or common budgets. It corresponds in general to the residential and economic unit known as *chip* in the village, but there are occasional differences. There was a household in the village in 1977, for example, made up of a husband, wife, their two children and the wife's child by her first husband (who had died). They all lived in the same house and pooled their resources just as any other family. The husband treated all of the boys similarly. Nevertheless, this single economic unit legally consisted of two *ka*: the *ka* of the husband, and the *ka* of the wife's former husband represented by her first son. But though the legal definition of the *ka* and the de facto composition of the *chip* did not correspond in this case, it is likely that, in fact, the second husband's eldest son (rather than his older half-brother) will take the responsibility of nurture of both his aged parents, as is his legal right and duty. Thus, although occasional discrepancies between the legal ideal and the folk reality can be found, in most cases the village ideal of the *chip* and the legal *ka* correspond: each consists of a house head, his wife, his eldest son and eldest son's wife and children, and his own unmarried other children. In other words, the household consists, in its most developed form, of a patrilineal stem family.

This *chip* is organized as an ongoing corporation made up of a head (*chuin*) and family members (*kajogwŏn*). The position of all the family members are reckoned from their relationship to the head, and the head, as the pivot of the family, is empowered to make the basic decisions about the use of household resources and the entry and departure of persons to and from the household. One becomes house head not because of any personality characteristic or talent, but because of one's structural position within the house. When one house head dies, his position automatically devolves upon his eldest son (or such substitutes for a son as may be designated in cases of sonlessness). Because of this mechanism of succession, the position of the house head, as indeed all the other positions of the *chip,* exists apart from the person who happens to be incumbent at any particular time. As each house head dies, he is replaced by another house head so that the family corporation may continue indefinitely.

The *chip,* then, is the most basic sociological unit of Sangongni because its structure defines the identities and roles possible for village residents, and because the villagers themselves think of all but intimate friends of the same sex as members of *chip* rather than simply as individuals with unique defining characteristics.[6] There is another sense, however, in which the *chip* is basic: those tasks most fundamental to human survival are all performed within its walls. Each household is organized as an independent economic unit that ideally holds the means of production necessary to sustain life. Food and other necessities are produced for household use with family labor. The means of production are ideally all under the direct control of the house head, but even if the household lacks land, labor, or capital and the family members have to work with borrowed tools on rented land, the household is still the unit of accounting and production. Since, moreover, the food and other necessities produced by the household are prepared within the household for consumption by the members of the household, the *chip* is also the basic unit of consumption.

In 1977, 95 (82.6 percent) of the 115 households of Sangongni had no significant source of income outside of peasant agriculture. Of the remaining 20 households, 11 practiced no significant agriculture, with 9 combining agriculture with side businesses. The nonagricultural households and those combining agriculture with a side business were, with a couple of exceptions, not native to the village and generally engaged in marginal occupations. Even the teachers, although high status individuals, had only indirect influence on village life because of their short tenure in the village (limited to five years), and because they commonly left their families in Ch'unch'ŏn and were usually out of the village on weekends and vacations, participating little in village life. Although many Korean villages nearer to good transportation routes are experiencing growth and diversification in their economy (Janelli and Janelli 1982:16–17; Kendall 1985:44– 48), this growth has, of yet, passed up remote villages such as San-gongni. Thus the occupational structure of the village in 1983, when 78 of the 97 households of the village (80.4 percent) engaged exclusively in agriculture, was little different from 1977 (see table 5.1). By and large, the agricultural households formed the political and social core of the village, and set the standards and tone of village life in both 1977 and 1983.

The Division of Labor in the Traditional Household

In the past, to ensure the survival of household members over time, a number of tasks had to be accomplished within the household walls: food for subsistence had to be provided, the house built and maintained, food produced by the household members processed and stored, domestic animals cared for, meals made and served, clothing provided and maintained, and the young who will provide the continuity of the family born, raised, and married. In the accomplishment of these tasks there was a clear division of labor between males and females. Men were responsible for growing the major field crops, operating and maintaining the irrigation system, taking care of the con-

TABLE 5.1
Nonfarm Sources of Village Income, 1977–83 (*by number of households*)

Occupation	1977			1983		
	No Farm Income	Some Farm Income	Total	No Farm Income	Some Farm Income	Total
Teacher	4	2	6	3	3	6
Civil servant	1	1	2	1	1	2
Store or winehouse	2	3	5	0	3	3
Mill or store	2	0	2	2	0	2
Religious specialist	2	0	2	0	1	1
Ferryman	0	2	2	0	1	1
Retired	2	1	3	1	2	3
Beekeeper	0	0	0	1	0	1
Total	13	9	22	8	11	19

struction and repair of the household buildings and the agricultural implements, and coordinating their activity with other households so that the irrigation, cow exchange, and labor exchange systems worked efficiently. Women were responsible for running the internal affairs of the household, managing food stores, growing vegetables for daily use, preparing meals, providing and maintaining clothing, and bearing and raising children (cf. Kim Chusuk 1985). Those tasks done primarily outside the house and which are the primary responsibility of the men are known as *pakkannil*—outside labor—while those tasks done primarily inside the house and which are the primary responsibility of the women are known as *annil*—inside labor. The house head, known as the *pakkat chuin,* or "outside master," and the house mistress, known as the *an chuin,* or "inside master," are each in charge of their respective spheres of activity and run them relatively independently of each other's control.

Legally, the house head is responsible for providing the income upon which the members of the household will live (New Civil Code, sec. 797), and the house head usually owns the land and house of the family as a personal possession that he can legally dispose of at will (see also Brandt 1971:52). The bulk of the household income usually comes from the major field crops, though in traditional times, cottage production of cloth and clothing by the women often made the difference between merely surviving and getting a little bit ahead. Gross agricultural production for all but the poorest families has normally been sufficient to provide at least a small surplus that can be exchanged for cash.[7] Whether this potential surplus has actually been available for exchange by the producer, however, has depended on land-tenure relations. During the colonial period, high tenancy rates led to the extraction of a large proportion of the crop from producing families in rent.[8] Much of the crop extracted by landlords entered the circulation system and eventually was exported to Japan, even while many farm families had to make ends meet through side occupations and foraging in the countryside (Suh 1978:86–89). The government-sponsored land reforms between 1945 and 1955 drastically reduced tenancy levels and thus reduced the proportion of the crop extracted through rents so that more production was retained for farm consumption.

Although women upon occasion do all agricultural tasks except those involving the use of animal or mechanical power,[9] most of the skill and labor in producing these crops is provided by the men. Males do virtually all of the construction and maintenance of irrigation facilities, all field preparation such as plowing and harrowing, and most other labor associated with rice agriculture (transplanting, harvesting, threshing), and all the construction and maintenance of dwellings and agricultural tools. During the winter they are responsible for cutting and gathering the firewood necessary for heating and cooking. Taking care of the draft animals is usually a male task (though it is often done by women and children as well).

The requirements and organization of agriculture are such that no household is self-sufficient in agricultural labor requirements. In this part of Kangwŏn Province, for example, although harrowing is done with a single cow (bulls or oxen are rarer), two cows are necessary for the plowing of both paddy and dry fields. Before 1983 in Sangongni, it was extremely rare for a household to have more than one adult animal. Thus, for the relatively brief periods during the year when plowing is done, cow exchange (*sokkyŏri*), was used to create a full yoke of cows. Labor exchange (*p'umasi*) is also necessary during peak agricultural seasons. The operation of the cow and labor exchange systems, as well as the operation of the irrigation system and the co-operative marketing of crops require coordination among the households of a village. Constant socializing and the exchange of information among men is necessary for its efficient operation. The kinds and amount of interaction among the males of the village and also directly with the government bureaucrats is conditioned by the political structure of the village and one's social status within this structure. To a great extent, then, a man's concern with village politics and social status forms an integral part of his economic role in the agricultural system. It is the special prerogative of the male to express his social position through correct linguistic usage, conspicuous consumption associated with hospitality to visitors, and correctly Confucian and properly lavish ancestor worship ceremonies (*chesa*).

A woman's most important responsibility is bearing children and nurturing the members of the household. Feeding, training, and disciplining of young children is done mostly by females and is the primary responsibility of the mother.[10] In complex families, the mother-in-law, if she is not dead or retired, supervises the domestic labor. She has the right to expect service from her daughter-in-law and to choose which, if any, of the household tasks she will undertake personally. Normally she chooses to take care of her grandchildren so as to free her daughter-in-law to concentrate on food preparation, laundry, and mending. The rural girl is brought up to expect that she will have to work hard and to know that it is her duty to take over all the household chores from her mother-in-law upon marriage. In earlier times, when daughters-in-law came into the household in their mid- to early teens, they learned how to manage most of their household tasks from their mothers-in-law. Sometimes mothers-in-law abused their daughters-in-law (Yi Kwanggyu 1981:40–63), though the opposite case is not entirely unknown, either. Now that an unhappy couple can move to the city or find land elsewhere, however, cases of abuse of daughters-in-law, never the norm (Brandt 1971:128), are rarer than they used to be.

The preparation and serving of meals is time-consuming for rural Korean women. The typical housewife is up an hour before her husband (and well before the sun in the winter) so that she can prepare the family meal before the rest of the family gets up. She must build the fire, draw the water,[11] heat the rice, heat the water for washing in the big cast-iron caldrons built into the stove, and chop and prepare the vegetables and side dishes that make up the balance of the meal. Convenience foods (except for instant ramen, which is occasionally used for lunch) are unknown. Everything must be made from scratch every morning. The diligent housewife, having prepared the food for her family, then gets her children up and dressed, and folds the quilts and sleeping pads to clear the floor where the meal will be eaten. The members of rural Korean families do not usually take their meals at the same time sitting together in a single group. Rather, the woman prepares separate small tables (*soban*) for the highest status members of the family and serves each of them separately. If she lives in a complex family, the woman must first serve her father-in-law and mother-in-law in their respective rooms. Other men are served in order of status and seniority. When all of the high status members of the household have eaten, the daughter-in-law will remove the tables from their rooms and eat her meal along with her children in the kitchen or some other ritually unimportant spot. Although she will have prepared enough of the soup and rice for the entire family, which side dishes she will eat very often depends upon how much the other diners have left over. When the meal is finished, the woman removes the trays, stores excess food, and cleans up. If the woman has arisen at 6:00 A.M., she may well not be done with these tasks until after 9:00. This task must be done three times a day most of the year, and five times a day during the rice transplantation season (which is also the silk-raising season).

The remaining housework of the rural Korean woman is as exacting as her meal preparation. These chores include sweeping (the whole house, courtyard, and grounds should be done once a day), mending, and doing the laundry. For the young housewife with children, laundry can be an especially difficult task. In rural areas the women do not try to keep their families in clean clothes all day every day. Clothes must be washed by hand and so will not be done until they look dirty. Washing can be done by drawing water with the household pump into a tub and washing them at home, but most women enjoy the conviviality and abundance of water at one of the stream or riverside washing sites (*ppallae t'ŏ*). The chief requirement of such a spot is a good supply of running water. Clothes are scrubbed vigorously on smooth laundry stones placed on the edge of the laundry site. Large quantities of soap are used and the clothes are periodically beaten with a wooden laundry paddle. Diapers, although known and used occasionally by all, are used sparingly. Children who have not yet been toilet trained are sent outside in dresses (girls) or pants with the crotch ripped out (boys) so that they won't soil their clothes when the urge hits them. In 1977, one woman, somewhat younger and more "modern" in outlook than the rest, used diapers regularly with her young son, but after watching her go out several times a day in midwinter, squat over the laundry stones, break the ice off the irrigation ditch, and launder soiled diapers with her bare hands in the ice-cold water, I came to the conclusion that perhaps it is easier and equally sanitary to just clean up the floor in case of accidents.

Quilts and sleeping pads are washed three or four times a year at most. These, and the quilted clothes that used to be worn in winter, are stuffed with cotton wadding and stitched with white (or some other solid color) covers. When they are washed, the covers must be unstitched, the cotton wadding removed, and the two parts washed separately. Thus quilts and quilted clothing have to be virtually unmade and remade during the washing process. Following the washing and drying of such clothes, the wrinkles used to be taken out by fulling (*tadŭmijil*). The clothes were placed on a fulling stone or board where they were rhythmically pounded with wooden fulling clubs. Old accounts of Korean villages mention the constant sound of the pounding from laundry pallets and fulling clubs, but in this age of modern fabrics and irons, fulling is not required except for the traditional regalia (*top'o*) worn by high status persons during ancestor worship ceremonies.

Agricultural labor is not in principle part of the female's *annil*, so women do it according to their ability to find spare time from other household tasks, and according to the supply of other labor in the household. It is common for women to gather work parties, for example, to weed the wheat and barley fields, but a young housewife with several small children and a large household to take care of may find it difficult to make time for this kind of activity unless there is a critical shortage of other labor in the household. Men as well as women participate in weeding (in separate work parties) so it is not necessarily part of the "women's work" per se. In Sangongni, in contrast to many less remote villages, women only participate in the cultivation of rice if there is a critical shortage of male labor. Although help in harvesting is not particularly unusual, it was quite unusual to see women transplanting rice in 1977, and in the few cases in which I observed women participating in this activity, the woman's household usually had a critical shortage of male labor. Women participating in rice transplantation always found it necessary to make some unsolicited comment to me such as, "See, women can transplant rice, too," when I came upon them. Since the fresh vegetables necessary for preparing meals can only be procured in Sangongni by growing them oneself, however, each woman finds it necessary to plant and cultivate a kitchen vegetable patch. Although men plow and prepare the soil, all other responsibilities for these gardens—choosing the crop, timing the planting, preparing the seed, weeding the plants—is a female responsibility. This is so much so that if a household includes no females, it will have no vegetables. In 1977, one man's vegetable garden went completely to seed and weed when his wife became too ill to cultivate it (though an occasional neighbor woman would sometimes do a little in the garden for his wife's benefit).

The only agricultural activity, apart from taking care of vegetable gardens, that was primarily a female responsibility was raising chickens, dogs, and silkworms. All of these activities, of course, are done in, or near the house. The care of these domestic animals is an extension of the woman's care for her family and children. The chickens are fed primarily on maize and sorghum grown in household fields. The woman of the house, who is in charge of the foodstuffs upon which the household members subsist, is by natural extension also in charge of the grain used to feed the chickens. The chickens provide the women with a little side income and are definitely a female responsibility.[12] For the same reasons, dogs are also a female responsibility. They are usually fed leftover human food. Silkworms, which provide the raw material for fabric, as mentioned in chapter 3, are raised by the women in the inner room.

Though the women in principle are not responsible for field labor, the story is different once the agricultural crops reach the gate of the household. In traditional times, when the men threshed the crops in the courtyard by flailing, the women would winnow the grain by tossing it in a winnowing basket. Now, with the advent of foot-powered and motor-powered threshers, only small amounts of winnowing have to be done to remove the last bit of chaff. Before the grain can be bagged and stored for the winter, it also must, however, be dried in the sun to reduce some of the moisture content, and the women take charge of spreading the paddy on mats in the sun in the morning and taking it in at night. Once the grain is ready for storage or milling, the house head decides, in consultation with the house mistress, how much of the crop will be sold immediately, and how much will be retained for family consumption. Arrangements for the sale of grain in large amounts (i.e., more than half a bag or so) are made by the house head.

That part to be used for household consumption is turned over to the control of the house mistress. Unprocessed grain, of course, cannot be used directly as food. At the very least, the grain must be husked to be edible, and often it must be reduced to flour as well. Nowadays, the husking of grain is universally done at commercial grain mills, but until after the Korean War in Sangongni these tasks were all done within the household by the women. Grain was husked in hourglass-shaped wooden mortars (*chŏlgu*) two or three feet in height with wooden pestles (*kongi*) of equal length. Larger and better equipped households might be equipped with a treadmill (*tidil panga*)—a long beam on a fulcrum with a stone pestle attached to one end. By stepping on a tread at the end opposite the pestle, the women could raise the end with the pestle as if it were the opposite end of a seesaw. As soon as they stepped off the tread, the pestle end would fall of its own weight and strike the grain placed in a mortar hole dug in the ground. Although using a treadmill to husk grain or reduce it to flour was easier than pounding it in a mortar, whichever method was used was hard work that took a long time. One informant of fifty-five reported in 1983, for example: "If I didn't work when I was pregnant, how was the barley going to be husked? I also reaped and threshed the barley and did it all one thing right after the other. There was nothing fortunate about it, I can tell you. When someone had a baby they went right back to husking barley. We didn't have a treadmill, you see, so it went like this: you'd get the unhusked barley and pound it to remove the husk, and make lunch and eat it. Then you would get some more unhusked barley and start with dinner."

Other tasks included pounding grain into flour for various kinds of rice cakes, grinding nuts or grains to make *muk* (a gelatinous food that could be made from a variety of grains, beans, or nuts), or preparing the various bean or pickled vegetable preparations mentioned in chapter 4.

In addition to this primary food processing, the women of the household usually manufactured the clothes of household members. Cloth was commonly woven from hemp, cotton, and silk. Hemp (sambe) and cotton (mumyŏng) were used to make clothes for the family, while silk (myŏngju) was usually woven for sale. Everything from growing the crop, spinning the thread, weaving and dyeing the cloth, to making the garments was done at home as late as the 1950s. Hemp, from which ordinary work clothes and mourning clothes were made, had to be cooked for a long time to turn it into usable fiber. The normal clothes worn at that time were all white (hence the large amount of work involved in laundry), but other colors could be made upon occasion. "We would weave cloth, pick leaves of the overcup oak (*Quercus dentata*) to boil, dye the cloth black in the resulting solution, and make Western-style clothes for those going to Japan as laborers [before 1945]," reported one woman of more than seventy in 1983. As late as 1977, cotton and hemp were still being grown in the village, though the weaving of cloth had died out.[13]

The female *annil* contrasts with the male *pakkannil* in a number of respects. Inside labor has to be done almost every day all year around, while male labor is highly seasonal with peaks when there is hardly time for sleep and troughs when there is only something to do every few days. Female labor is done in or near the house, while male labor is often done at some distance from the house. Except during weddings and funerals and during the rice transplantation season, each woman is self-sufficient in her household, while many agricultural tasks require the cooperation of men from different households. Most important of all, however, is that female labor is necessary for a household and cannot be done by the men (both because they don't have the necessary skills and because they would find it embarrassing to engage in tasks culturally defined as female).

The operating farm household in Sangongni, then, must include both males and females. Although many of the tasks that must be done to keep the Sangongni farm household going can be done by either males or females, there is a core of tasks for both the males and the females that cannot be done by the other sex. Women never use draft animals or motor-driven machinery and thus cannot plow or harrow or thresh the grain. Women never participate in the work teams that maintain the dikes and other parts of the irrigation system. They never take anything but a peripheral part in construction of buildings. These activities, moreover, are necessary for the production of the major income-producing crops. On the other hand, although men pursue the activities that in the normal course of events produce the income upon which the household must subsist, there are activities necessary for the maintenance of the household they do not do. Men don't cultivate the vegetable gardens that provide the fresh produce for everyday use. They don't cook meals (except in unusual circumstances), and they never do laundry. They participate only peripherally in child care, and they cannot produce the children who will take care of them in their old age and worship them after their death.

The Household as an Energy Flow System

The complementary nature of the male and female roles in the central Korean farm household can be vividly seen in the structure of household energy flows. In the simplest terms, we can think of the Korean household ecosystem as pictured in figure 5.1. The male's outside labor consists of two sets of tasks: creating an ecosystem favorable for agriculture, and working the land to produce crops. In their former capacity, they put in irrigation works, build up the soil by bringing in dirt from other areas (*kaekt'o*), and preserve the fertility of the soil by bringing in organic materials (*t'oebi*) such as unused straw, ashes, and the waste products of animals and humans. These long-term investments of energy create the ecological basis for the agricultural system and affect the productivity of their subsequent labors. Having created this ecosystem made up primarily of two kinds of fields—irrigated rice paddy, and rainfall fields—the men plow, weed, reap, and so forth to produce the raw agricultural crops that support the household. The fields themselves can be considered potential energy stored in the form of soil and nutrients, and are thus represented by a "storehouse" symbol.[14] By applying labor on the fields, the workers tap the stored energy of the fields, and by combining this energy with the sun and rain in growing crops, convert these sources of energy into raw agricultural produce. This produce can be considered another form of potential energy, and again is represented by the storehouse symbol. As long as the energy produced by the workers exceeds the energy put into the labor (or more accurately, as long as the energy produced by the work-

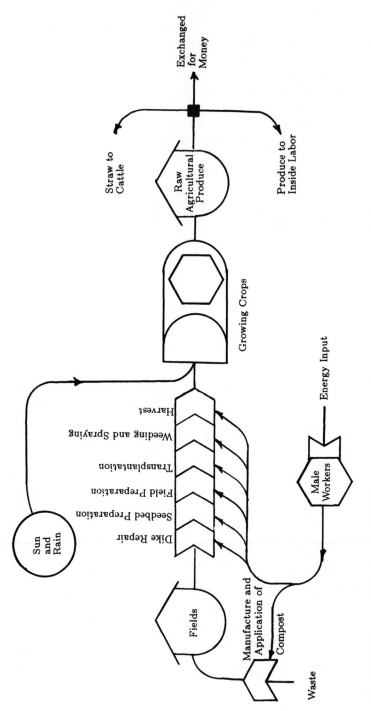

Fig. 5.1. The energy flow of outside labor

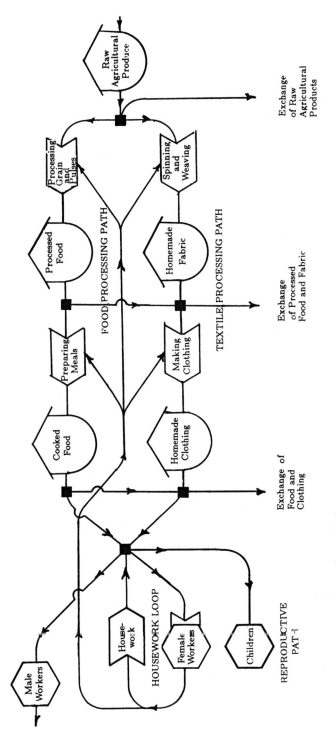

Fig. 5.2. The energy flow of inside labor

ers exceeds the energy necessary to maintain the workers plus the energy they expend in producing the crops), then the system is viable.

The production of the materials that support the members of the household, however, does not stop with the creation of the raw agricultural products. The potential energy represented by the raw agricultural produce must be transformed further, and it is the inside labor of the females that effects this task. It takes place along two pathways: food processing and textile processing (see fig. 5.2). Each of these pathways is similar in that it includes steps of primary and secondary processing of raw agricultural produce. In the case of food, such tasks as husking rice, grinding beans for *muk* or *meju*, or preserving vegetables by pickling are considered primary processing. Secondary processing, then, is the preparation of meals. Primary processing of textiles includes spinning and weaving, with secondary processing the making of clothes. In addition to these two pathways, there is a distribution node, a housework loop, and a pathway for the reproduction of household members (going through the children). A distribution node, represented by a solid square box, is a place where energy flows can be diverted in one of several directions through conscious decisions by household members. At each stage of the processing of raw agricultural produce, the women of the household have the option of selling or exchanging products in various stages of processing, and when the products to be consumed within the household are completed, the house mistress decides upon their allocation. Housework for the maintenance of the family members (laundry, sweeping, and so forth) takes energy, but it does not result in the transformation of sources of potential energy. Thus it is diagrammed as a separate loop. Finally, energy must be expended in the birth and nurture of the children that will eventually continue the family structure. These children are represented as net consumers of energy, though if the energy flow of the family is considered over a long enough time, production and reproduction should balance each other in conditions of no population growth.

The transformation of raw agricultural products, which is such an important part of the Korean farm wife's inside labor, should not be thought of as simply another aspect of housework. Housework, narrowly construed as those nonproductive tasks necessary for the household's maintenance, is a separate energy loop that forms only part of the complex energy flows controlled by the women through their inside labor. *Annil* includes housework, but it also includes productive labor complementing that of the males. If the role of the males is to apply labor to the fields to transform various sources of energy into other forms of energy useful to the household members, the role of the females is precisely analogous. They apply energy (work) to transform one form of potential energy (raw agricultural products) to another form of potential energy (food and clothing) through the primary and secondary processing pathways of both food and textiles. Thus in figure 5.2 as in figure 5.1 the flow of energy facilitated by work goes from one storehouse to another. The provision of energy to the members of the household is not complete until the final transformation of the raw agricultural products produced by the males is completed by the females.

We are accustomed to thinking of production as a linear process— one that begins with factors of production and ends with a product. When we think of the household as an energy flow system, however, the interrelationship of various factors of production becomes at once more complex and more concrete. Each work task controls the transformation of energy from a less usable to a more usable form. Energy is neither created nor destroyed, but rather captured and circulated. Until the energy captured by the outside labor is circulated through the household members, production has not been completed. By themselves, then, both the inside and the outside labor are incomplete: neither flow represents a completed energy circuit. If we combine the energy flow pathways of the males' outside labor as given in figure 5.1 with that of the females' inside labor as given in figure 5.2, however, a complete energy circuit is formed. This completed energy loop is represented in figure 5.3.[15]

The energy flow of the Sangongni farm household, thus, is characterized by an energy circuit that is completed within the household structure. In the abstract, this is not a necessary feature of the organization of farm households. In capitalist farming, or socialist farming, for example, energy circuits normally are not completed within the farm household structure (see fig. 5.4, or Smil 1979:120). In fact, households characterized by a completed energy loop are found primarily among family labor farms, such as those analyzed by Chayanov, where households are the units of production and consumption. However, given that the flow of energy within the household is a completed energy circuit, the energy flow of the household will exhibit all those properties characteristic of such systemic loops in general. The rate by which one form of potential energy is converted to another depends not only on the amount of energy applied at a workgate, but is also influenced by the amount of potential energy stored in other

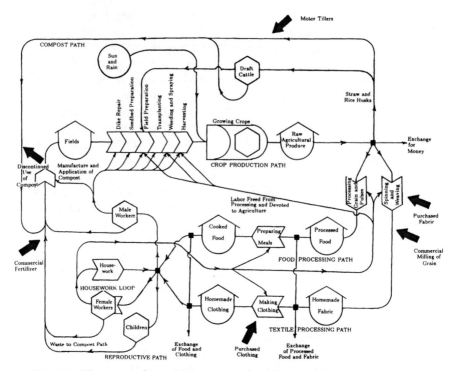

Fig. 5.3. The energy flow of a Sangongni farm household

places in the system. Since the flow of energy is organized as a completed loop, moreover, change in one variable ripples through the system to eventually feed back on that original variable.

These characteristics of the system help to explain the value of family labor farm organization. Up to a point, the possession of significant amounts of land tends to encourage production of crops and thus the application of household labor. Given a household goal of maximizing the flow of energy through the household energy loop, labor can best be applied on family land. When production is done on family land with family labor, all of the product can be circulated through the household energy loop to maintain household energy flow. Although aggregate production can be maintained with hired labor as easily as with family labor, the hiring of labor from outside the household diverts energy flows outside of the household energy loop, and reduces the rate of return on the family's investment of energy in im-

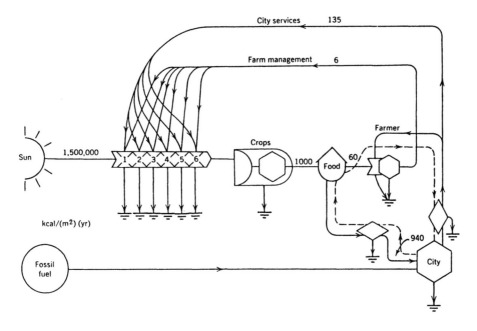

Fig. 5.4. The energy flow of a capitalist farm (diagram from Odum [1971:119])

provement on the land. At the same time, if household land is not sufficient to make use of household labor, the full use of household labor tends to be inhibited. Although it is possible to work on someone else's land, because of the necessity to pay rents on rented land, and because a landowner cannot afford to pay hired workers the full amount of the energy flow that their labor makes possible (or else they would make no profit), one's return for one's labor on others' land is drastically lower than on one's own land. Unless forced by an absolutely inadequate energy flow, the farmer has little incentive to make full use of his labor if his supply of land is inadequate and will tend to work less. On a peasant farm that is a unit of production and consumption—that is, on a farm in which household energy flows are characterized by a completed energy loop—the maximally efficient labor unit is one in which the land resources of the household exactly match its labor resources.

The energy circuit of the Sangongni household is open to flows of both energy and materials from the outside. Much of the crop is exchanged, as are certain of the products produced by the women. Open energy loops tend to have a self-regulating character. Because all of the elements (or variables) of the energy circuit are interdependent and mutually affect one another, a pulse in energy or materials coming from the outside very often results in the simultaneous adjustment of all the elements of the system to each other and the creation of a new steady state. One of these perturbations that has already been discussed involves variation in the energy flow introduced by sun and rain. This energy flow is highly seasonal, with maximums in the summer that allow the growing of crops and minimums in the winter that make agriculture impossible. This has led householders to expend more energy than necessary to produce their day-to-day subsistence during the growing season so that they have enough crops to tide them over the winter.[16] Thus, multiple adjustments in labor inputs at various points in the system allow the household to continue to function in spite of these pulses in the energy flow entering the circuit from the outside.

If we consider the energy flow of the household in the light of these considerations, the pivotal importance of the allocation of various kinds of household labor to a number of crucial tasks necessary to maintain the flow of energy in the household becomes apparent. If we think of production as the constant conversion of energy from one form to another, then with each transformation of energy there is a workgate (symbolized by an arrow) that controls this flow. The different elements of the energy circuit are interconnected and thus influence one another, but the allocation of energy to workgates is a conscious decision of household members made on the basis of flows of information, goals, and past experience; it is a strategy. It should not be assumed, therefore, that the state of the elements is an automatic result of exogenous forces and the structure of the energy flow as would be the case in a closed system. The energy flow diagrams do not demonstrate what people have to do, but rather illustrate the complex interrelations of alternative allocations of labor in the household.

Allocation of female labor into agriculture is possible, for example, but perusal of figure 5.3 reminds us that maintenance of the total energy loop is necessary for the farm household to operate successfully. If the allocation of female labor into agriculture results in less efficient processing of food, for example, the increase in energy flow consequent to the allocation of female labor into agriculture may be negated by a decrease in flow later on in the circuit due to a shortage of female labor for the primary or secondary processing of food. This particular allocation of female labor, then, may not result in a net increase in energy intake at the consumer level. The energy diagram reminds us that the workgates are not controlled simply by undifferentiated labor. They are connected to one another in a specific energy flow, and the person who provides the work that facilitates the energy flow at that spot in the energy loop occupies a specific role in the household. Thus, the household, in providing a labor supply for maintaining its energy flow, must provide one whose organization is appropriate to the tasks at hand.

If we assume for any short period of time that the technology is given and exogenous sources of energy[17] are constant, then the size of the energy flow of the system at any particular workgate is dependent upon the amount of labor of the right sort that can be applied at that workgate. Due to the structure of the household energy loop, moreover, this labor force must satisfy a number of conditions of size and composition. The labor force must include at least one able-bodied male and one able-bodied female, and they must apply enough energy at the workgates to maintain a flow sufficient to support themselves. Persons do not come in fractional units, so if the necessary labor force to maintain the household goes even fractionally above two persons, the household has to be prepared to generate an energy flow that supports that whole person, not just the fraction of that person's labor that the household really needs. Finally, for the household to maintain itself in the long run, an energy flow sufficient to allow reproduction of household members and support of the aged must be maintained.

Household Labor Requirements

In the last chapter we made an estimate of the minimum amount of land that could yield enough energy to support an Adult Male Equivalent. We did not consider in those calculations the amount of labor necessary to run a farm of various sizes. By specifying the labor requirements for various agricultural crops, however, we can estimate the approximate maximum farm size that a single adult male can cultivate. The figures for the labor requirements for agriculture are taken from field investigations by the author in 1977 in which the villagers of Sangongni were timed while spontaneously engaged in various agricultural tasks (Sorensen 1981a:535–61). For simplification, paddy agriculture has been divided into six basic phases (repair of dikes and irrigation ditches; seedbed preparation; field preparation including plowing and harrowing; transplantation of seedlings; weeding and spraying with pesticides; and harvest including reaping, gathering, and threshing). Rainfall crops can be considered in three phases (field preparation including plowing and seeding; weeding and spraying; harvest). Tobacco, the only cash crop included in this table, is sprouted in vinyl greenhouses erected in February and then transplanted in the spring. Since field preparation and transplantation take place at the same time for tobacco, both of these tasks are included under transplantation. Each of these tasks mentioned above has to be done by the farm household within a more or less restricted time period, and thus the amount of labor available during that time period limits that amount of land that can be cultivated by householders at the highest rate of return on labor and on capital.

In table 5.2 the number of man-days per hectare[18] necessary to do the important agricultural tasks for three of the major crops cultivated in Sangongni in 1977 is considered in relation to the ten-day period, or series of ten-day periods, within which each task has to be completed. For each task, the number of hectares that could be completed at the rate indicated during the time in question has been calculated. If we take rice as an example, dike repair takes place during the two ten-day periods between March 21 and April 10. If repairing dikes and irrigation ditches requires about 5.5 man-days per hectare, then in a twenty-day period 3.6 hectares could be managed by one man (if he did nothing else eight hours a day for twenty days). Time constraints on seedbed preparation are more crucial than for dike repair. Seedbeds must be done within the single ten-day period between April eleventh and twentieth. Given this time constraint, a single male could manage seedbeds for only 1.5 hectares of rice. Field preparation for transplantation can take place any time from the end of the seedbed period until transplantation itself (and, in fact, is often done immediately before transplantation). With a thirty-day period available for field preparation, 4.4 hectares could be managed. Transplantation of rice is the most labor intensive task of rice cultivation—requiring 26.7 man-days per hectare[19]—and it must be done within a twenty-day period for maximum yield to be obtained. Thus, the amount of land that can be handled by a single male during this period is drastically less than for other periods. Weeding and spraying of rice is done desultorily from the end of June to the end of August. Since the amount of labor involved is small and the time available large, no calculations were made. Finally, the harvest was done in the forty-day period between September 11 and October 20. At the levels of labor efficiency

Big Hamlet

Houses of Chang Yŏngun and of a neighbor

Terraces leading down Alder Pass

Overbridge from Nine Creeks

Midroom

Weaving spring thatch

Cleaning and grading spring silk cocoons

A labor exchange team cultivating a tobacco field

The fields for midsummer

Sangongni villager flailing beans

Mr. Kim and his rock garden

Garden for *kimch'i* vegetables

Storing daikon radishes

Stuffing the leaves of cabbage
to make *tong kimch'i*

Preparing leeks for *kimch'i*

November tombside ancestor worship (cultivators of *uit'o* in background)

Young men after a tombside ancestor worship ceremony finish leftovers in the village

Rice sheaves stacked in the fields

Reaping rice in 1977

Power threshing of rice in 1977

Shipping rice to town

Pounding rice in a *chŏlgu*

A treadmill for husking grain and making flour

Husking rice and making flour in a mechanical rice mill

New village hall in 1983

Plowing a vegetable patch with
a motor tiller

New ginseng fields

TABLE 5.2
Maximum Crop Area Manageable by a Single Adult Male
(*Time in man-days per hectare; area in hectares*)

10-day Period		Rice			Barley			Tobacco		
		Task	Time	Area	Task	Time	Area	Task	Time	Area
March	21–31	DR⎱	5.5	3.6	FP	21.6	0.5			
April	1–10	DR⎰								
	11–20	SB	6.6	1.5						
	21–30	FP⎱			WD⎱	22.5	0.9	TP	17.5	0.4*
May	1–10	FP⎬	6.8	4.4	WD⎰					
	11–20	FP⎰						WD⎱		
	21–31	TP⎱	26.7	0.7				WD⎬	9.0	0.4
June	1–10	TP⎰						WD⎬		
	11–20							WD⎰		
	21–30	WD	—	—	HV⎱					
July	1–10				HV⎬	12.0	2.5			
	11–20	WD	—	—	HV⎰			HV	4.5	0.4
	21–31									
August	1–10							HV	4.5	0.4
	11–20									
	21–31									
September	1–10									
	11–20	HV⎱								
	21–30	HV⎬								
October	1–10	HV⎬	12.0	3.3						
	11–20	HV⎰								
	21–31				FP⎱	21.6	0.9			
					FP⎰					

Key: DR = dike repair, SB = laying out of seedbeds, FP = field preparation, TP = transplantation, WD = weeding and spraying, HV = harvest. During unmarked periods, little significant labor need be done on the crop in question.

*Cultivators of tobacco are required by the government to cultivate 40 ares.

prevailing in 1977, approximately 3.3 hectares of land could be harvested during that period.

The procedure for the other crops is similar to that for rice, and need not be described in detail (see table 5.2). The amount of labor required for each of the tasks of the various crops and the amount of time available to accomplish each task varies. However, the maximum amount of land a single adult male could manage by himself is determined by the most labor intensive task. For rice, this is transplantation of seedlings. Although when other tasks are considered, a single male—even with traditional technology—could easily manage well over a hectare, the transplantation of rice seedlings is so labor intensive that a single male could only manage about 0.7 hectares. Many and various crops with different labor requirements and different timing constraints are cultivated on rainfall fields. Barley, however, may be considered typical of rainfall crops (including pulses, but excluding vegetables, tobacco, and mulberry) in its labor requirements, but not necessarily in its timing.[20] The most critical period for barley is the March field preparation time according to table 5.2, but, in fact, since most barley is planted the previous fall and allowed to lie dormant all winter, the table is deceptive in that respect, and the 0.9 hectare limit on wheat and barley that is caused by the shortage of time to do the first weeding on those fields is the operative limit. Because the timing of the planting of other rainfall field crops is so various, I have not put them on the table. Since most of the rainfall crops require either field preparation or weeding during the March 21 to May 10 period, I have let the limit on barley represent all of the rainfall crops, excluding tobacco. Since the acreage of tobacco is fixed at precisely 0.4 hectares by the government, farmers have no choice about how much tobacco they will plant. Thus the labor constraints on tobacco run opposite to the other crops. For most crops we have assumed that labor shortages will limit the area planted. For tobacco, however, the labor requirements limit the application of labor to other crops and thus limit the area of cultivation of these other crops rather than of itself.

Based on the above figures, then, a single adult male in 1977 could manage at the maximum a farm consisting of approximately 0.7 hectares of irrigated riceland and 0.9 hectares of rainfall field, for a total of 1.6 hectares.[21] Since a farm of this size would make use of all a farmer's labor at the best return for labor possible if he owned the land, this figure also defines the most efficient landholding unit from the point of view of the household.

The above limits, based on the most labor-intensive task for each crop considered—transplanting rice seedings in the case of irrigated riceland, and doing the first weeding in the case of rainfall fields— would have been operative in the past as well as in 1977. These particular tasks had not in 1977 been subject to changes that would make them more efficient than in traditional times in Sangongni. Significant agricultural innovation had taken place, of course, but such innovation involved primarily the use of manufactured fertilizer, vinyl greenhousing (a more labor intensive technique), and improved seedstocks.

None of these factors had decisively affected the efficiency of labor in the crucial labor bottlenecks. Thus, at a given level of productivity, the limits of labor efficiency limited the size of the household energy flow in traditional times in much the same way as in 1977. In the 1948–49 period, 0.7 hectares of irrigated riceland could have produced enough rice to support some 9.9 AME, and 0.9 hectares of rainfall field could have produced enough field crops to support around 5.3 AME. By 1977, the corresponding figures were 15.6 and 9.1, with an assumed 7 percent increase for 1983.[22]

The labor requirements for inside labor cannot be specified with the same precision for the traditional period as those for outside labor. Most of the primary processing of raw agricultural products was no longer done in the household by 1977, and only an impression of the amount of time involved in each activity could be gleaned from interviews. The time involved in other household activities, such as the preparation of meals and the care of the household and laundry depends to a great extent upon the size of the family and its age structure, and it is difficult to determine how much of any particular activity is devoted to a particular person. Finally, standards of housework vary a great deal more than standards of agricultural performance. In some households, where the inside labor situation was favorable and the house mistress concerned with appearances, much time was spent in providing domestic services of the highest quality. In other households where the inside labor situation was less favorable, and the house mistress had little status to uphold, standards were very much lower.

If we consider food processing first, rural women spent about two hours in the morning and evening and about an hour during the day in secondary processing (preparation of meals and cleaning up after them) for a total of five hours. During rice transplantation, the addition of two extra meals into the schedule added at least two hours to this schedule. Some seven hours a day could thus be spent on this task alone. Studies of some rural households have revealed that, on the average, 3.5 hours per day are spent in meal preparation (Song and Lee 1970), but meal preparation for Sangongni housewives seemed much more time consuming than this. In Sangongni no foods apart from *kimch'i* could be fully prepared before a meal. Thus, to prepare a meal, each housewife had to first light the fire, heat the rice, chop the vegetables, and prepare each dish from scratch. Only when meals were prepared in the field, or for lunch, were reheated foods eaten in the best-run households. Although I was not able to observe traditional primary food processing directly except in a few marginal instances, it seems likely that if grains had to be husked before each meal, it would add at least 30 percent to the time of meal preparation. Thus, during the traditional period, it is likely the food processing pathway required some 6.5 hours per day of labor.

We will have to leave aside the textile processing pathway, since all textile processing except for the ordinary repair of purchased clothing had died out in the village by 1977. Sewing machines were common, but they were used mostly for mending and often not touched in a particular household for weeks on end. In any case, textile and clothing production is something that did not have to be done every day, and could be fitted into time left over from more pressing activities. Women who reported making fabric and clothing often mentioned working late at night so we can assume that these activities were done in spare moments.

The housework loop consists primarily of three activities: cleaning the house and grounds, doing the laundry, and in recent years marketing. Sweeping and house cleaning took about an hour a day (if we include cleaning up after meals in food preparation). Laundry didn't have to be done every day, but on days when it was done, it required three or four hours. In addition, small amounts of washing—such as rinsing out socks muddy from field labor—were done almost every day. One would estimate that washing averaged at least to an hour and a half a day—depending, of course, on the size of the household, whether the household included any infants, and the level of cleanliness required by the house mistress.

Marketing was done primarily on the market days held every five days at the local periodic market. Few women went to the market each five days, however. In Sangongni, the market town was about a two- to three-hour walk from the village, and going to market took, on the average, about six or seven hours, a major expedition usually planned in advance with other village women. If a villager needed only one or two things, often she could prevail on a friend who was going to market that day to pick them up for her. I would guess that most women went to market about every fifteen days (judging that about one-third to one-half of the women of the village were gone on market day). This would make an average of about one half-hour a day for marketing. A newly married woman with young children, however, might seldom see the market at all.

Although the time figures for inside labor are only approximate, they point very strongly to a single conclusion. Inside labor required the full-time services of at least one adult female every day. If we add the time for secondary food processing and housework together, we already get eight hours of work. By including primary processing of food, we add another hour and one-half. During the period when textiles were produced at home, the time required for doing this had to be in addition to these other requirements. We have not, moreover, included any time in these figures for child care, or the care of domestic animals, or for the cultivation of kitchen gardens—all things that every housewife in Sangongni did. Although there are many agricultural tasks that, according to the cultural division of labor, women can and will do, it is inescapable that in a household that did not have more than one female worker, no labor could be spared for such activity. For a large household, moreover, it is quite likely that more than one female worker was necessary in traditional times to take care of all of the necessary inside labor. The words of a fifty-two-year-old housewife interviewed in 1983 express these time constraints vividly:

Our family in my early marital home was quite large. There were ten or eleven people when I first came here. We had workers, father-in-law, mother-in-law, grandfather-in-law, grandmother-in-law. I would pound the grain in the mill and carry water home from the stream on my head. I did it all. I did the laundry, too. I did sewing—skirts and vests, trousers and vests. I made lined Korean socks and Western socks. In the old days everybody lived that way. We made clothes out of *kwangmok* [white cotton broadcloth]. We would plant a field and pick it.

We had to launder everything, boil it, and then full it. The women had to do all the skirts and vests, too. During the day we would go around working, and then at night we would stay up late doing needlework. Aiyu! I can hardly talk about all the work we did. We hardly had time to sleep. We would work long hours like this and then if we became drowsy we would sleep for a minute and then it would be dawn again.

Changes in the Flow of Energy

The model we have been developing of the Sangongni agricultural household has been based on the assumption that the major energy flows are within the household. For the fifties and sixties, this was largely true. More than two-thirds of the production of most households must have remained within the household energy loop. Today, however, very few households remain for which this is true. Exchange occupies a much more central place in the household economy than it did in the past, and a much smaller proportion of household production—less than half in most cases—flows through the household food processing pathway. Even for those food items that remain in household possession, moreover, much of the processing takes place outside the household. If we were to list the basic changes in household energy flow in the last generation they would be (in approximate order of their appearance) as follows: (1) discontinued growth and processing of textile products and substitution of purchased fabrics for homemade ones; (2) commercial polishing and (when needed) grinding of grains; (3) substitution of purchased for homemade clothing (although some housewives continue to make some of their clothes, and the making of sleeping quilts and sleeping pads is still commonly done in many homes); (4) continuous substitution of purchased commercial fertilizer for homemade compost, so that by 1977, only small amounts of compost were added to fields; (5) the beginning of the introduction of mechanical power for draft power.

Since each of the elements of the energy flow circuit of the Sangongni rural household are interdependent, it is difficult to picture the implications of these changes in sources and flows of energy for the organization of the household. All of these changes, thus, have been marked on figure 5.3 with solid arrows. If we consider the earlier changes first, we can see that all of them involve the substitution of mechanical power outside of the household for manual labor within the household. This mechanical power is purchased with surpluses of agricultural products produced with the outside labor. Thus, the textile processing pathway of the inside labor disappeared first. In addition, with the turning to commercial milling and grinding of grains, much (but not all) of the primary processing of food products in the food processing pathway is being done outside the house. All of these early changes in the energy flow of the household, then, involve the substitution of mechanical labor for female labor used in the primary processing of agricultural products. We would expect this to free some of the female labor for other activities.

During traditional times, it seems unlikely that very much female labor could have been available for agricultural activities without jeopardizing the completion of the household energy loop. Even today, a rural housewife with small children has little time to devote to agriculture. With the gradual lessening of the number and arduousness of the female inside labor tasks, however, in households with more than one adult female member, some female labor can be spared for agricultural labor. In 1977 in Sangongni, young girls, in fact, were important contributors to household agricultural activities (in many cases, more important in this respect than their brothers, who were often sent off to school).

Other changes in the energy flow of the household have, as yet, had fewer important sociological implications. Commercial fertilizer has gradually over the past generation been substituted for compost made in the household, but the labor involved in the manufacture of most compost was spread out in small quantities over the year (with much of it added to the field preparation time). Thus, although discontinuing compost manufacture has saved the agricultural household labor in the aggregate, since the labor has largely not been saved during periods of peak labor need, it has made little difference in the size of farm one man can manage. The same thing may be said of motor tillers. Although they represent an overall saving in the amount of farm labor, this saving has, until now, largely been in field preparation and threshing. Neither of these tasks has been a labor bottleneck in Sangongni, and so the introduction of motor tillers has not expanded the size of the farm one man can manage except in the sense that by saving time in field preparation for rice, more time can be spent in weeding and other tasks that must be done in the rainfall fields during the same period.

We have noted in previous chapters that the amount of labor in Korean villages has been falling ever since the mid-1960s in spite of there being no particular surplus of agricultural labor, even during the periods of peak rural population density. The migration out of rural households that has caused the reduction in the amount of labor available in village households would have been impossible if the application of labor to agriculture had not been getting more and more efficient. The increase in farm labor efficiency, moreover, started well before the mechanization of agriculture began. As mentioned in chapter 2, part of this increase in labor efficiency seems to have come from the introduction of modern factor inputs such as pesticides and commercial fertilizer, and part seems to have come from more effective complementation of the labor requirements of various crops due to the introduction of vinyl greenhousing for rice seedlings. This analysis also leads us to expect that increases in farm household landholdings, by increasing the amount of land for which the maximal return on labor is available, would encourage the application of more existing household labor into agriculture. Part of the increasing efficiency of labor also, however, seems to be due to a restructuring of the allocation of male and female labor within the household. If direct mechanization of agricultural tasks doesn't seem to have increased the size of farm cultivable by a single household because such inputs have, as yet, not been applicable at the labor bottlenecks of Sangongni agriculture—the transplantation of rice and the weeding of rainfall fields— the mechanization of many of the traditional tasks of primary processing has freed female labor not available before for allocation to agriculture. This labor, moreover, can be allocated to labor bottlenecks. We have mentioned, for example, that the weeding of rainfall fields can be done either by males or females, but that it tended in 1977 to be a task in which a good deal of female labor was used. This freed the males, during a period when many agricultural tasks competed for his attention, to concentrate on field preparation for rice agriculture, and increased the amount of land that the household could manage. Paradoxically, the interdependence of the workgates controlling household energy circuits led to a situation where the efficiency of outside labor was increased by the mechanization of inside labor.

Although today women are contributing a larger share of their labor to agriculture than in the past,[23] the cultural division of labor remains the same. Unlike Japan, where women are expected to make a contribution to agriculture on a more or less equal basis with men (Embrée 1936:97), and are expected to consequently finish their household tasks as quickly as possible (Beardsley, Hall, and Ward 1959:228–29), men are still primarily responsible for the outside labor and women for the inside labor in Korea.[24] Within this framework females now are now able to give more attention to agriculture because of changes in the value of the variables in the system. Changing circumstances have led to new strategies of labor allocation within the traditionally structured household.

CHAPTER 6

The Changing Family Cycle

The *Classic of Poetry* says:
Oh Father! You gave life to me. Oh Mother! You raised me.
Poor, poor parents who suffered so in caring for me.
I want to repay that deep parental grace, but the high heavens are infinite.

The master said:
To be filial is to serve one's parents. When living with them be respectful.
When providing for them, make them happy. When they are sick, comfort
them. At their funeral, wail for them. At their sacrifices, be reverent.

As we have seen in previous chapters, the Sangongni household is a
unit of production and consumption. It is also a unit of reproduction.
If, as we have contended, the householders of the village try to produce household needs on household land with household labor, then
the principles that govern the entry and exit of members to the household, interacting with demographic parameters, determine the size
and composition of the household labor supply, and thus affect the
efficiency of household production. Since the household organization
generated by the interaction of the principles of household structure
with concrete circumstances must be suitable for providing the needs
of household members, we would expect villagers to modify their re-
productive and other family strategies in light of local conditions.

Modernization theorists have generally expected the forces of industrialization and urbanization to lead to the convergence of traditional family systems on a "conjugal" model similar to that found in
the West (Goode 1963:10; Ember and Ember 1983:334). Japan,
where the traditional corporate stem family, the *ie,* was abolished as a
legal entity in 1947, and where the frequency of stem family households has been falling steadily since World War II (Fukutake 1982:

124) has come closest to confirming these expectations in the Far East. Statistical analysis of patterns of household organization, however, can be misleading. In a stem family system such as that of Japan, for example, the proportion of conjugal families is partially a consequence of the proportion of younger sons born twenty to thirty years before who must form branch households, as well as of the age at marriage of successors and the age of death of their parents. Changing frequencies of household type may reflect demographic rather than structural change. Large-scale surveys, moreover, are seldom able to distinguish residential households from economic and legal families (cf. Kim Namje 1985). Diversified families with a unified economy but dispersed residence, thus, may be treated as independent households. Recent detailed work on rural Japanese families, in fact, has revealed that many of the features of the traditional household succession system are still being retained (R. J. Smith 1978:55). Studies of Hong Kong (Salaff 1981) and Taiwan (Harrell 1981; Gallin and Gallin 1982), have shown Chinese joint families positively thriving under industrial conditions as well. In Sangongni, too, complex family organization does not seem to be disappearing. Modifications of patterns of household organization have been largely the result of changing demographic patterns, and changing strategies of household labor allocation, rather than changing principles of household structure.

For the peasants of Sangongni, the household is not simply an economic universe, it is also an ethical universe. Rural Koreans tend to think of the principles that structure their households as preeminently moral principles that, whatever their practical usefulness, are worth upholding in and of themselves. Since there are several ways that peasant households can be organized in a rice-growing economy, including both the patrilineal stem households of Korea, the patrilineal joint households of China, as well as the bilateral housholds of Southeast Asia, the principles that structure household organization cannot be derived solely from economic analysis. They have to be studied in their own right.

The two quotes that open this chapter, the first from an eighth-century B.C. poem in the Chinese *Classic of Poetry (Shī Jīng)*[1] and the second from the fifth century B.C. *Classic of Filial Piety (Xiào Jīng)*, open the section on filial piety in a primer used in Sangongni's traditional school of Chinese classics, or *sŏdang*. This primer, known as *Exempla for Illuminating the Mind (Myŏng Sim Pogam)*, is a collection of aphorisms in classical Chinese that epitomizes the traditional

Confucian values, which to a large extent govern village behavior to this day. In traditional times, in spite of the Korean language having been reduced to writing with a simple and ingenious alphabet in the fifteenth century, classical Chinese was the literary language of government and the elite, and a modicum of ability in written Chinese was necessary for all males who desired any status above a commoner. Throughout Korea, villages commonly had schools of Chinese classics run by older men of learning.[2] Education in the Chinese classics was inextricably entwined with education in Confucian moral principles, which were thought to distinguish civilized men from wild beasts. Thus, study of Chinese in such books as *Exempla for Illuminating the Mind* mostly entailed memorizing morally uplifting phrases in classical Chinese. With the opening of a modern middle school at the local market town in 1971, the Sangongni *sŏdang* no longer operates, but many villagers over the age of forty in 1983 could still remember studying from this primer and could quote phrases taken from it in classical Chinese (with Korean pronunciation). A *sŏdang* was still operating up the valley in a neighboring village as late as 1977, though by 1983 the old man who had last taught it had died and the school had been discontinued.

The quotes above illustrate the two cardinal concepts of traditional Korean Confucian morality: parental grace (Korean, *ŭn;* Chinese, *ēn*), and filial piety (Korean, *hyo;* Chinese, *xiào*).[3] As in other Asian countries where the influence of the Confucian world view has been strong, the foundation of the moral order has been conceptualized as the well-ordered family, and moral relations have been thought to reside in the "five relations of humanity" (*oryun*) classically expressed by Mencius in the fourth century, B.C.: ". . . without a doctrine, people are like wild beasts. The sage [Emperor Shùn] was concerned about this, and sent Xìe as Minister of Instruction to teach with the relations of humanity: between father and son is love; between ruler and subject is righteousness; between husband and wife is differentiation; between older and younger is ordination; between friend and friend is trust" (*Mencius:*III:i:4:8).

The placement of the relationship between father and son at the head of the five moral relations is not accidental, for this relationship is the foundation of the Confucian family and thus the foundation of the whole moral universe. Children incur a debt to their parents because of the parental grace they have received by having been given birth and nurture. From this debt comes the obligation of filial piety.

Filial piety entails treating parents with respect at all times, taking care of them in their old age, mourning them well at a proper funeral, and offering sacrifices to them after their death. The two concepts of parental grace and filial piety are reciprocal in principle—parents take care of their children, and their children in turn take care of the parents—but the cultural emphasis is much more on the obligation of the children to the parents than of the parents to the children. The obligation of filial piety is not thought to be conditional. Whatever one's feeling about what is reasonable, there is no cultural support for the idea that a child whose parents fail to nurture him or her by that fact no longer has a debt of filial piety. On the contrary, in such cases, the fulfillment of this obligation is even more exemplary. Though in real cases villagers may tolerate a son who moves out of his father's house, or even one who marries against his parent's wishes, they would never tolerate public abuse or ridicule of parents by children no matter what the provocation. For traditional Koreans, in fact, even doing anything to oneself that will make one incapable of carrying out one's duties of filial piety is a cardinal sin. "Don't wander to far-off places while your parents are alive, says the master, and if you do go, you must tell them which direction" (*Analects:*IV:19).

The obligation due to parents is the heaviest and most serious of all debts recognized by society. It is so great, in fact, that it is impossible to repay the debt completely by being filial to one's parents; "the high heaven is infinite." One can only fully discharge the debt to one's parents by treating them with filial piety, having children, and continuing the family line. Of the various kinds of neglect or disrespect to parents that are considered breaches of filial piety, by far the most serious is childlessness (*Mencius:*VI:1:26). In part this is because continuity of ancestor worship depends upon the continuity of the family line, but it is also because the reciprocity between generations set up by *ŭn* and *hyo* requires family continuity. By caring for one's own parents, one repays them for part of their trouble in raising one, but the reward will be forthcoming and balanced reciprocity maintained only if the debt is passed along to one's children who will nurture one in return.

Corporate *chip* organization in Korea provides for succession in the male line, and requires, as part of the obligation of filial piety, patrilocal residence for the eldest son, on whom the obligation of filial piety is especially strong. This kind of family organization has both a moral and an economic aspect. Maintaining patrilineal household structure is, especially among the elite, considered a good in itself—the triumph of principle (*lǐ*) over chaos. In a society where the accumulation of capital is difficult, however, survival depends upon labor power (Meillassoux 1981:102), and one effect of the reciprocity between generations maintained through parental grace and filial piety is the maintenance of an adequate labor supply throughout the family cycle. This point, of course, is not lost on rural Koreans. Women, for example, who have scant concern with patrilineality as an abstract principle,[4] when asked if boys or girls are better will always answer boys. This is not because they hold women in contempt or hate their daughters, but because they recognize that in the household system instituted in their country their future welfare depends upon their giving birth to sons and raising them to maturity so as to maintain the household patriline. If they have no sons, there will be no one to take care of them in their old age. Men and women, thus, will go to great lengths to secure sons. Much of the folk religion revolves around practices to promote fertility or the birth of sons, and traditionally any man with much land who was sonless after a lengthy enough marriage was virtually required to take a concubine by whom he could produce sons. Although this sort of concubinage is dying out as daughters' position in rural areas has improved, there was still one polygynous family left in 1983 (the first wife was considerably older than her husband and had borne no children), and there had been several other such cases in the past.

Patrilineal corporate family organization has its practical side, but the values of the family and of filial piety are strongly felt as ethical imperatives in their own right, too. Although all villagers of Sangongni were not in the habit of quoting from the *Classic of Poetry* or *Myŏng Sim Pogam*, the values expressed in these classics were universally known and deeply felt. Filial piety, above all, is still felt to be a cardinal virtue, and maintaining the continuity of the family line a worthy goal. Several of the most famous Korean folk tales deal with filial sons (*hyoja*) or filial daughters (*hyonyŏ*), and the villagers of Sangongni were apt to discuss general ethics in terms of "maintaining the way of filial piety" (*hyodo rŭl chik'ida*). Any mention of filial piety will always elicit positive responses whether the mention is in the context of concrete examples or abstract principle. When old people gather together on festive occasions in the village, like old people everywhere they are apt to talk about their own and other people's children, and one can often overhear persons who had treated their parents well—perhaps providing them with a few creature comforts, or an especially nice sixtieth-birthday celebration—referred to approvingly as *hyoja*, filial sons.[5]

The Family Cycle

Since the household, or *chip*, is organized corporately—that is, each household is organized around a head, has a defined group of members who belong to no other household, and has a mechanism of succession by which household roles can be passed from one person to another—it can theoretically maintain the same structure forever. Although the incumbents of household roles change as new people are born, married, and die, the roles themselves and the household structure remain. Succession is preeminently to the role of house head, and this form of succession is recognized in law (New Civil Code secs. 980–995). The equally important role of house mistress (*an chuin*), though not recognized in the law, can also be seen as maintained by succession. Explicit succession to the role of *an chuin* symbolized by taking up residence in the inner room, seat of the house mistress, has been found in some parts of southeast Korea (Yi Kwanggyu 1975a: 12). Although formal exchanges of rooms as part of succession are not found in Sangongni, the house mistress has certain economic and ritual responsibilities that are usually performed by no other household member, and are passed down from house mistress to her eventual successor, her eldest daughter-in-law. The identity of the house mistress, thus, is almost always clear (Sorensen 1983).

Patterns of succession to the house headship are quite rigid and have been fixed in the Korean legal code since the turn of the century.[6] The house headship devolves on the oldest, most closely related lineal male descendant of the previous house head—that is, the previous house head's eldest son (secs. 984–985). If the eldest son has moved to town and his widowed mother, younger brother, and sister-in-law all live in the ancestral house in the village, succession still passes to the eldest son. During the time the father and son are both alive, the father's residence in the village and the eldest son's house in the city are legally but branches of the same *ka*. With the death of the father, this is still true, except that the family headquarters, so to speak, has moved to the residence of the new house head in town. In case of sonlessness, family continuity can be maintained through adoption.[7] Women, although they are able to succeed to the headship of houses in the absence of brothers or children (sec. 984), are not normally capable of passing that headship along in their own right. The devolution of the headship on a female almost always is the last step before the extinction of a household line. Uxorilocal marriages, colloquially called *taeril sawi*, can be made in cases of sonlessness, but as normally done in Korea these do not result in the provision of a successor. The husband of such marriages cannot take the house headship, and the children, who usually take their father's name, by that fact cannot succeed to the headship of their mother's house (Chŏng Kwanghyŏn 1967:33). *Taeril sawi* marriage was said by the villagers to have been common in past times, but the participants in such marriages were almost certainly propertyless households with no nearby agnatic kin and little status to uphold.[8]

House heads and house mistresses in Korea gradually hand over tasks to their successors as they became too old to handle them. Thus, by the time they reach sixty or so, most Korean house heads and mistresses are retired de facto and were said by the villagers to have "transmitted the house" (*chŏn'ga*) to their successors. When *chŏn'ga* has taken place, the future successors to the roles of house head and house mistress take over the day-to-day running of the household. Unlike in Japan, where retirement (*inkyo*) usually involves the legal relinquishment of the title of household and formal handing over of household control (Nakane 1967:13), however, Korean *chŏn'ga* is not legally recognized (see also sec. 980). Eldest sons must wait for the death of their fathers to obtain full and undisputed control of the house headship.

Household property, unless it has been explicitly registered in the name of a household member, is considered the personal property of the house head, who can use or dispose of it however he wants to (sec. 796). After his death, the property of the house head is divided according to his will (sec. 1012), although the actual division may be delayed for a number of years. In the absence of a specific will or declaration of intent by the house head, inheritance follows customary practices. According to village custom, the household estate is divided among sons with the daughters being excluded (see also Brandt 1971:132).[9] Division among the sons is not equal as in traditional China, nor is it by primogeniture as in prewar Japan. The rule of thumb is that the eldest son shall receive twice as much as the other sons, but in any case not less than one-half of the estate.[10] This rule, of course, is modified in practice to take into account the economic situation of the family. If division of the household land would threaten the survival of the main household, the land will not be divided. On the other hand, if household landholdings are large, division of them was sometimes more equal than the above rule would indicate.

Family members are acquired through birth, marriage in, and adoption. Family membership is reduced through death, marriage out, divorce, fission, and adoption out. All lineal ascendants and unmarried, legitimate lineal descendants of a house head belong to the *ka*, unless they have entered another family through marriage or split from it. Adult males capable of self-support can be forced to split from the family, but lineal ascendants and the eldest son of the household cannot be split from the family (sec. 789). Eldest sons, in fact, can do nothing that would jeopardize their eventual succession to the house headship including split from the family (sec. 788), adoption out (sec. 875), waiver of succession (sec. 991), or making an uxorilocal marriage where his wife becomes house head (*ippuhon*) (sec. 790). Since a house head must pass the line of succession to his eldest son, all other children of the house head have eventually to leave their natal household. Daughters leave their natal household (*ch'in'gatchip*) for their husband's household (*sijip*) at the time of their marriage. Even if their natal household has no sons, Sangongni daughters have traditionally married out, with the inheritance of property and succession to the household line being taken by a son adopted from an agnate (preferably a father's brother). Such adoptions have usually been done after the death of the previous house head (*sahu yangja*). In traditional times, a wife was brought into the house for each of the sons. Younger sons, after marrying in their natal household, split off with their wife and children typically after five to ten years of marriage to form a branch house. This process was simply called "setting up housekeeping" (*segan nada, sallim ŭl nada*) and was often a gradual process of separation lasting a year or more (Ch'oe Paek 1981).

The traditional process by which the younger sons split off from the main household to form branch households before 1966 was similar in many respects to the Chinese process of *fēnjīa* where, classically, the estate of the father is divided up equally among the sons and each son forms a separate household. In fact, the technical term for the splitting off of younger brothers, *pun'ga*, is simply the Korean pronunciation of the characters in *fēnjīa*. However, there are several major differences between the processes in the two countries. In Korea, only the eldest son is thought to continue the line of his natal house and only he has the primary responsibility of supporting his parents in their old age. This house of the parents and eldest son, colloquially known as the *k'ŭn chip* or "big house," is considered the main house. The younger brothers, when they set up housekeeping on their own with their wives and children, are thought to form new lines dependent on the main line, so their houses are colloquially known as *chagŭn chip* or "little houses." Only the eldest son is qualified to perform household ancestor worship ceremonies, so even though the *chagŭn chip* gradually achieve economic independence, they remain ritually dependent upon the *k'ŭn chip*.

The villagers of Sangongni reported that before 1966 the house head of the *k'ŭn chip* decided when and under what terms the younger brothers should set up independent housekeeping. If the father was still alive several years after his younger sons' marriages, then it would be he that made the decision, but if he had died, his eldest son succeeded to his position, and in that case the oldest brother made the decision. From about 1920 until the land reform of 1950, the tenure status of rural Koreans continually worsened, and splitting of the land often threatened the survival of the main house. Although many villagers received an allotment from their fathers or brothers according to the rules of thumb noted above, many others received nothing, or, if they were somewhat less unfortunate, received only a house and a year's supply of food.

In China, by contrast, the role of the house head and of the eldest brother is less important. No one son regularly has sole responsibility for the parents in their old age or has a monopoly on ancestor worship. Thus there is little feeling that the younger sons are branching off from a main line. All the sons inherit relatively equally and no brother can be singled out as the sole successor to the main line. While Koreans speak of big and little houses, or more formally of root and branch houses (*pon'ga* and *pun'ga*), the Chinese tend to speak of all the brothers' households as the spreading branches of the same tree (Cohen 1976:246). In Taiwan, the decision to split the household can be made by the father before his death or agreed on among the brothers after his death. In either case, however, it does not come out of the blue the way some Sangongni *chagŭn chip* described the timing of their splits, but rather is the culmination of growing tension between the competing economic needs of the brothers within the household. Because of tension between brothers involved in the distribution of the estate, a disinterested third party such as a mother's brother is often called in to assist. Among Korean brothers, on the other hand, where there has never been any pretense of equality between them, relations seem less fraught with tension. Although every village, including Sangongni, has cases of brothers on bad terms because of inheritance disputes (see also Brandt 1971:200; Han 1977:55, 91–92;

Janelli and Janelli 1982:103–4), in general, villagers agree, brothers tend to remain on good terms (Brandt 1971:139; Janelli and Janelli 1982:104).

All the brothers of a Chinese house usually split at the same time with a formal division of property drawn up in legal form. The *fēnjīa* is a point in time; before it, the household is joint; after it, each household is separate. In Korea, on the other hand, not only was the setting up of separate housekeeping often a gradual process, but also each younger brother left the main house individually when the house head thought he was ready. Thus, the process of *pun'ga,* from the point of view of the *k'ŭn chip,* stretched out over a number of years until the last younger son left the house.[11]

In rural Korea, the principles governing the acquisition and departure of members from the family, and the succession to family roles, lead to a regular sequence of structural types over the developmental cycle of the household. A newly formed *chagŭn chip* will consist of a nuclear family made up of a married couple and their children. As the children grow up, the daughters marry out—each at the proper and conventional age. When the eldest son is ready to marry, a wife will be brought in for him, making the family stem in form (if the parents are still living). In the traditional system, wives were also brought in for the younger sons as they reached the conventional marriage age. From the time of the marriage of the second son until the splitting off of the last son and his family, the house was in joint form. As younger sons of the branch family set up separate housekeeping, they become *chagŭn chip* to their natal house, which itself is *chagŭn chip* to the household from which *it* originally split. Relative to these newly formed *chagŭn chip,* however, the natal house of these younger sons has become a *k'ŭn-chip.* After the last nonsucceeding son forms a branch family, the main family reverts back to either nuclear or stem form depending upon the longevity of the parents and the amount of time each of the younger sons spends in his natal household. Succession of the eldest son takes place upon the death of the father, bringing the cycle to a close with the family either in joint or stem form depending upon the number of sons, their relative age, and the father's age at death. (If the father dies young, succession can even take place while the family is in nuclear form, since the eldest son may not be married by this time.) The branch house, thus, starts in nuclear form and gradually develops through more complex forms until it becomes a main house in its own right.

The cycle of the main houses, the *k'ŭn chip,* starts where the branch houses leave off. This cycle begins with the devolution of the house headship on the eldest son at the death of his father, or in the absence of natural sons, its devolution on a son adopted from an agnate of the previous house head. The timing of succession in the case of natural sons is dependent solely upon the timing of the death of the previous house head, but it usually occurs after the marriage of the successor and the formation of at least a stem and, in the past, a joint family. Each brother splits from the complex family at the appropriate time, so that some time after the succession takes place, the joint family reverts back to stem form, and with the death of both parents becomes nuclear. The nuclear form will be succeeded by joint form with the marriage of the son of the new house head, and the cycle will be repeated again when the old house head is succeeded by his eldest son. For main houses, then, as long as a successor to the house headship is found, each cycle is a repetition of the previous cycle, and as long as there are no major changes in demographic parameters, an infinite number of these cycles can be repeated.

The system we have described so far was found in rural Korea up until the 1960s. In 1966, however, important revisions were introduced into the New Civil Code and the Family Registration Law, which provided that all sons but the eldest are automatically split from their natal household at the time of their marriage (sec. 789; Kim Chusu 1985:85). This is known as "legally fixed splitting of the house" (*pŏpchŏng pun'ga*), and has been part of a series of revisions of traditional Korean family law that have been designed to reduce the power of house heads and improve the position of women. In spite of these changes, most of the fundamental features of household organization mentioned have remained. Thus, for both main and branch households, family continuity is still maintained through the succession of one natural or adopted son to the position of house head. The eldest son still has legal responsibility for his parents and commonly resides with them. Nonsucceeding children must marry into other households, or eventually split off to form branch houses of their own. Only the timing of the splitting off of younger sons has been changed. In the old system, nonsucceeding sons married before splitting from their natal household, while now they split at the time of their marriage or before.[12] These differences of timing mean that prior to 1966, families with more than one son would usually go through a joint phase in their domestic cycles, while since that time, the creation of joint families has been in principle (and in fact) impossible.

Thus no joint families remained in Sangongni in 1983, and in 1977,

only one marginal case of joint family organization existed.[13] Most of
the older villagers, however, could recall periods in the past of living
in large joint households of as many as twenty people made up of a
house head, his several married sons, and their families. Although
these large joint families are no longer found, branch houses still develop from nuclear forms to stem forms, and main households still
develop from stem to nuclear and back to stem. If one uses the age of
the house head as a crude measure of the point of the family developmental cycle, for example, we can see that for *k'ŭn chip,* complex
families are found largely among the younger and older house heads,
with nuclear families predominating among the middle aged (see fig.
6.1). This general pattern is expected, since for a son to succeed to the
house headship at an early age, his father must either have died young
or given birth to him late in life, and under those circumstances, it is
likely that the house head's mother or unmarried brothers or sisters
still remain in the household. As these people die or move out of the
household, it tends to become nuclear in form. Later on, with the
marriage of the house head's eldest son, we expect the family to again
develop into a complex form. Branch houses by definition begin in

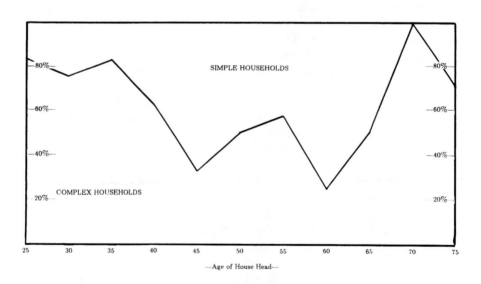

Fig. 6.1. Relationship of *k'ŭn chip* household complexity to age of house head

nuclear form, on the other hand, and we thus find them predominantly nuclear early in their cycle (see fig. 6.2). As the house head becomes older, we find that some do develop into complex families, but this tendency for the development of complex families is not nearly so marked as it is for the older ages in the *k'ŭn chip*.

Continuity and Survival

Although in figures 6.1 and 6.2 our general expectations for the development of family types over the family cycle seem to be confirmed, the details of each family are unique, and there seem to be many exceptions to the rules. In the case of *k'ŭn chip*, the untimely death of the father and mother may result in a nuclear family when we would expect a complex family. Or, as in one village household, a *chagŭn chip* may include an aged mother because the eldest son has died and his widow and children, the *k'ŭn chip*, are too financially pressed to maintain an aged dependent. For branch households, moreover, even late in the family cycle, when we would expect most of them to include married successors, the rareness of complex family formation

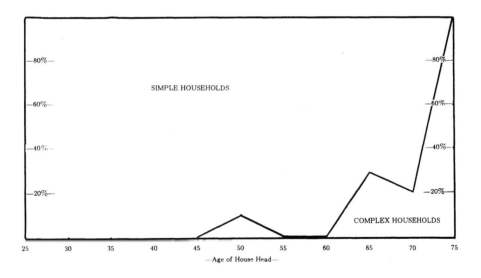

Fig. 6.2. Relationship of *chagŭn chip* household complexity to age of house head

seems to indicate that the principles of household formation outlined above don't tell the whole story. In fact a characterization of the family cycle of big or little houses as a sequence of structural types can clearly be only an approximation. In traditional times, a family could only go through a joint phase if more than one son was born and married before the death of the parents. Today, a stem family can be formed only if a son is born early enough in the father's life to be married before his death. Any particular sequence of structural types, then, is not a fundamental feature of the system, but rather is the result of the intersection of principles of family organization with demographic and economic variables. Some of these variables, such as the mean life span of individuals, are largely out of the control of family members. Others, such as marital fertility, can be controlled, but only unreliably and with great effort. Many factors, however, such as the timing of migration from the household or the timing of marriage, are subject to simple human manipulation. It is reasonable to suppose that where such manipulation is possible, it will be done so as to enhance the fortune of the family or its individual members. Such manipulation will be a strategy rationalized toward the attainment of family goals, and conditioned by the family's adaptive requirements and external socioeconomic forces.

We have defined the adaptive requirements of the household as those conditions that must be met for household energy flow to be maintained within a viable range. We have taken the value of 3000 kilocalories per day per adult male equivalent as well within the range of viability for members of Korean households, given the stature of the villagers of Kangwŏn Province and their level of activity, but have not tried to specify the precise boundary below which household survival would be impossible. Nevertheless, for an energy flow of at least the above level to be maintained, certain conditions have had to be met by Sangongni households both in traditional and more recent times. Householders have had to have access to the factors of agricultural production (including land, seedstock, and agricultural implements), and householders have also had to have access to sufficient labor of the right sort to work the land and process the raw agricultural output that is produced on the land. The amount of land necessary to support an adult male equivalent has been estimated for various periods in table 4.9, while the amount of labor necessary to maintain an agricultural household and cultivate various amounts of land has been estimated in table 5.2.

The values in these tables illustrate some of the constraints of household organization in Sangongni, but they are not absolute. Although it is desirable for a household to own enough land to provide for its own needs, for example, there were and are alternative methods of gaining access to land, and, failing that, gaining access to other means of production. Land can be rented in, labor can be hired out, or income augmented through handicrafts, trading, or animal husbandry if the land owned by the household is insufficient for subsistence. Similarly, although it is desirable for a household to be able to work all of its own land with its own labor, if labor is insufficient to cultivate household land, labor can be hired, or land can be rented out. The return on one's labor, however, is highest on agricultural land that one owns oneself. If land is insufficient, the amount of labor necessary to support the household increases, because the proportion of the energy flow maintained within the household energy loop falls. For the same reason, if labor must be hired, then one's return on one's investment in land is lower than if household labor is used. If both land and labor are insufficient, then the viability of the household as a continuing social unit is in grave danger. What the figures in tables 4.9 and 5.2 indicate, then, is not the boundaries of household viability, but rather the conditions under which the household operates with maximum efficiency. Although it is not necessary for mere survival that households operate at maximum efficiency, the more efficient village households have an advantage over the less efficient ones and will be more likely to thrive and continue in the village than their less favorably composed counterparts.

The figures in the tables are relative also in another sense. Since they are constituent elements of a system, they are dependent on other variables whose values are not constant. The amount of land necessary for household subsistence is dependent upon the number of adult male equivalents in the household. Likewise, the maximum amount of land cultivable by the household is dependent upon the amount of labor resident in the household. These values in turn are dependent upon the previous success of the household in production and reproduction. Until we understand the factors that govern family size and composition, then, our understanding of the ecological organization of the household is incomplete.

For the family to maintain itself, and provide replacements for aging family members over time, it is obvious that the successor to the house headship must marry at some point. The timing of this marriage is crucial, too. If the marriage is made too soon, children may come too soon and too fast, placing a heavy economic burden on the family, which must nurture and eventually marry them off. Delaying the marriage can also create problems. The longer one waits, the fewer years of fertility one has to make use of in giving birth to heirs. In addition, if one waits too long, even if a successor is born that successor may not be old enough to take over the farm when the house head becomes too old to work, or dies.

Just as individuals pass through regular stages of development from birth to childhood to old age and death, families, in acquiring and socializing the members that will provide family continuity, also pass through stages of development. These stages have been characterized by Fortes (1958) as *expansion* (from the marriage of two people until the completion of their family of procreation), *fission* (from the marriage of the first child to that of the last), and *replacement* (from the marriage of the last child until the death of the parents). In the Korean family cycle, we can see that all of these stages are going on simultaneously in different subunits of the traditional rural families. Since the eldest son remains in his natal household, his marriage marks not only the beginning of the fission period, but also the beginning of the expansion period of his own conjugal unit, which will eventually provide for the continuity of the family corporation. As the nonsucceeding brothers and sisters leave the household by the various means described above and reduce household membership, the growth in the successor's conjugal family adds to household membership. One expects, thus, the fissioning of the siblings of the original family to be offset by the simultaneous growth of the succeeding conjugal family.

For the farm households of Sangongni, maintenance of the family labor supply was an important determinant of household adaptation and thus an important concern. No household can operate for long, for example, without at least one adult male and one adult female to manage the work gates of the household energy loop. The timing of various demographic events such as births, deaths, and marriages determines the timing of entrances and departures to the family labor and consumption pools, and determines the relationship of the expansion, fission, and replacement stages of the various subunits of the rural family to one another. The size and structure of the household at any particular time, thus, is determined partly by rules of household organization, which specify the ways in which persons may be added to or sent out of the household, and partially by the value of various demographic parameters. Some of the families created in this way by the intersection of culture and demography will be well adapted to manage the functional requirements of farm household organization, and will be efficient units of production and reproduction. One expects that other families, however, will be less well adapted to the requirements of agricultural production and thus less efficient. At any point in the family cycle we can assess this adaptation by measuring three characteristics of the household: (1) the adequacy of its labor force to maintain the household energy loop; (2) the relationship of the size of the labor force to the number of household consumers; and (3) the requirements of the household to reproduce itself.

In a population like that of traditional Sangongni, which did not use contraceptives, fertility was basically uncontrolled except by the age of marriage. Death rates were likewise outside the villagers' control. Thus, most of the demographic parameters that interacted with the principles of household organization to create household structure were outside forces, which rather than being objects of simple human manipulation were forces to which people had to adjust themselves. In the following pages we will investigate how village demographic parameters interacted with the principles of family organization to create certain possibilities of family organization, and how villagers adjusted their resultant families in the interest of improving their economic well-being.

The Traditional Family and Household Labor

The date of the partial revision of the New Civil Code, 1966, is a convenient watershed for distinguishing the traditional and transitional periods of Korean family organization. Although the original New Civil Code of 1958 already provided for changes in the system that reduced the power of house heads and improved the position of women, the institution of "legally fixed splitting of the household" at the time of the marriage of nonsucceeding sons laid the basis for the demise of the joint period of traditional family organization. To investigate the family cycle of Sangongni for the traditional period that ended before fieldwork commenced, it is necessary to use ethnohistorical methodology to reconstruct the developmental cycle of a number of families. I was able to do this for twenty-five families from Sangongni for the period of 1918 to 1977. In all of these families, the last marriage of the successor was before 1965, and thus before the changes in the civil code were effective in the village. These reconstructions were made on the basis of personal interviews, inspection of family registration records (*hojŏk*), and inspection of residential registration records (*chumin tŭngnok*). Inspection of variations in family size and composition over the ten-year period before and the ten-year period after the marriage of the head of the main or branch household confirms the supposition that the fissioning of siblings from the family was offset by the growth of the conjugal family of the successor. There was gradual growth in the size of the family from 6.4 to 8.2 members during the first ten years following the patrilocal marriage of the successor in spite of this being the period when younger sons were beginning to leave their natal households and parents were dying off.

In the 1918–77 sample, males married when their parents were still alive at a mean age of 20.6 years.[14] Females married at a mean age of 19. Although there was some variation between families on the age at which sons and daughters were married, within families the age of marriage of siblings was remarkably constant. Both males and females seemed to be married when they reached the "proper" age.[15] Since the successor was invariably the eldest son, the departure of most siblings took place after the successor married and began to have children. The average age of younger sons at the time of their splitting from the household (*pun'ga*) was 31.3. Thus the growth in family size after the marriage of the successor reflected not only the growth of the successor's family, but also that of his younger brothers, who didn't formally split from their *k'ŭn chip* until seven, eight, or more years after the marriage of their older brothers.

Figure 6.3 charts the fluctuations in the size of the family male labor force of the 1918–77 sample over the same period of the developmental cycle. Labor has been calculated in terms of adult worker units: males between twenty and fifty-five have been figured at a value of one, with smaller amounts for those between eleven and nineteen, and over fifty-five to take into account the diminished, but not inconsequential labor power of the young and old. Both before and after the marriage of the successor to the headship, one observes a steady labor force.[16] By marrying their children at a relatively young age, and by retaining younger brothers with their wives and children in the main house for a number of years, a large male and female labor force was obtained just at the peak period of labor need—the years when the children are young and consume without contributing to the household labor force. The father and sons could work together to provide the food for the large family and to obtain the capital to finance the departure of the younger sons. The mother-in-law and daughters-in-law could help each other during the peak period of domestic labor when young children must be cared for in the household, and when the oldest of the children were still too young to help around the

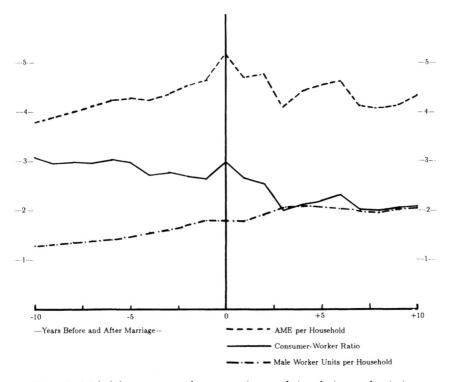

Fig. 6.3. Male labor power and consumption needs in relation to the timing of the marriage of house heads, Sangongni, 1918–77

house. In addition, the large labor force ensured that such disasters as sickness or death of the father or of the successor would not prevent the family from being able to provide for itself with its own labor.

The relationship between family consumption needs and family labor supply can conveniently be expressed by the consumer/worker ratio. Since we are interested in households that produce their own food supply, the number of consumers in the family has been expressed in adult male equivalents. Workers have been expressed in adult worker equivalents. The result of our calculations for the 1918–77 sample has been presented in figure 6.3. Although for individual houses the value of this figure ranges from 1.8 (a household made up of a single couple both of working age) to 5.7 (in a large household where the son died at an early age, leaving his wife and children, aged parents, and only a fourteen-year-old adopted grandson to do the work), for the households as a whole, the value of this ratio runs between two and three for most of the family cycle. The lower the consumer/worker ratio, the more favorable the household's economic situation. Based on the information in table 4.9, we would expect that for a family that owned enough land to make use of all the labor of the household, one adult worker could support seven, or possibly eight AME consumers with 1948–49 levels of productivity. Few households, however, approach this limit unless they have been struck by disaster and all of the adult males have unexpectedly expired. On the other hand, for tenant farmers whose labor productivity is half that of owner-cultivators (because of the need to pay rent), the much more conceivable consumer/worker ratio of three or four would bring the family close to the subsistence level, even assuming that the tenant could find enough land to rent to make full use of his labor. Thus although a landowning household with such an unfavorable consumer/worker ratio as five or six might survive with just a little belt tightening, it is highly likely that a tenant household would have to respond to such a situation with more drastic actions, such as marrying underage daughters as child brides (*min myŏnŭri*), putting daughters into service in richer houses as maids (*singmo*), or sending sons to become live-in agricultural servants (*mŏsŭm*) for land-rich, labor-poor households. The consumer/worker ratio as we have calculated it is much more sensitive to fluctuations in the labor supply of the household than to fluctuations in the number of consumers. This underscores the fundamental importance of the family labor supply in determining the adaptive position of the household. Since too unfavorable a consumer/worker ratio might lead to household demise, it is clear that maintaining this ratio within manageable bounds for the duration of the family cycle—something that was a consequence of the rules of family organization in traditional times—was important for household adaptation.

Although the village grew only moderately during the period, the households of the village were able to produce a large supply of children. Between 1918 and 1975, the difference between the birth and death rates in the village would have led to a population growth rate, in the absence of migration, ranging from 1.2 to 3.2 percent, with most values being in the 2 percent range or above (Sorensen 1981a:348). During this time, most women bore at least three and more usually five or more children. Thus the family cycle seems to have provided for the functional requirements of the household: most households had a stable supply of labor, most households had a stable consumer/worker ratio well within what could be supplied by house-hold labor even at 1948–49 levels of productivity, and most house-holds were able to reproduce very successfully.

The traditional family cycle, then, can be thought of as a successful one for the villagers of Sangongni. The beneficial consequences, how-ever, were not simply the automatic result of the intersection of de-mographic parameters with the rules of household organization. Vil-lagers were not content to simply let nature take its course. There was much migration out of the households of the village, and this migra-tion seems to have been at least partially motivated by the desire to alter the size and composition of household membership. A crucial aspect of understanding the reasons for the size and composition of the household in Sangongni, then, is understanding the relationship of migration strategies to household organization.

We might begin to approach this problem by asking what the family cycle of Sangongni would have been if migration had not taken place. Since most families have already been modified by migration, this, of course, cannot be found out by observation. One can, however, con-struct a model of the interaction of rules of household organization and demographic parameters, and use a computer to generate house-holds structured according to these rules and the demographic param-eters characteristic of the village. The rules of Korean household or-ganization have already been given above and need no repeating. As demographic parameters, we will take the characteristics of the cohort of villagers born between 1930 and 1939. This cohort was the largest ten-year cohort of the adults in the village both in 1977 and 1983, and the men from this cohort accounted for more than 30 percent of all the house heads in the village during both periods of fieldwork. Because of the size and dominance of this cohort in village life and politics, its characteristics are close to that of the village as a whole. In addition, its size has made it possible to get a better sample than in other cohorts of measurements from which to calculate demographic parameters. Estimates based on this cohort, then, are the most reliable available.

The men in this cohort married at a mean age of 19.6. Their wives on the average were 1.9 years younger. The first surviving child was born when the husband was 24.2 and subsequent children were born every 3.1 years until an average of five surviving children were had. Younger brothers split from the main household at the average age of 31.3 when their older brothers were, on the average, 35.8. Since most of the members of the 1930–39 cohort from whom I collected data are still alive, I cannot calculate their average age of death. Based on deaths in other cohorts, however, I estimate that before 1955, the average age of death for males and females was around 50. Since 1960, males have died in the village at an average age of 61.2 and females at 68.9. For our model, these figures, taken from an actual cohort in Sangongni, have been rounded off, and only one of a number of variations in sibling order has been chosen. Thus, we have assumed that males marry at 20, have their first child at 24, split from the main household at 30 and die at 62. We have assumed that females marry at 18, have their first child at 22, have subsequent children every three years until they have five, and die at 68. It is assumed that each sibling cohort is made up of three females and two males born in alternating order starting with females (this allows the succeeding son to be born when his father is 27, just slightly above the mean age calculated for the cohort).

If the villagers governed their domestic lives according to this model with no attempt to manipulate the timing of births, marriage, or migration from the household, the number of AME consumers would range from 5.6 to 8.0 over the domestic cycle. The number of male worker equivalents would range from 2.00 to 3.85 and the consumer/worker ratio would range between approximately two and four (see fig. 6.4). In many respects, the values for these various measures of consumers and male workers resemble what was actually found during the traditional period as revealed by our 1918–77 longitudinal sample. However, if we directly compare the consumer/worker ratios for the sample and for the model, some interesting differences are revealed (see fig. 6.5). During most of the period before the marriage of the successor in Sangongni, the consumer/worker ratio was in actuality more favorable than that generated by the model.

During the period from approximately a year before the marriage of the successor until approximately six years after his marriage, on the other hand, the consumer/worker ratio found in Sangongni was worse than that generated by the model. This difference may be due partly to deliberate manipulation of the timing of family events to create a favorable consumer/worker ratio, but a more important cause is that the demographic parameters upon which the model is based do not correspond precisely to those found during the whole of the 1918–77 period. Before the Korean War, for example, death rates seem to have been much higher than after the war, when modern medicine began to be introduced into country districts. Those deaths before 1950 for which I have records occurred mostly when people were

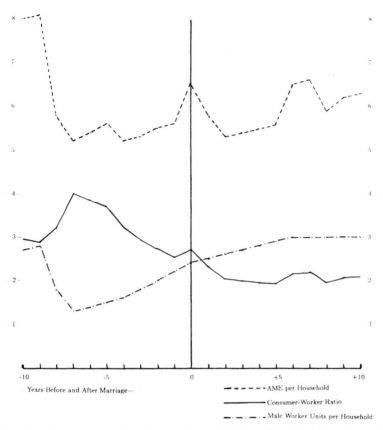

Fig. 6.4. Consumers and workers in the pre-1960 model of the domestic cycle

in their late forties and early fifties. This contrasts with the model in which the post-1960 death rates found in the village were used. If one's first surviving son is born when one is twenty-six, then that son will become a full-fledged worker when one is forty-six. During the pre-Korean War period, my records show an average male age of death of forty-seven. Thus, there would have been little overlap in the labor contribution of the son and the father at that time. In the model in figure 6.4, where the death rate of males is assumed to be sixty-two, on the other hand, during the nine years when the father is between forty-six and fifty-five, both the father and the son will be at the peak of their labor powers. Thus, the favorable consumer/worker ratio in the model is due to an assumption of more labor power in the household than actually was the case.

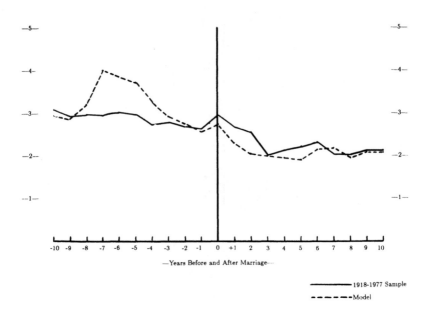

—Years Before and After Marriage—

———— 1918-1977 Sample
‑ ‑ ‑ ‑ ‑Model

Fig. 6.5. Model and sample consumer/worker ratios

The less favorable performance of the model during the ten years before the marriage of the successor is due to similar demographic circumstances. The worst consumer/worker ratio of the modeled family cycle comes seven years before the marriage of the successor. The high consumer/worker ratio of this period is due to three factors that converge at this time: (1) the father dies eight years before the marriage of his grandson, and thus ceases to contribute even a small amount of labor to the household; (2) the younger son splits from the household and withdraws his labor; (3) the aged grandmother is still alive and adds to the consumer burden of the household. Although in the 1918–77 sample the father and brother usually had split from the household by this time, because of the early death and a longer spacing between children, the consumer burden was lower, making the consumer/worker ratio more favorable in Sangongni than predicted by the model.

Changing Demographic Parameters and Household Size

The value of the preceding model of the family cycle does not lie in its being a precise replication of what each family in Sangongni (or anywhere else in Korea) actually has done or will do, though, of course, it was designed to resemble the characteristics of Korean families. Its value lies in helping us refine our understanding of the implications for the domestic cycle of the interaction between cultural and demographic factors. Demographic factors have been rapidly changing in Korea. The age at which people die has risen steadily, patterns of fertility have become more similar to those found in developed countries, and the age of marriage has steadily risen. All of these phenomena are interrelated, but because they interact with each other in complicated ways, the adaptive implications of demographic changes are not always easy to fathom. The direction of change in the value of the consumer/worker ratio, for example, is difficult to predict when multiple demographic changes that individually work in opposite directions are taking place. Is the increase in male life span found in rural Korea a help to household production, or an additional burden for households to bear?

We have already observed that the villagers of Sangongni do not simply "let nature take its course" and allow demographic factors to determine the size and composition of households constituted according to the rules of rural Korean social structure. Household size and composition is the result of the interaction of cultural rules and demographic factors, but only as modified by migration strategies designed to enhance household adaptation. Simple observation of changes in household size and composition, then, cannot give us a good idea of the independent effects of changes in demographic parameters, because all observed change is partly the result of strategies of migration designed to overcome disadvantageous household sizes and compositions that may be generated by maladaptive demographic events. If we can make a good guess as what would happen if people did not modify their behavior to take into account the demographic changes, however, we can approach this question with a clearer idea of which consequences are demographic and which are due to other factors. It is this question that mathematical modeling of the domestic cycle can help us answer.

Death Patterns

As we noted when comparing the 1918–77 longitudinal sample with the model in table 6.1, the death rate has an important influence on the family cycle. This is not only because the timing of the death of the house head determines the timing of succession in the *k'ŭn chip* cycle, but also because it influences the efficiency of the household labor supply by affecting how much overlap there is in the labor contribution of the father and the son. If the average age of a man's death is below the average age of men at the time of the birth of their successors plus the age of their successors when they marry, then the average family will not go through a full stem or joint phase. On the other hand, the greater the longevity of the house head, the longer the stem or joint phase of the family cycle. If, for example, men usually live to see the marriage of their eldest grandson, the family will never revert from stem or joint back to nuclear form. If the father lives significantly past sixty, moreover, his declining labor contribution to the household will tend to increase the consumer/worker ratio and make it less efficient. Before 1949, the former case in which complex families were seldom formed, and when formed did not last very long, seems to have been close to the truth in spite of the family cycle encouraging the formation of complex families. With the dramatic rise in village life expectancy since the Korean War, the latter case is coming closer and closer to realization.

Fertility Patterns

The fertility of the population of Sangongni has been high. Before the late sixties, rural crude birth rates ran around forty-five per thousand (implying an annual growth rate of almost 3 percent), and in Sangongni, at least, they have only fallen since then to about thirty-five per thousand.[17] Since the birth of children in the households produces new consumers, and if they are male will eventually produce the male farm workers of the household, it is obvious that patterns of fertility are important for the family cycle. The age at which a man produces his eldest son and successor determines the length of the main house family cycle, and this age is obviously dependent upon the age at marriage and of the birth of children in general. The spacing of children affects the timing of peak household consumer demand. The relationship between the age of onset of childbearing, the length of the bearing period, and the spacing of children ultimately determines the size of the family. These parameters for ten-year birth cohorts of Sangongni women are given in table 6.1.

The figures in table 6.1 display a clear trend for the establishment of the mother's age at the birth of her first surviving child. Between about 1915 and 1965, when the members of the first five cohorts were marrying and beginning their families, the mother's first child was born, on the average, at an earlier age in each succeeding cohort. Moreover, the variability of the age at which this first surviving child was born was reduced. Since the female age at marriage was rising during this period, one must conclude that infant mortality was falling and children born early in a woman's childbearing life were becoming more likely to survive.

TABLE 6.1
Selected Fertility Parameters of Sangongni, 1910–80
Age of Mothers at Birth of First Surviving Child

Birth Cohort	Mean Age	Standard Deviation	Number of Cases
Before 1910	25.8	4.82	15
1910–19	23.3	5.19	12
1920–29	21.7	4.11	30
1930–39	22.6	4.06	43
1940–49	20.9	3.47	22
1950–59*	21.3	1.76	18
Spacing of Surviving Children (Years)			
Before 1910	4.0	2.34	26
1910–19	4.6	3.34	35
1920–29	3.9	2.20	119
1930–39	3.1	1.42	165
1940–49	2.8	1.27	65
1950–59*	2.4	0.83	9
Completed Family Size for Male House Heads			
Before 1910	2.9	1.71	23
1910–19	3.2	1.91	20
1920–29	5.0	1.72	32
1930–39	5.0	1.87	40
1940–49*	3.8	1.13	23
1950–59*	1.4	0.73	20

*Because most of the people in these cohorts have not completed their families, the figures are for *average* family size for those resident of the village in those cohorts who were married.

If we look at the figures for the spacing between surviving children, the trend is again clear. Between about 1915 and 1965, the spacing of surviving children comes closer and closer together, and the variability of that spacing is reduced. The production of children has become less erratic. This adds further strength to the inference that infant and childhood mortality rates were falling (as would be expected with the improved public health measures, improved nutrition, and improved access to medical care that developed during this period).

The male completed fertility rate increases from 2.9 to for the pre–1910 cohort until it reaches 5.0 in the 1920–29 cohort. After the figure of 5.0 is reached, however, the data reveal no unequivocal trends for male completed fertility. The members of the 1930–39 cohort, although they have the highest total fertility rate of any of the cohorts in our data (primarily because of the unprecedented baby boom that followed the Korean War and lasted until the mid-sixties) seem to have had fertility in reserve which they did not use. After the age of thirty, the age-specific rate of reproduction of this cohort is consistently below that of earlier cohorts even though before the age of thirty, it was higher than for any previous cohort (Sorensen 1981a:340). A completed fertility rate of five is moderate by the high fertility standards of many populations. Women born around 1910 in Taiwan, for example, averaged almost seven children (Wolf 1985:169), and the extremely fertile Hutterites have averaged more than ten (Henry 1961). Although it seems likely that the 1940–49 cohort will have substantially fewer children after the age of thirty than the 1930–39 cohort, it is not clear that their completed fertility will be smaller than for the previous cohorts, since their reproduction rate up until the age of thirty is higher than in previous cohorts.

Household Size

In the absence of migration, most of the changes in the demographic parameters in table 6.1 would lead to an increase in the mean size of both main and branch households. The rise in the average age of death increases the number of years that each person spends in the household and, in the absence of other changes in the family cycle, increases the amount of overlap in the life cycle of the constituent units of the corporate family. The fall in the age of women at the birth of their first surviving child tends to lower the age of the house head at the birth of his successor and thus shorten the length of the family cycle. Shortening the length of the family cycle, similarly to greater longevity, increases the amount of overlap between the constituent units of the corporate family and thus tends to increase household size. In addition to these changes, spacing of children has narrowed, and the completed family size per male house head increased until the early seventies, though it has fallen somewhat since then.

Only two trends that have appeared during this period would have the effect of leading to a decreased household size: the steady rise in the age of marriage—especially for males—and the abolition of the joint family stage of the domestic cycle. Of these, only the institutionalization of legally fixed splitting of the household (*pŏpchŏng pun'ga*) has actually led to a decrease in household size. This is because, in the absence of migration, a rise in the age of marriage will lead to the retention of daughters or sisters in their natal home. So long as the average completed family exceeds two, the number of extra years the daughters will spend in the household will exceed the fewer years the single daughter-in-law of the successor lives in the house. Delaying marriage will lower household size, then, only if this delay is substantial enough to raise the age of birth of first children and lengthen the total family cycle. This, as yet, has not taken place.

In spite of the changes in demographic parameters that almost uniformly have the effect of increasing the mean household size, a notable feature of the township in which Sangongni is situated is that mean household size has changed very little. The total population of the township grew from 8,101 in 1925 some 28.7 percent to 10,429 in 1966, and then fell 18.6 percent to 8,486 in 1975 for an annual change of 0.85 percent per year over fifty years, yet there were no significant changes in average household size or the distribution of households of different size (for those censuses where such data is available) during this whole period. Given a knowledge of the demographic parameters characteristic of the village population, we can derive formulae that will allow us to compute what the mean household size of main houses and branch houses would be if demographic parameters were allowed to play themselves out according to Korean cultural rules for an indefinite period in the absence of migration. These formulae also give us a basis for estimating the effect of changes of each of the different parameters on the mean household size. A comparison of the results of projections by formula and census figures are given in table 6.2.

Before 1944, the projected average household size is smaller than that found in the census, while for the period after 1944, the projected average household size is substantially larger than that found in the

TABLE 6.2
Actual and Projected Population and Household Size
for Sangongni's Township

Date	Census Population	Projected Population	Number of Households	Actual Mean Household Size	Projected Mean Household Size
1910	6,326	—	1,245	5.08	—
1925	8,101	—	1,517	5.34	4.62
1930	7,683	8,684	1,466	5.27	4.75
1935	8,297	8,483	1,532	5.42	4.70
1940	n.a.	9,161	—	—	—
1944	8,513	9,877	1,586	5.37	5.40
1949	n.a.	9,726	—	—	—
1955	n.a.	10,263	—	—	6.20
1960	9,337	12,014	1,720	5.41	6.40
1966	10,429	11,149	1,840	5.68	6.96
1970	9,083	11,628	1,545	5.88	6.87
1975	8,486	10,127	1,514	5.61	6.80

NOTE: Projections of township population were made using each previous census population and the estimated growth rates for village population in each period. Projections for mean household size were made using demographic parameters for the appropriate cohorts in the village and township census data to estimate the age distribution of the population in 1925, 1930, and 1960 through 1965. For 1935, 1944, and 1955, for which age distribution data was not available, the age distribution of 1977 was arbitrarily chosen for use in the projections. See Sorensen (1981a: Appendixes C through G) for details of the projection techniques used.

census. The reasons the projected household size before 1944 is smaller than that actually found are likely to be two: the parameters for the earlier cohorts may be unrealistically low due to small sample size and aged informants neglecting to mention children long married out, dead, or split from the household (though I specifically asked for all born children); and people may have been delaying *pun'ga* because of the smallness of the household and the need for household labor. In this case the value for the *pun'ga* parameter, which was not differentiated by age cohort in the model projections because of the small number of cases available, may have been unrealistic for these particular cohorts. Whatever the case with earlier households, however, the reasons the projected household sizes after 1944 are bigger than those found in the census are clear. Beginning in the thirties and increasingly in the sixties, seventies, and eighties, large numbers of young people have migrated to the cities. This migration has reduced household size at least 15 percent from what it would have been in the absence of migration and has operated to improve household consumer/worker ratios.

Patterns of Migration and the Family Cycle

Since migration from Sangongni has reduced village population growth and stabilized household size for at least a fifty-year period, it obviously is not a recent phenomenon. Women, of course, have always left their native villages in great numbers to take their place in their marital households. Tenant farmers and landless laborers have traditionally been geographically mobile. For the last fifty years, in what we have chosen to call the traditional period, the villagers of Sangongni have had rates of fertility and mortality that would lead to population growth rates of 2 percent or more, yet the township in which the village is situated grew at an annual rate of only 0.7 percent from 1925 to 1966. Most of the population growth generated by the village in the twentieth century, thus, has been absorbed elsewhere. During the colonial period, some of the excess population, with the encouragement and sometimes coercion of the Japanese authorities, colonized underpopulated rural areas. In 1977 there were still at least three older men in the village who had been sent to Manchuria before 1945. Even during the traditional period, moreover, the growth of cities absorbed significant amounts of rural population growth (Kwon, Lee, Chang, and Yu 1975:62). The migration that began in the sixties and continues unabated in the eighties is of an entirely different order, however. Because of it Sangongni, and indeed all of rural Korea, has been losing population not only in percentage terms but also absolutely.

This latest migration has been almost exclusively a rural-urban migration. From 1963 when 2.7 million workers were employed in the nonfarm sectors of the economy, nonfarm workers grew by leaps and bounds to 6.7 million in 1977 and 9.7 million in 1982. Since most of these jobs have been in urban areas, the acquisition of nonfarm employment has typically involved migration to urban centers, which have in turn grown at an astonishing rate. Whereas Korea's population was 28.3 percent urban in 1960, it was 50.9 percent urban in 1975, and 57.3 percent urban in 1980. This huge migration from the villages has naturally reduced their population. Sangongni's population, which had been around 850 in the early sixties had already fallen some 20 to 30 percent to 594 people in 115 households by 1977. Outmigration continued at a high rate throughout the rest of the seventies and into the early eighties, so that by 1983, it had fallen an additional 34 percent to 391 people in 96 households with little sign that the exodus was ending.

Although at times it has seemed as if the cities must certainly be completely overwhelmed by the influx of rural villagers, by and large the provision of jobs and urban services in Korea has not lagged too far behind the influx of migrants. Urban unemployment since the mid-sixties has been kept down to reasonable levels, and the shanty towns that appeared in the late sixties and seventies have gradually been replaced by government-sponsored apartment blocks and other more substantial housing. Although Korean cities are far from paradisiacal, there is no question in the mind of most Sangongni villagers that urban life is preferable to rural. Many of the remaining villagers express the desire to move to town. The only thing still keeping many of them in the village is their knowledge that they lack the skills (*kisul*) to acquire desirable urban jobs, and their knowledge that the factors of production (including land), which they have painstakingly acquired over the years of agriculture in the village, will be difficult to duplicate anyplace else. As in other migrations, the differential strength of urban attractions for people in different situations has made some more likely to migrate than others.

Cities are attractive for their amenities, and for their educational and occupational opportunities. With the phenomenal growth of Korean industry, the urban job market has been fairly good for migrants but it is extremely competitive. To obtain the best jobs as government bureaucrats (*kongmuwŏn*) and "salary men" (*saellŏri maen*) in corporations (*hoesa*) today, a good deal of education—preferably through college—is required. To succeed in small business, perhaps as the proprietor of a "hole in the wall store" (*kumŏng kage*) or as an independent taxicab driver, capital is needed—in the latter case several million wŏn (several thousand dollars). Capital is also needed for living space that must be either purchased for cash (loans for more than 10 or 20 percent of the purchase price of a house or apartment are rare) or rented on a long-term lease (*chŏnse*) in which a substantial amount of cash is put down for the interest-free use of the landlord who will return the principal at the end of the rental period. Even for blue-collar occupations that do not require capital for entry, such as for drivers, mechanics, and the like, training is necessary to make a successful urban career, and training takes time and money. Thus, although the city has its attractions, it is not for everyone. Whether the city beckons or not depends as much on one's position in the village as on the amenities and opportunities of the city. As we have already seen, a number of factors partially determine the efficiency of households as units of production and consumption in village agriculture. Households that are poorly equipped to survive in the countryside may find the city an attractive alternative at the same time that better adapted village households, while conceding the attractions of urban life, find migration an impossible alternative.

If the conditions that make village life more or less attractive were independent of those that make city life more or less attractive, the conventional analysis of push and pull factors would be appropriate for understanding migration from Sangongni. This, however, is not the case. A villager who possesses fixed capital in Sangongni, and thus is in a good position there, can also convert this capital into urban advantage by a number of routes. Landowners of course, can directly convert village capital into cash by selling their house and land and using this capital to set themselves up in the city or, if they are not sure whether they want to remain in town, they can rent their village properties and be freed from worry about food sources. Alternatively, they can use their capital resources to provide either themselves or their children with technical or educational qualifications that will aid them in the urban job market. Since rural Korean families are corporate entities, moreover, the migration of eldest sons and of unmarried children of the household does not by that fact remove them from household membership. Migration of selected family members from the household may simply set up a branch of the household in the city so that the total labor power of household members may be efficiently used. Depending upon who leaves the household at what age, this kind of migration has various effects on adaptive capabilities of the village household as a rural unit of production and consumption. None of these factors in and of themselves pushes or pulls people into the city, however, though they certainly condition the attractiveness of different kinds of family adaptive strategies.

Since migrants from the household still remain household members, their structural position within the household is a crucial datum conditioning their migration strategy. We can conceptually distinguish two kinds of migration—that of individuals and that of households. These two types of migration are taking place at different rates. If we refer to the figures for village population change between 1977 and

1983 given above, we can see that over those six years, the number of individuals in the village fell 34.2 percent while the number of households fell only 16.5 percent. Perceptions of the relative advantages of village and city life vary according to whether one is a house head or not. House heads are less likely to migrate than other members of the family. There are good structural reasons why this should be so. The house head is responsible for family property and income, so a move of the head from the village involves a complete change in the family's means of livelihood. The whole family almost always accompanies a house head when he moves,[18] so the move of a house head often leads to the disappearance of the entire household from the village.

For those other than the house head or house mistress, the move to the city is in general less momentous. Since the importance of such migration for the organization of the household varies a great deal with the precise structural position of persons within the household, here, too, household structure strongly conditions migration strategy. Daughters, who do not carry on the family line, must marry patrilocally by their mid-twenties at the latest. We should find, then, that the proportion of daughters remaining in the household will fall from the ages of eighteen or nineteen until about twenty-five, when virtually all of them should be gone. Younger sons who must split from their natal household at the time of their marriage are in a similar position. We expect them to find the city especially attractive as a source of livelihood, since they are entitled to only a small inheritance. All younger sons should be gone from their natal households by the age of about thirty, when most of them will be married and will have to have established themselves in some nonfarm occupation. The obligation of filial piety, on the other hand, falls very heavily on eldest sons. It is legally impossible for them to split from their *ka* in any way. They inherit the obligation to maintain the family line and care for their parents in their old age, and they inherit the bulk of the household estate. We thus expect them to migrate less frequently than other children, and if they do migrate, we expect many of them to return to the village at the time of their succession to the house headship and their inheritance of the family farm.

These expectations are in general supported by data collected in the village in 1977 and 1983. Children of all ages and both sexes remain in their natal households until after they have finished middle school, or until they reach the age of about fourteen. After this, most children of both sexes leave the village. Few of the girls return to the village for more than a year or so after leaving, because they marry and enter their husband's household. Oldest sons do remain in the village more frequently than their younger brothers. While fewer than 20 percent of the younger brothers between the ages of fifteen and nineteen remained in the village in 1983, at least 36 percent of the oldest brothers of each age group remain in the village (see table 6.3). Thus, our supposition that structural features of family organization strongly condition migration patterns from the household seems confirmed. Puzzling features, however, remain. Although eldest sons remain in their natal household at a greater rate than younger sons, well over half of them in every age group above fourteen have departed from the household. In addition, the age at which migration takes place does not seem to be predicted by structural features of the household. Daughters leave the household long before the ages of nineteen and twenty, when they are beginning to get married. Younger brothers leave the household long before their late twenties when they marry and legally split from the household.

Although for those over eighteen, the motive for moving to town may be factory employment, the motive for those of younger ages is almost always education. As Korea has rapidly developed, educational standards have risen sharply. In 1977 there were many village natives who had completed high school and several who had completed college. With the exception of the village schoolteachers (most of whom, due to government policy, are not village natives) only one of these high-school graduates lived in the village. Even as late as the mid-seventies, anyone with a high-school education could get a fairly decent job in the cities where wages were higher and life inherently more comfortable (an assessment of city life explicitly shared by the villagers). The majority of even middle-school graduates at that time

TABLE 6.3
Percentage of Children of Sangongni Households Who Were Living in the Village in 1983 (*by age and structural position in the household*)

Age Group	Eldest Sons	Younger Sons	Daughters
0–4	100.0	80.0	100.0
5–9	100.0	100.0	96.4
10–14	100.0	94.1	92.0
15–19	36.4	18.2	13.8
20–24	35.7	25.6	6.7
25–29	47.8	36.4	30.8

usually had a good shot at a decent blue-collar job. With the rising educational standards in Korea, however, the siblings of those who had found good urban employment in 1977 and earlier had to get more education just to stay in the same level of the job market in 1983. Today, without a high-school education, a girl will have a poor prospect of making that desirable urban marriage, and without at least a technical-school education a boy will not have a chance at a good urban job. For those youngsters who are planning on making the transition to urban life, then, the necessary training begins well before structural factors in the household necessitate their departure. Since the closest trade or high schools are in the county seat or the provincial capital—both some twenty-five kilometers distant—obtaining a technical- or high-school education, let alone a college education, necessarily entails a move to town within a year or two of completing middle school.[19]

This migration of younger villagers from the household has led to the creation of population pyramids with the hourglass shape characteristic of populations from which large numbers of young people are migrating (see fig. 6.6). The pyramids for both 1977 and 1983 clearly show the effects of the high migration rates of the young out of the village. Those between fifteen and forty form a smaller proportion of the population than the cohorts immediately above or below

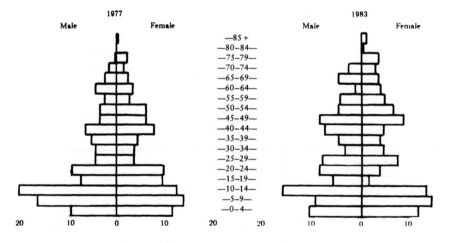

Fig. 6.6. Sangongni population pyramids for 1977 and 1983

them, because migration has been heaviest in those age groups. When we compare the shape of the 1983 pyramid with that of 1977, many of the characteristics of the 1983 age pyramid simply reflect those of the 1977 one lagged five years, but other characteristics cannot be so explained. In 1983, proportionately more children had left the village in the fifteen to nineteen age category and between twenty-five and thirty-four than in 1977. In the twenty to twenty-four age category, on the other hand, we find more villagers have remained than we would expect, given the size of the village cohort of fifteen to nineteen year olds in 1977. Young house heads are still leaving the village, but there seems to be a significant return migration of young men who, having gone to town and acquired their education, or tried factory work, are returning to the village. For those that have acquired an education, the attraction that has induced them to return is clearly the substantial landholdings of their households. The average landholding of the eight households that have had high-school graduates return to the village by 1983, was 191.3 ares—well above the village mean landholding of 110.9 ares. Those returnees who did not have substantial landholdings to lure them back to the village, on the other hand, did not have education past middle school. Some of them had managed to acquire capital through factory work and buy land when they returned to the village, however.

Selective migration by household status and age out of the village has not only had an important effect on the village's age pyramid, but it also has had an important influence on the size, structure, and family cycle of the households remaining. With the continued migration of sons out of the household, total household size has fallen from 5.2 (SD = 2.1) in 1977 to 4.2 (SD = 1.7) in 1983.[20] This fall in household size is not primarily due to a fall in fertility. If we compare the household size at various stages of the domestic cycle that would be generated by our model with those found in Sangongni in 1977 and 1983, for example, the sharp differences between the expected and actually found household size are not in the early years of the family cycle, or the expansion stage, but most clearly in the middle and later years of the domestic cycle. The fall in mean household size is not caused so much by a fall in the number of children that villagers are having, but in the migration of these children from the household to the city in their early teens.[21]

That a large proportion of Sangongni households have failed to retain their successors in the village can be seen in figure 6.7. The per-

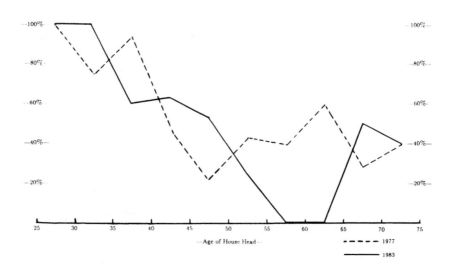

Fig. 6.7. Percentage of eldest sons at home by age of house head

centage that have eldest sons resident in the household falls consistently with the age of the house head until they reach their sixties and are ready to retire. Although some migrant eldest sons eventually return to the village, the vast majority, at least until recently, have not. Having once married and established themselves in town, they have few incentives to return. The work in the village is arduous and backbreaking—especially for the women—and only a large landowner can offer a standard of living comparable to that of those who have managed to find a decent urban job. The migration of labor out of the household has led to a substantial rise in the consumer/worker ratio for the middle period of the domestic cycle (see fig. 6.8). Whereas in the traditional period the most favorable part of the family cycle—when the consumer/worker ratio was lowest—was shortly after the marriage of the successor, today this period of the family cycle is the one in which the consumer/worker ratio is the most unfavorable. Since the successors that increase the family labor supply at this time are mostly migrating from the household, the labor supply continuously declines (on the average) from a peak some fifteen years after the marriage of the house head until there is some slight improvement at the end of the family cycle.

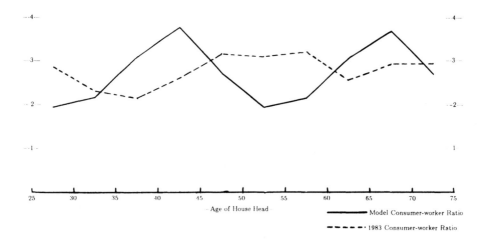

Fig. 6.8. Model and actual 1983 consumer/worker ratios

Social Change and the Family

For many social scientists the evidence given would be enough to justify announcing the decline of the agricultural village and the destruction of the corporate farm family. Certainly at the level of patterns of
behavior, the changes in the family organization of the village seem
striking. The authority of the house head has been eroded. Large joint
family households are a thing of the past, and younger brothers no
longer routinely live in little houses built near the house of their parents and older brothers. Adoption of agnates seems to be a dying custom, and females, even, sometimes inherit property. Love matches
made in town without the permission of the parents and the use of an
intermediary no longer scandalize the villagers (though arranged marriages are still the norm). Eldest sons normally don't spent the entirety
of their life in the house where they were born and raised, and (most
shocking of all), even eldest daughters-in-law may never have the experience of serving their parents-in-law.

It would be a mistake, however, to try to seek the basis of the traditional Korean farm family at the level of patterns of behavior. The
most fundamental features of the traditional Korean farm family lie
not in any one custom or set of statistical norms, but rather in the
basic assumptions about what a family is and how people are related
to one another. These assumptions include the corporate conception

of the family in which each family has a head, a fixed membership, and mechanisms of succession by which the fundamental roles of the family can be passed along the generations; the patrilineal method of reckoning kinship; and the conception of reciprocity between generations symbolized in the concept of filial piety. Given these principles of family organization and given the traditional farm economy where survival could best be ensured by a family cycle that above all else provided for continuity in the household labor supply, certain rules of thumb, or patterns of behavior, came in the past to be statistically normal. We have already seen how the rules of thumb that created joint family households had, in the context of traditional agriculture, certain functional advantages in the provision of labor in the household. These functional advantages were not accidental—not because culture in some mystical way always generates adaptive customs—but because these customs were *not the most fundamental and basic features that they seem, but rather were one of a number of possible permutations of cultural rules contingent on socioeconomic conditions.*

I would contend that traditional patterns of family behavior were not cultural norms, but strategies aimed at attaining culturally appropriate goals in a culturally appropriate manner. Strategies, being aimed toward recognized concrete goals, must always change with circumstances. That that which works to attain goals in one circumstance may not work in other circumstances surprises no one. With changes of circumstances, sources of socioeconomic success and prestige also change. If the goals toward which behavior is rationalized change, and if the circumstances in which they operate change, then typical patterns of behavior must also change. In the midst of this change, however, there can be basic continuity in culture—assumptions about how the world works, about the constituent units into which the world can be divided, and the basic ways these units are related to one another.

With the declines of morbidity and mortality in rural Korea, the safety value of having excess labor in the farm household is less crucial than it was a generation ago. As the improvements of traditional agricultural practices described in chapters 2 and 3 have increased the efficiency of household labor, the labor requirements for the successful running of the family farm have fallen, as have the usefulness of a large family labor force. At the same time that the requirements for household labor have been falling, the requirements for household capital have been increasing. Capital has become necessary not only for investment in the improved factors of agricultural production that have increased the efficiency of household labor, but also for the training expenses of the many children of the household who must compete in urban labor markets. The sacrifices and expenses that farm families often endure to provide for the education of their offspring would inspire the sympathy of even the most hardhearted. One of the more prosperous villagers in 1977 was spending well over 10 percent of his gross annual income of around five thousand dollars on tuition for the public high-school education of his eldest son, the technical-school education of his third daughter and the middle-school education of his second son. When the cost of room and board in Ch'unch'ŏn for the two older children is added into the bill, another 10 percent bite is taken from his income. This farmer was in the top quintile of village landowners, so the strain on the family budget of ordinary farmers for providing as much education as they can for their children with academic ability can be imagined.

In a situation where the traditional family cycle provides for large amounts of labor in farm households that no longer need this much labor, and in a situation where household needs for capital are increasing at exponential rates, it is no wonder that adjustments in the family domestic cycle have had to be made. By sending surplus labor out of the household to take the jobs available in the urban economy, the economic situation of all household members can be dramatically improved. The migration of labor that is truly surplus out of the household does not harm household productivity, and because that labor becomes engaged in productive activity, the total family income increases.[22] The migration of members out of the household reduces total family consumption but, as we have seen above, since those who are old enough to migrate from the household are also old enough to work, this process has increased the consumer/worker ratio. If per capita productivity had remained at 1948–49 levels, this phenomenon might have been a problem that would have made selective migration from the household a much less beneficial strategy, but with the 1977 or 1983 levels of productivity of twice the 1948–49 level, any household with one adult male worker and one adult female worker can, with access to land, produce enough to support as many adult male equivalents as are likely ever to be found in one natural household. This even applies to tenant farmers.

Because migration of surplus labor from the household is an adaptive strategy that benefits all household members, we should not consider it in a negative light as the destruction of the traditional Korean family, but rather as positive evidence of the basic resilience of the traditional principles of Korean family organization and their adaptability in new situations. We will leave the detailed analysis of the relationship between land, labor, and household organization to the next chapter, but we can anticipate by saying that in most farm households in Sangongni in 1977 and in 1983, all adult labor above the minimum to run the farm household had migrated. Most households were left with precisely one adult male worker and one adult female worker. Most often these workers were husband and wife, but the presence of precisely one adult male worker and one adult female worker in many households was not simply that it takes one man and one woman to consummate a marriage. Many of the households for which this was true, for example, did not include a married couple, but consisted of such combinations as a widow or stepmother and her unmarried adult son, or a widower and his oldest daughter, or even a retired grandfather, his still-active wife, and their adult oldest grandson.[23]

Family Migration Strategies

Although in the discussion of migration I have so far emphasized the importance of preserving the labor supply of the household, with the development of Korea's new urban-industrial economy opportunities are various and families don't always come up with a strategy that maximizes all aspects of the farm economy. There are, for example, cases in which migration of labor out of the household has left the household with an inadequate labor supply. Sometimes this kind of migration is just a prelude to household demise, but in other cases, it should be seen as a short-term deleterious consequence of a long-term family diversification strategy. The Chin family, who moved to Sangongni from a nearby village in 1968, are one interesting example of this kind of strategy. They chose to move to Sangongni because the wife of Old Grandfather Chin, who at the age of seventy was still house head, was originally from the village, and they could get some land through affines who were moving from Sangongni to yet another village where they owned land. In addition, the younger brother of Old Grandfather Chin had successfully formed a branch family in Sangongni some years before. At that time Chin's three sons of forty-one, thirty-five, and thirty-two had married, but none had yet formed a branch family. Mr. Chin died only a year after they arrived in the village in March 1969, but even more calamitously, his youngest son died that same year in May, leaving a widow with three young children—a daughter and two sons. They had one-third of a hectare of irrigated riceland and two-thirds of a hectare of dry field. For an ordinary family this would have provided what would have been considered a good livelihood in 1969, but it was inadequate for the nineteen members of this complex joint family.

Normally in such situations in traditional times, the head of the main house would have forced the younger brothers to split from the household taking what little land they were entitled to, but in this instance, a strategy of diversification had already been in operation. Although the second son's family had remained in Sangongni, he had moved to town some time before. He eventually obtained a college degree and got an excellent job with a good company in Seoul. Meanwhile, his father's younger brother died without male issue and the second son was adopted to this line. His wife moved into the house into which her husband had been adopted to accompany the remaining widow, and to take over management of the land that was inherited as a consequence of the adoption. The widow of the youngest brother stayed in the village without formally splitting from the main household until after 1977. The dual residence pattern of the second brother with his adoptive house in the village and his residence in Seoul was arranged in 1971, and it continued through 1977 and 1983, though the households of each of the brothers had been split by this time. One family residence was in Seoul where the college-educated husband lived and worked accompanied by his older children who thus had a place to live while attending secondary school and perhaps college. The other family residence was in Sangongni, managed by the wife using her own and hired labor. Although the efficiency of the farm was hindered by this arrangement, the total position of the household was enhanced by their maintenance of a dual urban/agricultural strategy.

Although joint-family organization is no longer found, similar strategies of diversification of the family economy are extremely common in the village. Most of them do not involve the splitting of the conjugal unit but rather the splitting of the generations of the stem family. Kim Yŏn-ho, for example, has been a very successful farmer who inherited little land, yet became wealthy while at the same time managing to send five sons through at least two years of college. Back in the late forties or early fifties when elementary education had just been introduced into the village, Kim raised a calf and sold it for money that he invested in a house in Ch'unch'ŏn. Part of the house he rented most of the time, but the rest of the house was reserved as a residence for his sons as they went to Ch'unch'ŏn to attend school (cf. Mintz 1977:187–88). Each of his sons completed their education and, because at this time educated people were rare, most of them got extremely good jobs. Although by 1977 the house was no longer needed for the education of the children, it still functioned as a branch house of the family, with the eldest son resident. Even though the eldest son lived in the house, the house was considered part of the family estate and proved useful when the wife of the youngest son, who was resident in the village in 1977, was pregnant. She was able to go to town toward the end of her pregnancy and have the baby in a hospital—a routine occurrence for city folk, but extremely rare even for well-off country people who continue to give birth to their children unattended at home.

Most diversification strategies for today's households involve the placement of children in urban occupations. Some of these children send remittances to the main family, but this is neither the norm nor the main motivation in most cases.[24] Parents who do not need the money will usually not ask for remittances from children and, in any case, if the parents have been unable to provide the children with secondary education—a situation common among the poorer third of farmers—children seem to feel less of an obligation than if such an education has been provided.

In fact, diversification seems most often to provide opportunities for education. Most cases known to me involved reciprocity between siblings in the provision of education for each other. In a typical case, an older sister or brother took a job after completing high school with parental support, and used the salary to pay for the education of a younger sibling whom the parents could not afford to send through school (see also Mintz 1977:187–88). Sometimes these arrangements are managed by the father through remittances sent to him, but in other cases, the siblings make the arrangements among themselves.

In the case of eldest sons the provision of education can, in fact, be a delayed migration strategy for the household. One fifty-one year old female informant, for example, when questioned about future plans answered: "Farming is back-breaking work and I would like to not have to do it. My eldest son is going to college and won't be a farmer. My second is like the first, but I don't know what he's going to do. I'll tell him not to farm. I'd even tell a dog not to farm. When our Chŏng-sik gets out of there [college], he'll find a position, he won't farm and he'll make a living. Maybe we'll be able to accompany him. Later on he might earn a lot of money. I don't know if city life is good or not, but I hope it will turn out that way."

Since the mid-sixties Koreans have no longer formed joint families on the Chinese model, but the corporate structure of the stem family remains. The mere migration of a family member out of the village and into an urban occupation does not in and of itself mean the family has disintegrated or broken up. If the migrant is the eldest son, it is impossible for him to split from his natal family, and whatever the residential arrangement, father and son form a legally corporate unit.

Of course there are many cases when, whatever the legal situation of the household, the migration of eldest sons is a de facto breakup of the family. If the household has substantial holdings of land, retired couples often remain in the village and live off their rents while their other sons and daughters make separate lives elsewhere. These parents may join another child's house, if at all, only when they are alone and unable to take care of themselves. The opposite case also occasionally happens. Sons sometimes migrate out of the village when their father is in his prime, only to return when the father retires. In the past, this pattern has not been common. When sons are born early in their father's life, they will be in their forties when their father is ready to retire. By then, their roots in the city are often too deep and they will not want to return to the country. When a son is born late in a father's life, however, the time of the father's retirement comes just about the time when the son is ready to marry and settle down. In this situation the father may well "transmit the house" (*chŏn'ga*) to his son shortly after his marriage and the son will be able to manage household affairs almost from the beginning of stem family formation, avoiding the awkward years when father and son are both in their prime yet the son has no say in the running of the household. All of the sons who returned to stem families in the village after urban residence fall into this category. In spite of a migration rate that reduced mean household size in Sangongni between 1977 and 1983 one full person, from 5.2 to 4.2, the return of these sons to form stem families with their fathers and mothers actually raised the proportion of stem families in the village over the six-year period (see table 6.4).

Although there has been a tremendous increase in the number of patterns of behavior in villages like Sangongni,[25] the traditional Korean farm family is far from dead. In adjusting to changes in labor requirements for agriculture, household needs for capital and increasing life spans, Koreans have found new strategies of adaptation, to be

TABLE 6.4
Family Type in Sangongni, 1977–83

	1977		1983	
	Number	Percentage	Number	Percentage
Single	9	7.8	8	8.2
Nuclear	66	57.4	53	54.6
Stem	37	32.2	34	35.1
Other*	3	2.6	2	2.1
Total	115	100.0	97	100.0

*Includes households made up of grandparents and grandchildren, or two unrelated grandparents, and a single polygynous household.

sure. The basic principles that structure these strategies of adaptation, however, have remained intact. Rural Korean families are still the basic units of village social structure. They are still organized corporately according to patrilineal principles. Membership in households is still fixed and definite, and succession to household roles still allows for the continuation of the house line generation after generation. Rural households are still units of production and consumption that adjust their size to family labor needs. The moral worth of filial piety is still deeply felt. What has changed is not these principles, but rather the circumstances. Farming requires less labor, families require more capital, and diversification strategies allow family goals to be attained in numerous ways. In a stable agrarian society where economic opportunities and the goals of family organization are limited by circumstances, a few rule of thumb strategies may be adequate for family needs, and a description of these strategies may suffice for a description of the principles of household organization, but in a complex society where numerous goals and strategies are possible and where numerous factors select for different characteristics in different families, a more abstract characterization of the principles of household organization that take into account the conditioning effect of socioeconomic circumstances is called for. A change from a simple rule of thumb system to a more complex system should not be seen as breakdown but as development.

CHAPTER 7

Industrialization, Migration, and Land-Tenure Patterns

That peasants should adjust the size of their farms in accordance with both family consumption requirements and family labor supply is expected in Chayanov's model of agriculture with family labor farms and, as was noted in chapter 2 (nn. 15 and 16), there is good evidence that the peasants of Sangongni do indeed make these kinds of adjustments. This model of peasant agriculture can operate so long as the size of farms may easily be adjusted to conform to demographic changes in the family. In those Russian villages that continued the tradition of periodic repartition of farmlands, this condition of his model was met. In other villages, Chayanov felt that rental of land would provide the necessary flexibility (Chayanov 1966:111). As Skalweit noted two generations ago, however, the land-tenure regime of many countries—particularly those with impartible inheritance—does not allow such flexibility. Where this is the case, rather than adjust the size of their farms to accord with their family labor supply, families may very well adjust their labor force to accord with the available farmland by taking in agricultural servants and wage laborers (Skalweit 1924) or by manipulating the course of the family cycle, as McGough has observed for China (1984). As Kautsky noted, moreover, under these kinds of land regime, industrialization can alter land-tenure patterns and lead to large-scale migration out of the countryside (1899:164–74,216–17).

Agricultural servants could be found as late as 1977 in Sangongni, and hiring labor for wages is common. For Sangongni, too, migration is also a process through which an equilibrium between farm size and family size can be achieved. In chapter 6, for example, the selective migration from the household between 1977 and 1983 in which mean family size fell one full person from 5.2 to 4.2 while the amount of labor within the household and the proportion of complex families remained stable,[1] was interpreted as the result of villagers adjusting their migration strategies in accordance with relatively unchanging fundamental principles of household organization and in accordance with the functional needs of those households.

Most agricultural land in South Korea is privately owned, and can be bought and sold subject only to the limitations of the land reform law of 1949.[2] Land is expensive, however, and cannot simply be bought when the need arises. Households thus frequently find that the amount of land they own does not correspond with what they need to produce their subsistence needs or make efficient use of household labor. In most cases, villagers try to keep at least one able-bodied female and one able-bodied male in the household to manage the inside and outside labor, respectively. Failure to do this almost always is a sign that a family is following a diversification strategy that will eventually lead to their departure from the village. The precise amount of female and male labor required in the household, however, is dependent upon the size of the farm and the crop mix cultivated. Unlike many horticultural societies, where a correspondence between farm size and consumer/worker ratios is also observed (Sahlins 1972:102–23), the land in Korea is fully occupied. Households cannot simply expand their farms onto unused land as they grow. Neither can they abandon surplus land with the expectation of taking it up again when it is needed. There are various ways of gaining access to land and of using surplus land (which will be treated in more detail below), but, as is typical of peasant societies, the rate of return on agricultural labor and capital investment depends upon land-tenure relations. Returns are highest when household members cultivate land owned by their household. In other situations part of the surplus generated using household capital or household labor is directed outside the household energy loop.

Though in rural Korea in traditional times, adaptation to farming in poor households may have been primarily a question of finding enough land to make use of household labor or, in rich households, of finding enough labor to work household lands, the successful industrialization of Korea has now added a new factor to this equation: the rate of return on capital and labor. In the past, opportunities for the use of capital were confined to conspicuous consumption, usury, and investment in land. There were few realistic alternatives to the use of family labor in farming. Today, however, industrialization provides rich and poor alike with choices. Those with capital can consider investment in their children's higher education to enhance urban job prospects, or investment in urban-based family enterprises that can provide a good living for family members. Even those without skills may well make a better return on their labor in an urban factory than in agriculture. These alternatives have been taken up by countless villagers from the length and breadth of Korea. Each of these choices, however, has important consequences not only for the future size, prosperity, and location of the family, but also for village social organization. Taking advantage of the options provided by industrialization requires migration to the cities. Decisions whether to remain in the village and whether to invest in village land, thus, have come to depend upon a complex calculus of relative advantage. What skills does one possess (or can one realistically expect to acquire) that are applicable in an urban context? How much land does one own and how does this affect the return on the agricultural labor done by household members? Where will one get a better rate of return on one's capital and labor: in the city or in the village? Since the amount of land owned by a household is an important determinant of the rate of return on household labor (something Chayanov did not consider), it is a prime factor conditioning strategies of migration that affect village social organization and is the third important factor that peasants consider in determining their cropping patterns.

The relationship between migration and land tenure is a feedback one: migration strategies are dependent upon land tenure, but land-tenure patterns are also dependent upon migration strategies. Land, of course, is a form of fixed capital, but it can easily be converted into liquid capital by sale. Just as villagers are faced with variations in the amount of labor available to their households and choices in its allocation, they are faced with variations in the availability of capital and choices in its allocation. Given the level of labor productivity and the amount of labor available, some households are better able to produce a surplus through agriculture than others. Investment in land will improve the return to labor better in some households than others. In some households, investment in education makes sense, while in others where children have little academic ability or inclination, such investment is not possible. Some migrants from the village simply abandon their houses and land if they are not worth very much, while others rent out their holdings to friends or relatives they can trust. Since making a successful transition to urban life requires large amounts of capital, however, most migrants from the village eventually sell out. This provides opportunities for those who are able to produce a surplus and who elect to remain in the village to purchase additional land. Thus, the land-tenure patterns of the village are the result of numerous long-term decisions about the allocation of family labor and capital that have resulted in the migration of households with certain characteristics and the retention in the village of house-holds with other characteristics.

The Distribution of Land

Because of the intimate connection between migration, land tenure, and the functional needs of the household, land-tenure patterns are conditioned by the abilities and needs of farm households. This can be seen in table 7.1, where the distribution of landholdings of various sizes in 1976 and 1982 has been given. This distribution is fairly typ-ical for rural Korea in its general features.[3] It is bimodal: a large per-centage of the farmers own no land at all (i.e., are tenant farmers),

TABLE 7.1
Land Ownership in Sangongni in 1976 and 1983 (*in ares*)

Amount of Land	1977		1983	
	Number of Households	Percentage	Number of Households	Percentage
Not available	2	1.9	2	2.2
No land	24	23.1	19	20.9
0.1 to 24.9	2	1.9	3	3.3
25.0 to 49.9	7	6.7	5	5.5
50.0 to 74.9	13	12.5	4	4.4
75.0 to 99.9	16	15.4	15	16.5
100.0 to 124.9	14	13.5	6	6.6
125.0 to 149.9	8	7.7	12	13.2
150.0 to 174.9	8	7.7	6	6.6
175.0 to 199.9	3	2.9	3	3.3
200.0 to 224.9	1	1.0	3	3.3
225.0 to 249.9	1	1.0	4	4.4
250.0 to 274.9	3	2.9	4	4.4
275.0 to 299.9	—	—	2	2.2
300.0 and more	2	1.9	3	3.3
Total	104	100.1	91	100.1

NOTE: Eleven households in 1977 and six households in 1983 have been excluded because they neither own nor cultivate land. Landowners who are not residents of the village have been excluded.

but those households that do have land tend to have substantial amounts. Very few landholding households own less than 50 ares, and only a small number own more than 150 ares. More than half of the landholding households own between 50 and 125 ares of land. In Sangongni, the smaller landowners tend to concentrate their holdings in irrigated riceland rather than rainfall field. The superior productivity of rice, the surety of crop provided by irrigation, the high prices rice commands, and the preference for rice as the major food staple all tend to encourage concentration of scarce capital in riceland as long as the household labor supply is adequate for its cultivation. The difficulty of getting enough labor to cultivate large tracts of riceland make it a less attractive investment than rainfall fields, however, for the larger landowners who cannot manage all of their land with household labor. Thus, as household landholdings increase, the proportion of irrigated riceland to total land falls.

Apart from this tendency for householders with less land to concentrate their holdings in irrigated riceland, and those with more land to have a larger proportion of rainfall field, the distribution of riceland and rainfall field within households is relatively equal.[4] Households must possess both types of land to produce the crops required for subsistence, and since the peak labor requirements for the crops grown on the two different types of land complement each other, distributing one's holdings over both types of land makes for efficient use of household labor. As with total landholdings, holdings of each type of land tend to be concentrated within a narrow range. On the one hand, few of the landowning households own less than the 11.4 ares of irrigated riceland and the 25.1 ares of rainfall field the mean Sangongni household of 3.8 adult male equivalents needed in 1977 to produce enough crops for subsistence (see table 4.9). On the other hand, few holders of land own more than the 70 ares of irrigated riceland and the 90 ares of rainfall field which we, based on table 5.2, have estimated a single adult male can cultivate using prevailing hand techniques of cultivation.[5] As can be seen in table 7.2, for owned riceland and owned rainfall field, as well as for total owned land, over 70 percent of the households who owned land in 1977, and more than half of those households who owned land in 1983 (with the exception of owners of rainfall fields), owned amounts that fell within the limits defined by subsistence needs and the amount of land one male can cultivate. This can also be inferred from the mean size of landholdings and their standard deviation. The mean in each case is well within the above limits, and the standard deviation such that almost all house-

TABLE 7.2
Landholding and Farm Size (*ares per household*)

	1977			1983		
	Mean	Standard Deviation	Percentage Within Limits*	Mean	Standard Deviation	Percentage Within Limits*
Owned riceland	60.8	42.4	70.1	80.8	53.6	53.8
Farmed riceland	59.0	40.7	73.0	74.8	38.1	56.4
Owned rainfall field	63.1	38.1	71.2	81.6	65.1	47.6
Farmed rainfall field	61.7	36.6	72.6	74.0	56.8	57.3
Total owned land	119.9	75.5	72.4	148.5	103.6	57.1
Total farmed land	114.7	70.1	76.9	135.6	82.3	58.3

*The lower limit of 36.9 ares is the estimated amount of land the mean family of 3.8 adult male equivalents would need for subsistence in 1977 based on the information in table 4.9. The upper limit of 160.0 ares is the estimated amount of land one adult male can cultivate based on the information in table 5.2

holds would be above the minimum needed for subsistence and below the maximum that can be cultivated by a single male.[6] Since, from the point of view of the household, renting land out or cultivating it with hired labor are, as mentioned in chapter 5, less efficient than cultivating one's own land with household labor, landholdings outside the subsistence minimum and labor maximum tend to be less common.

Methods of Adjusting Household Labor

Although there is a correspondence between the average amount of land that a household can manage on its own and the amount of land that people tend to own, this correspondence is a statistical tendency rather than an absolute requirement. Although some 70 percent of the landowners of 1977 and almost 54 percent of the landowners of 1983 owned amounts of land that fell within the "ideal" range, more than a quarter of the landowners owned more—sometimes a great deal more—land than could be managed by a single adult male. In addition, 20 to 30 percent of the agricultural households of the village were completely landless tenant farmers. A good half of the households in the village, thus, have to find a way to adjust their access to land so it corresponds with the amount they need for subsistence and the efficient exploitation of household labor.

Some householders, it is true, are able to accumulate enough capital to buy any extra land they may need to provide for family members. The price of irrigated paddy land in 1983 ran five to eight times the annual gross productivity of the land, however, so this requires careful long-term planning, saving, and a commitment to remain in the village.[7] Tenant farmers pay 50 percent of their gross crop in rent. If they have the same mean number of consumers and workers in their household as the rest of the villagers, they will have to cultivate at least a hectare of land to generate much of a surplus. Even then, given the other demands on family income, it is almost impossible to accumulate a surplus sufficient to allow the purchase of land. Unlike their landowning counterparts, then, tenant farmers are seldom able to improve their living conditions by acquiring land.[8] Since consumption needs and labor supply vary over the household developmental cycle, moreover, even families with ideal amounts of land find themselves with a labor surplus or deficit at times. Thus many households have to find short-term strategies that will either adjust their labor supply to meet the requirements of their landholding, or adjust the labor requirements of their farm to correspond with the labor supply of the household.

Adjusting Labor Supply

Labor Exchange (p'umasi). This mechanism is simple and direct in concept: a person borrows a day of labor from another household for which he is obliged to return the favor some time in the future. Although it is individuals who participate in the system, debits and credits are calculated in terms of the households to which these individuals belong. One household member may substitute for another. Both men and women exchange labor, and to a certain extent male and female labor are interchangeable within the system (at par), but most exchange tends to be within rather than between the "inside" and "outside" spheres. Thus, for example, if a house head has a large project that he is expediting through labor exchange, as host he is obliged to provide the exchange laborers with food and drink. The house mistress may exchange labor with other housewives to accomplish this part of her household responsibility while her husband exchanges with men from still other households to accomplish the main task.

Work Teams (ture). These are thought of as something from the past in Sangongni, and are no longer a regular feature of labor mobilization. Such teams used to be systematically organized to transplant all the fields in a certain area as a single job. Costs to landowners were figured out later according to each individual's holdings in the area transplanted. Work teams are associated with the prereform land-tenure system where large numbers of landless householders had to cultivate fields for the landlord leisure class. In recent years work teams have been revived in some places in Korea where severe overall shortages of agricultural labor have developed. Work teams are more efficient than labor exchange in mobilizing labor because all workers participate whether or not their particular household circumstances require them to make adjustments in their household labor supply. In 1977, some newly converted paddy was transplanted this way in San-gongni, but, in general, work teams are not a favored labor mobilization technique in the village today.

Live-in Laborers (mŏsŭm). Among large landowners, a common way of augmenting the household labor force used to be taking in *mŏsŭm*—live-in agricultural laborers. Such workers lived and ate with the family, and typically were given a small wage. In addition, members of the gentry, who in the past found physical labor demeaning, rather than mingle with *mŏsŭm*, often had whole families of hereditary servants known as *ha-in* (low ones) installed in small houses adjacent to their own. Although *mŏsŭm* were fairly common up to the sixties, the last of the *ha-in* are said by the villagers to have left around the time of the Korean War. They mostly moved to the city where their former servile status would not be known, though one high status villager remarked that if he met one of them on the street he would still use low forms of reference. There were no *mŏsŭm* in the village in 1983, and only one in 1977 who, being an old kinsman, was not the typical live-in laborer. He lived and worked in the house of one of the larger village landowners whose single son was living in town and going to high school. With large landholdings and a severe labor shortage, this landowner had to rent out some of his best land, but with the help of his live-in worker, he cultivated the major portion of it himself. The worker, when not busy with other tasks, could also do hired labor for other villagers.

Buying and Selling Labor (togŭp, p'ump'ari). Households with a labor surplus can send excess workers to do agricultural work for wages (*togŭp* or *p'ump'ari*), and use these wages to supplement an insufficient family income. Those with a labor deficit can hire workers for wages to get over labor bottlenecks. Both strategies are popular in the village, but their frequency is limited by the extreme seasonality of labor peaks and the availability of short-term labor. Very often both exchange and hired labor are used together on the same project.

Because of the opportunities for alternative employment provided by industrialization, rural wages have risen considerably and even extremely wealthy landowners can no longer afford to make use of agricultural servants or live-in laborers. Work teams are also a thing of the past. Their spontaneous development depended upon prereform land-tenure conditions in which large amounts of land were held by noncultivating landlords and many peasants were landless. For tasks that one man cannot do alone, or tasks that must be completed within a short period of time (such as plowing, seeding, transplanting), on the other hand, labor exchange is efficient and commonly used. Since borrowed labor must be paid back within a relatively short period of time, however, labor exchange cannot overcome gross household shortages or surpluses of labor. The situation for day labor is similar to that of labor exchange: it is useful to tide the household over short-term labor bottlenecks, but running a whole farm with hired labor would be difficult. One adult male, for example, can manage twice as much irrigated riceland during most of the year as he can transplant by himself. If he can hire enough labor during the six-week period of harvest, he can double the amount of land he can manage with only a moderate outlay of cash. The frequency of this pattern is reduced, however, by the shortage of available labor and by agricultural wages being twice their normal rate when transplanting of rice is to be done. Labor exchange and the buying and selling of labor, thus, only redistribute modest amounts of labor at peak seasons and are not very efficient ways of adjusting gross disconjunctions between household landholdings and labor supply.

Adjusting Labor Requirements

*Crop Mix.*The mix of crops cultivated by a particular household (especially on rainfall fields) can be adjusted to take into account the labor resources of the household. Households with insufficient riceland or a large amount of female labor may raise silkworms on an unusually large scale. Households with a large male labor force may cultivate tobacco.

Rental of Land (sojak). Rental arrangements (*sojak*) include both sharecropping (*t'ajak*)[9], and fixed-rate rental (*toji*). In sharecropping, the tenant provides the capital for farming and pays the landlord a fixed share of the harvest. The standard share is 50 percent, although shares as low as 30 percent are sometimes found on poor land, or between kinsmen.[10] Fixed-rate rentals are usually paid in advance in bags of husked rice. Although fixed-rate rentals can be found on irrigated riceland (one farmer, for example, was paying 500 *kŭn* of husked rice for 7 *majigi* of irrigated land),[11] the most typical cases of fixed-rate rental in 1983 involved rainfall fields upon which cash crops were being grown. Typical rents in 1983 ran about a bag and a half of husked rice per third of a hectare.[12]

Adjusting Labor through Rental

For the landowning household with a labor surplus, sharecropping can be attractive. A small landowner, for example, who is using only part of his household labor on his own land, can easily and cheaply cultivate more land with the seed and equipment he already has. Although the return on the rented land is low, capital costs are also low, and the farmer has few alternative ways of making use of excess household labor. Recently, fixed-rate rentals have also become popular for householders in this category. The popularity of fixed-rate rentals for owner-tenants is related to their subsistence usually being assured by what they cultivate on small amounts of their own land, so they can consider risky money-making crops without jeopardizing their survival.

Full tenants, as opposed to owner-tenants, most typically rent by sharecropping subsistence crops even on rainfall fields, because in this system rents don't become due until after the harvest. From a capital-use standpoint, tenancy arrangements are not so attractive to completely landless households as to owner-tenants. Full tenants cannot pay off any of their capital costs on land they own themselves with its superior rate of return. Since landless householders have few alternative uses for their labor, however, they most commonly make a living as tenant farmers. Day labor, when it can be found, is fairly well paid today, but it is also very seasonal. It is hard to provide oneself with a year-round living solely on the basis of wage labor. Such side occupations as keeping a wine house, running the village ferry, or caring for the village chestnut trees[13] can make an important contribution to family income, but can seldom guarantee subsistence. Sharecropping, on the other hand, may provide a low return for one's labor, but through it one can usually produce enough for subsistence.

Land for rentals comes from two sources: landowner households with a labor shortage and ancestor land. Ancestor land has been donated as *wit'o* to a lineage organization to provide income to finance the autumn tombside ancestor worship ceremonies. Since the main purpose of tombside lineage ancestor worship is to raise the social status of the households that hold them, the senior members of the lineage who donated the *wit'o* do not want to lose face by cultivating it themselves. Thus, this land is invariably rented out—though the renter is often a poor agnate whose genealogical position is such that he can raise his status very little through participation in the ceremonies, even if he could afford to. About 5 percent of the village land is in this category. Another 25 percent of the land of the village is rented out either because the owner of the land has too much land to cultivate with one or two persons, or because the household has a temporary shortage of labor. Long-term renting of land was made illegal during the land reform, although villagers continued to rent discreetly to kin and neighbors. The 1981 Constitution of the Fifth Republic recognizes the legality of "leasing or managing by consignment in order to raise agricultural productivity or rationalize the use of agricultural land" (Kuramochi 1985:23). Even so, villagers are somewhat reluctant to acknowledge this kind of arrangement, and some of the larger landholders claimed to be personally cultivating impossibly large farms. Renting out land provides a poorer return than cultivating land with wage laborers, but for the household with a goodly amount of land and a severe shortage of labor (such as a retired couple, or a widow with young children), renting out land in a sharecropping arrangement has several attractions: the renter provides his own tools, seed, and fertilizer (unless special arrangements have been made with the landlord who may provide such input for an extra amount of rent), and the renter totally manages the land, leaving the landlord with few responsibilities.

The net effect of rental strategies is to adjust farm size in the light of the consumption needs of the family and the male and female workers available to work the land. Thus, the amount of land cultivated by farmers (defined as all land owned and cultivated oneself plus all land rented and cultivated oneself) is in every instance closer to the limits imposed by consumption needs and labor availability than the amount of land owned by the house. This can be seen in table 7.2. The mean amount of land held by those who own land is more than the mean amount cultivated because large landholders are obliged to rent out excess land. Rental arrangements in each category of land increase the percentage of households within the subsistence and labor limits mentioned above.[14] In fact, most of the variation between the size of household landholdings and the size of the farms cultivated can be explained as adjustment to the amount of male and female labor in the household and the number of consumers. Large landowners rent out enough land so that what they have left can be cultivated by household labor with small amounts of hired help. Small landowners and tenant farmers expand their holdings with rented land at least to the point of covering their subsistence needs, and ideally to the point that all of their household labor is being used.[15] Thus, the concentration of farm sizes, and to a lesser extent landholdings, between the amount needed to support a family and the maximum amount of land that can be worked by family labor is not accidental, but related to the functional requirements of the agricultural household as Chayanov had predicted.

Distribution of Landholdings

Farm size can be interpreted as an adaptation to contemporary household needs, but land-tenure patterns cannot. Although the demographic situation of the household affects the ability of the members of the household to accumulate capital and acquire land, one cannot account for land-tenure patterns primarily in terms of demographic differentiation, as Chayanov attempted to do (1966:68–245). Because of the amount of time it takes to accumulate the capital for substantial land purchases, landownership is a legacy of past strategic decisions made in response to past social and economic conditions, rather than in response to immediate conditions visible to the field worker. Land-tenure patterns, thus, are the present manifestation of historical processes that have been working for some time. The most important of these processes or events for the land-tenure patterns of Sangongni have been the post-World War II land reform, inheritance patterns, strategies of land acquisition and sale, and household migration strategies.

Post-World War II Land Reform

High rates of tenancy had probably been characteristic of late nineteenth-century Korea, but during the Japanese colonial period (1910–45) conditions deteriorated even more. In Korea as a whole, the percentage of landless agricultural households rose from 39.4 percent to 55.7 percent over the thirty-five years of colonial rule. By 1945, 63.3 percent of the agricultural land of the country was owned by noncultivating landlords (Pak 1966:88), and tenancy was seen in most quarters as a serious social problem responsible for much political unrest.

This situation was reflected in Sangongni, where most families reported being tenants or small-scale owner-cultivators before the land reform. Few had enough land for subsistence without entering into some sort of tenancy arrangement or engaging in side occupations. There were no Japanese landlords in Sangongni, but a number of prominent families no longer resident in the village controlled a good deal of the village land. When younger sons set up housekeeping, most received no land from their natal household. Even if their natal household had land, the amount was often too small to allow division.

After liberation in 1945, there was considerable domestic political pressure to pursue land reform. In the immediate postwar period, however, the political situation was too complicated for orderly land reform, such as took place in Japan. The peninsula was occupied by two rival powers, the United States and the Soviet Union, and both of these powers eventually set up competing states in the south and the north, respectively. There was much political agitation during this period, and, for a time, even guerrilla warfare.[16] In spite of political obstacles, however, between 1945 and 1955, 61.9 percent of the total agricultural land of South Korea was transferred from landlord hands to those of owner-cultivators. Although most landlords in Korea were ethnic Korean, over the colonial period Japanese had come to own large amounts of some of the best agricultural land. This land was confiscated by the American military government in 1945 and sold in 1948 to tenants (with a limit of two hectares) for 20 percent of the crop over fifteen years.[17] A year after the founding of the Republic of Korea in 1948, moreover, the National Assembly managed to pass a comprehensive land reform law. The Land Reform Act of 1949 provided that land not cultivated by the owner, but in any case holdings over three hectares,[18] was to be purchased by the government for 150 percent of the annual yield. Landlords were to be paid with government bonds to be redeemed in five annual installments equal to 30 percent of the annual yield of the land. The transfer of lands was just about to begin in 1950 when the Korean War broke out, but in spite of the war, by 1954 much land had been transferred.

One difficulty in the land reform law of 1949 was its weak provisions for enforcement. The land reform was supposed to be administered by land committees comprising the heads of the relevant administrative organs, with members appointed from the citizenry made up of half landlords and half tenants. This left the door open for much landlord maneuvering in many places, and private land sales as well as government-sponsored transfers became extremely important just before and during the land reform period. Landlords, who had bene-fited greatly from Japanese economic policies, had been discredited with liberation. With the agitation against landlords, the talk of land reform, and the political unrest of immediate postwar Korea when rents were difficult to collect, land became a less attractive investment to the monied classes, and prices began to fall relative to the produc-tivity of the land. When land reform itself came to be implemented, moreover, inflation wiped out much of the value of the government bonds. Landlords, thus, had good incentives to make private land sales when they could, even for cheap prices. Nationwide, 10.3 per-cent of the total cropland was confiscated from Japanese nationals in 1945 and sold by the military government in 1948, 24.1 percent was transferred by private sale during the land reform period, and 27.5 percent was transferred in the land reform proper (Ban, Moon, and Perkins 1980:286).

Although I systematically surveyed all landowners in the village in 1983 on the source of their landholdings, I could find none who would admit that he acquired any land in the land reform proper. Land re-form did take place in the village, and informants would say such things as, "There were those who paid off all their installments and made the land their own, and there were also those who sold it to eat." Most of the households of present-day village landowners were landless before the land reform, however, and only began to acquire land during this period.[19] Even though land was very cheap at this time, it was usually purchased with money earned by both males and females from side occupations rather than with profits from agricul-ture. Typical strategies for raising capital included weaving cloth or raising a cow for sale. Many of these older farmers who acquired their first land during the land reform period freely commented that the drastic fall in prices due to the land reform and the political turmoil of the period made it possible to acquire land by purchase for the first time. One informant reported, for example:

In the old days people were generally poor. Here in Sangongni there were about 200 households at that time. People who were rich may have numbered three or four households. Those people had several hundred bags each [an-nual harvest of grain],[20] but those who lived below that were all poor. Many were sharecroppers. The share was usually one half with the remainder being what I could eat, but it was terribly inadequate. By the time of the June 25th incident [the Korean War], I had all the land which I possess today. I didn't receive even one *p'yŏng* [3.3 square meters] in the distributions [of the land reform], but earned money with my own strength and bought my land. If you ask why land prices were so low in those days, I'll tell you. Since there was going to be a distribution due to the land reform, the landlords sold off their land cheap. So with land being so cheap, I raised cows, sold them and bought land. Lots of land was sold. Right before the land reform, a lot of land was sold, and I'm saying that's when I bought my land. At that time I bought something more than 1300 *p'yŏng* [43 ares] of irrigated land and about 2000 *p'yŏng* [66 ares] of rainfall field.

Inheritance Patterns

Inheritance is partible among all legitimate or recognized[21] sons of a man, but the eldest son, who legally must succeed to the house headship is favored. According to the Civil Code of 1958, he who succeeds to the house headship receives one portion of the estate in his own right and one half portion extra as successor to the house headship (Kim Chusu 1985:495). This rule causes the eldest son to receive half again what other sons receive. Its justification, of course, is that the successor must provide for his parents in their old age and worship them after their death with periodic sacrifices (*chesa*). The legal rule is only a moderately accurate summary of traditional village practices, where the rules of thumb outline in chapter 6 prevailed. As the owner of household assets the house head can divide his land according to his own wishes either during his lifetime or by will, and in this case the proportions given to various heirs is at his discretion.

Although I have too few fully documented cases of inheritance by siblings to treat them statistically, investigation of those cases that I was able to document[22] seemed to reveal two tendencies: (1) if the subsistence of the main house was threatened by the division of household property, none of this property was divided among the younger sons; (2) among the larger landowners, where division of the property "by the book" would have created a main house with more than it could cultivate with its own labor, and branch houses with barely enough for subsistence, the division of the land was somewhat more equal than called for by the provisions of the civil code. No estate smaller than 50 ares, to my knowledge, has been divided by inheritance in the last generation. About thirty years ago, an estate of 16.5 ares was left entirely to the older brother, with his younger brother becoming a tenant farmer (though, since this was right about the time of land reform, the younger son was able to begin acquiring land and now has substantial holdings). Somewhat later, an estate of 50 ares was divided among two brothers with two-thirds going to the eldest brother and one-third going to the younger, exactly according to the pre-1958 rules. This left the eldest brother's household right at the subsistence level (in the absence of side occupations or the rental of land), and his younger brother's household only slightly better off than a tenant farmer (though he, too, has managed to acquire more land). The largest estate of which I have a precise record was one of 165 ares divided twenty years ago. Since the eldest son had died leaving only a grandson, the father divided the land on his deathbed. Of the 66 ares of irrigated rice land, 33 went to the eldest grandson and 16.5 ares to each of the two remaining sons. This was precisely according to rule. The 99 ares of rainfall field, on the other hand, were divided equally among all three heirs, with each receiving 33 ares.

In the case of the smallest landowner, the younger son got nothing. In the case of the medium landowner, the younger son got 50 percent of what the eldest son got—the amount specified in pre-1958 inheritance law for intestate persons. In the final case of the larger landowner, the younger sons got 75 percent of what the eldest son got. Although present landholdings of various households are, because of the buying and selling of land, no longer directly proportional to what each household obtained in inheritance from its natal household, due to unequal inheritance among sons, main houses in general own substantially more land than branch houses in Sangongni.[23]

Strategies of Land Acquisition and Sale

If the adjustment of the size of inheritance portions in light of household subsistence needs and labor supply indeed is a general characteristic of inheritance in rural Korea, inheritance patterns have contributed to the concentration of landholdings within the range that will provide for subsistence yet allow cultivation to be done primarily by household labor. Large estates will tend to be split into units manageable by the labor of one household, and small estates will tend not to be split below the level that they will be able to provide for the subsistence of a single household.[24] The effect of this tendency on land distribution in the village is limited, however, by so much land being bought and sold every year. Most of the land of the house heads who succeeded between 1977 and 1983 was inherited, but it was unusual for as much as half of the landholdings of those who succeeded to their house headships before the seventies to be made up of inheritance. In 1983 40 percent of the land owned by house heads was inherited from their fathers, but 60 percent was purchased from both kin and nonkin. Between 1976 and 1983, at least 25 percent of the land in the village changed hands. Although today tenant farmers find it extremely difficult, if not impossible, to begin acquiring land, during the land reform prices seem to have been cheap enough to allow even them to begin to purchase land. Today, only if a farmer has a modest stake of land is it still possible to augment his holdings to improve his economic position.

Some of the buyers of land were small farmers who were trying to augment their holdings so as to reduce the amount of rent paid. Others were large landholders intent on expanding their holdings and moving into the owner-landlord category. One or two were clearly trying to acquire holdings large enough so that, when split, more than one son would have a substantial farm (though only the top 15 percent or so of the landowners can contemplate this).[25] Households that bought land between 1977 and 1983, however, had two things in common: they already owned some land, they included more consumers (both young and old) than average, and they included more workers than average. Although the circumstances of the household in 1977 gave one a good basis for predicting farm size in 1983, one could not have predicted on the basis of 1977 landholdings or household structure which householders were going to purchase more land, or the amount of land that they would purchase.

Those households that remained in the village yet sold land between 1977 and 1983 were also a diverse lot. Some sold land to acquire capital for an important project outside the village—such as education of a son, or setting up a married younger brother in a business.[26] Others simply represent the discharge of a financial responsibility to a brother or sister. In many cases, however, such sales are preliminary to the departure from the village of households that have failed to retain enough labor to efficiently manage their land. Many of the larger landowners have successfully placed sons in good situations outside the village and need to retain only such land as will provide them with income in their old age through rentals. These older villagers will either join their eldest sons in town or, when they die in the village, no successor will remain. Which families will do this, however, depends as much on the ability of sons to find outside opportunity as any characteristics of the household in the village.

Household Migration Strategies

Although there is a statistical correlation between the number of adult male equivalents in the household in 1977 and the amount of land acquired between 1976 and 1983,[27] it would be a mistake to interpret this correlation as a "cause" of the acquisition of land. After all, the size and composition of the family can as easily be adjusted by migration to fit the amount of land available to the family as vice versa. Rather, that those families that purchased more land between 1977 and 1983 were more complex and larger in size in 1977 (but not necessarily larger landowners) than the majority of Sangongni farm families is an indication of a household economic strategy already focused on the village rather than migration. This can more clearly be seen if we keep in mind the characteristics of those households that migrated from the village between 1977 and 1983.

Since the amount of land a household owns is the chief determinant of return to labor, it strongly influences migration strategy. Even though farming can provide one's subsistence, smallholders and landless tenant farmers have found that an ordinary factory job in town provides a better standard of living than agriculture in the village. Job prospects for larger landowners, on the other hand, have to be more attractive before migration is justified. Migrants from the village between 1977 and 1983, thus, were overwhelmingly from the ranks of the landless and smaller landowners. Eleven of the twenty-four tenant farmers in the village in 1977 had left by 1983. Those landowners who left the village during the same period owned only 67.3 ares of land, on the average, while those that stayed averaged 127.1 ares. The households that left were, on the average, smaller than those that remained and they had fewer male and female workers. The differences in family size and composition between those families remaining in the village and those that left, moreover, were not due to differential birth and death rates, but to previous migration. Departure from the village of many of the migrant households was not just a sudden uprooting of the whole family, but rather the culmination of a series of decisions made in the past. Capital had not been invested in agriculture, previous household members had already been sent to the city, and, in many cases, the urban success of these previous migrants had precipitated the departure of the entire family.

Strategies of Household Adaptation

The adaptive strategies of households in Sangongni between 1977 and 1983, then, can be divided into two types: those predicated on remaining in the village and those predicated on eventual migration to the city. Those planning on remaining in the village maintained households averaging five residents and retained, for the most part, at least one male and one female worker in the household. Although not all families pursuing this strategy were landowners, most of them owned at least an hectare of land and either maintained the same landholdings in 1983 that they had in 1977 or had increased their holdings. Those who sold land between 1977 and 1983, on the other hand, were significantly different from the households pursuing a long-term strategy of remaining as agriculturalists in the village. They had smaller households with fewer workers and consumers than other villagers. In fact, those households that sold land between 1977 and 1983 were indistinguishable in 1983, in most structural aspects of household organization, from those households in 1977 that had left the village by 1983.[28] Those villagers who sold land between 1977 and 1983 had taken the first step in a strategy whose ultimate conclusion, as far as the village is concerned, will be the sale of all their land and departure from the village.

Migration and Village Social Organization

Thus, although rental arrangements provide villagers with enough flexibility to adjust their farm size to their consumption needs and labor supply, by determining the return to labor in agriculture, and thus conditioning migration patterns, land-tenure patterns have also had a decisive effect on village social structure. In the short run, families can reach a satisfactory equilibrium between consumption needs, labor availability, and access to land through such mechanisms as selective migration from the household and rental of land. In the past, when alternatives to agricultural strategies did not exist for most villagers, these short-term mechanisms had to do. Although acquisition of land could improve the position of the household, this seems to have been almost impossible for the majority of peasants in the economic climate of the past. Land reform changed much of this by breaking the power of the landlords and bringing the price of land within reach of the ordinary peasant.

Because of the land reform, Korea entered her period of rapid industrialization with a quite equitable distribution of land. Since the fifties, however, the conditions of agriculture in the village and the larger Korean economy have made different economic strategies rational for different landholding strata. Since those with little land can only make a meager return for their labor and have little prospect for increasing their landholdings, direct migration to the city, even in the absence of skills, will raise their standard of living, and, by improving access to education, raise the chances of social mobility for their children. Those who have substantial holdings of land and few skills applicable in urban contexts, on the other hand, can get a much higher return on their labor in the village than they could expect from an ordinary urban job. Their best strategy, then, is to remain in the village unless they can get the qualifications that will allow them upward social mobility in the urban world. These larger landowners can still invest their capital in education and other activities to enhance their urban prospects, or (more likely) those of their children, or they can use their superior returns on agricultural labor to generate a surplus for investment in increased landholdings. These strategies are not mutually exclusive: many of the landholding households are now both sending their children to school and acquiring land. If the eldest son of these households manages to find a good urban position, then the whole house may move to town. If he doesn't find an urban position with a return to labor as good or better than he can get on the farm in the village, then chances are he will return to the village.

The net result has been that the smallest landowners have gradually been selling their land and moving to the city, while many medium and larger landowners have been adding to their holdings. In addition, those large landowners who have been successful in placing their children in urban positions have been pursuing a strategy of delayed migration. As they have passed their prime and can no longer manage their farms themselves, they have been gradually selling land. Although the present old couples who live in the village without their successors may well remain for a while, with their children gone it is just a matter of time before they sell the rest of their land and disappear from the village.

This migration and sale of lands by small landowners and by those larger landowners who have successfully implemented an urban strategy has made the land distribution in Sangongni gradually less equal. Even over the relatively short period between 1976 and 1983, there was a significantly increased concentation of land. The Gini index, a statistical measure of inequality that varies between 0, a distribution in which everybody owns the same amount, and 1, where one person owns everything and nobody else owns anything (Allison 1978:869), went from 0.424 in 1977 to 0.479 in 1983.[29] When considered in a worldwide context, a figure of 0.479 indicates considerable equality of land tenure even for East Asia where all the countries experienced land reform after World War II.[30] It may point toward a future in which class lines are again to be deeply drawn across the countryside, but the nationwide significance of recent increases in tenancy rates is not unequivocal. Kuramochi, citing a 1977 survey by O Hosŏng (O Hosŏng 1981:57) in which owner-tenants were found to be cultivating larger farms than full owners, attributes much of recent increases in tenancy rates to the desire of owner-cultivators with surplus labor to rent the land of recent migrants to the city to increase the scale of their agriculture rather than to any new tendency toward proletarianization of existing landowners (Kuramochi 1985:19–20).

In fact, the increasing concentration of land in Sangongni, as evidenced in the rising Gini index between 1976 and 1983, is not due to increasing inequality among landowners. A large number of landowners of all farm sizes added to their holdings during this period, and many of the larger landowners actually sold land. There was no statistically significant correlation between the size of household landholdings in 1976 and the amount of land bought or sold by the household between 1977 and 1983. The rise in the Gini index thus does not seem to represent the squeezing out of the middle peasants that Kautsky and Lenin envisioned as a consequence of industrialization. It reflects, rather, the increasing gap between those who have any amount of land and those who have never had land at all. Although many landowners in Sangongni started out as tenant farmers as few as fifteen years ago, land prices are now much higher relative to productivity than they were during the land reform period and the Korean War. None of the villagers who were tenant farmers in 1977 had acquired land by 1983, and almost half of them had left the village entirely. Even in 1977, tenant farmers were recruited largely from outside the village. Of those nonnative villagers who left after 1977, many were replaced by other landless farmers from nearby rural districts (and in one case, even Seoul) who seem to form a sort of floating rural proletariat. Those who entered the village between 1977 and 1983 can be primarily characterized by their landlessness, their relative youth, and their lack of education. Many of them are at the beginning of their family cycle, and perhaps during the period from 1945 to 1965 would have been able to acquire land. That none has recently done so attests to the difficulty even today of producing a significant surplus when no labor can be employed at the highest rate of return, i.e., on one's own land.

Land Tenure and Social Organization

The land-tenure patterns of Sangongni, as we have argued, are closely related to the functional requirements of peasant family labor farms. Being the result of the operation of socioeconomic processes over a period of time, however, these patterns cannot be interpreted simply as the result of adaptation to the conditions that can be observed in any "ethnographic present." Just as the landholdings of individual households today are partly the result of their resources of labor and capital during the crucial land reform period, the aggregate patterns of land tenure in the village are partly a result of land distributions in the past when conditions were different from those observed today. Land-tenure relations do not directly control the size of farms, but by determining the distribution of the agricultural products produced by household labor, land-tenure relations determine how much household labor can be used at what rate of return. A consequence of this is that the labor supply of the household is partially determined by strategies of migration based on a calculus of relative return for labor. In the long run only two strategies are available: a household can try to acquire enough land so that the return to labor for agriculture will rival what family members with their particular level of skill could make in town, or it can send labor out until eventually the whole family leaves the village.

Given the political commitment to the family farm that has guided much government policy in South Korea since 1948, the distribution of not only the amount of land cultivated, but also the amount of land owned has been molded by household adaptive requirements. Processes of land transfer sometimes deliberately—as in inheritance patterns, or in the land reform program—and sometimes because of the operation of rational processes of strategy formation—as in selective migration of households—take into account the amount of land necessary for subsistence and the maximum amount that can be cultivated by a single able-bodied male. Land is too scarce and too expensive for most households to be able to maintain holdings that will justify the constitution of families that permanently maintain two or more able-bodied agricultural workers, but at the same time, no household can last for long unless it can maintain the minimum labor supply of one able-bodied female and one able-bodied male. The amount of land necessary to support such a family defines the minimum farm size. The maximum farm size is limited by the amount of land the family can cultivate using primarily household labor, and thus is limited by the typical size and composition of the households that are created by the rules of family organization interacting with the demographic parameters characteristic of the village and the division of labor of the household. With current techniques and levels of production, one able-bodied male can cultivate only about 1.6 hectares of land at the maximum, so the most efficient family landholding runs between 1 and 1.6 hectares.

Industrialization has not directly touched Sangongni, yet by providing alternatives to agricultural work for household labor, it has profoundly affected household strategies of adaptation. For the first time, villagers can send excess labor out of the household on a large scale with a reasonable expectation that it will be self-supporting. This allowed them to take into account not only consumption needs and labor availability in their adaptive strategies but also the return on household labor. This has led to migration patterns conditioned by land-tenure patterns. Holders of little or no land have left, while among those with land, a strategy either of remaining in the village or of stepwise migration could be employed. Those who remained added to their landholdings; those who migrated did so first by setting up their children in the city and then gradually selling off their land as the householder's village labor supply fell and as the capital needs of the urban-based family members increased. In the past, the process of outmigration of smallholders, and consolidation of the position of medium and large holders would have led either to a fall in the efficiency of farming or an increase in the size of the tenant class, as more and more farms increased beyond the size manageable primarily by household labor. Since tenants have urban opportunities, however, the size of this class has not increased dramatically. Efficiency has fallen, but so perhaps have rents and land prices. With mechanization over the horizon, moreover, a fundamental change in labor requirements is bound to come and the relationship between the factors introduced here will change. Industrialization, by providing alternative uses for village labor, first made the return to labor an important criterion for deciding who will and will not remain in the village. Now, if mechanization is introduced on a large enough scale to solve village labor problems, a full-scale revolution in the relationship of land and labor in Sangongni may take place, and the margin between profit and loss rather than the productivity of labor and the distribution of product may determine the rationality of village agricultural and migration strategies.

CHAPTER 8

Organization, Structure, and the Explanation of Social Change

We have been using an analysis of social change in Sangongni, a village in the mountains of Korea, to address the question of rural adaptational response to conditions of rapid urbanization and industrialization. Sangongni and other villages like it in industrializing societies present us with an interesting problem of explanation because, although they have not been directly touched by the institutions of urban-industrial society which are thought by many to bring about social change, they have nevertheless been profoundly affected by the urbanization and industrialization that has taken place elsewhere in their societies. Numerous theories have been proposed to account for the change in total societies, or the change in the urbanizing and industrializing sectors of societies, that should follow from industrialization, but comprehensive theories dealing with what should happen to nonurbanizing rural areas during a process of rapid urbanization and industrialization in the society surrounding them are rarer.

Those comprehensivie theories that do exist are built on the expectation that the penetration of markets and wage labor into rural areas will lead to profound changes in traditional economic relations and thus social organization. For Kautsky (1899), for example, the shift to cash cropping from subsistence farming was expected to lead to immiseration of the peasantry, their alienation from the land, and a switch to capitalist farming based on large-scale enterprises using wage labor. The transformation of rural society and the break-up of traditional extended families and Gemeinschaften, then, would not depend upon the urbanization or industrialization of rural areas themselves, but simply their incorporation into international markets. Others who have not worked with explicitly Marxist frameworks, such as Goode (1963), have expected the requirements and opportunities of industrial society—geographical mobility, the expansion of anonymous instrumental relations, the emphasis on achievement over ascription—to be decisive elements leading to the demise of traditional complex family systems and their convergence on a conjugal system that is thought to be functionally more compatible with industrialism.

The expectations of these theories, however, have not for the most part been met in Sangongni itself. Although some people have lost or sold their land in the village and become wage workers, for example, most have not and wage labor is not increasing in importance in the village. It is difficult to characterize the total economic changes that have occurred in the village as immiseration and proletarianization, moreover, when almost everybody's living standard has been palpably improving. The many who have left the land have not necessarily done so to become proletarians, and they have not, by and large, been forced to do so (in the sense of having to do so to survive). Although conjugal families are common in the village, the stem family exhibits surprising vitality in Sangongni and does not seem to be in any immediate danger of extinction. In fact, there has been unexpected stability in village social structure in spite of the startling changes that have overtaken the rural Korean economy.

It is possible to understand how the villagers of Sangongni have adapted the way they have to the forces of urbanization and industrialization by clearly distinguishing between social structure—fundamental values and principles for organizing society—and social organization—the observed pattern of concrete activities. According to this view, social organization is created by members of a society in the course of manipulating social structural rules to attain desirable goals in changing socioeconomic circumstances. The social organization that can be observed at any point in time, then, has no fundamental or explanatory importance except insofar as it provides evidence for underlying rules of social structure, goals, and strategies for manipulating these rules. Since strategies are situational, and different people at any particular point in time find themselves in different circumstances, we do not expect to observe all people behaving the same way at all times. As circumstances change over time, people's repertory of rational strategies and the frequency of their use should also change. Statistical investigation will reveal these changes, but such changes in social organization reflect flexibility that is built into the social structure and thus does not necessarily signify a fundamental shift in the principles and values for organizing society.

How social organization will change with changing circumstances depends upon the social structure and the goals toward which behavior is rationalized. Social structure molds decision making by defining a system of meaning through which new social forces and possible strategies to cope with them may be interpreted, and by defining a structure of functionally interrelated elements that limit the amount of variation that can be introduced into the system. Most changes in the forces that impinge upon village life are not, of themselves, meaningful; that is, they require no particular course of action. Refracted through the lens of social structure, however, these social forces acquire significance and can be dealt with through goal-directed activity.

Social change is often conceived as a process in which old social institutions are shaped to conform to the requirements of new social forces. This is essentially the view of Kautsky (1899) and Steward (1955:14). But no society is a blank slate upon which social forces operate. Old institutions determine the context within which new social forces operate; social structure provides a framework within which the desirability of various goals and the available behavioral options can be evaluated. If the existing social structure thus defines the significance of, and shapes social responses to, new ecological, economic, demographic, or political forces, then new circumstances may not require modifications in social structure as we have defined it here. What seems like fundamental structural change in a society can be seen simply as change in strategic choice within a stable social structure. In such cases, the anthropologist must demonstrate how old patterns of behavior are no longer rational under new circumstances. He must outline the constraints that the old institutions impose on the formulation of new strategies, and he must show how these new strategies are rational means of attaining old goals in new circumstances.

In Sangongni, because of the fundamental role family organization plays in Confucian ethics and because of the fundamental role the family labor farm plays in ensuring the welfare of the individuals of the village, I believe the household today plays the leading role in supplying the structure through which social forces are interpreted, constrained, and ultimately dealt with through goal-directed strategies in rural Korea. The peasants of Sangongni, in other words, respond to the changing economic circumstances introduced by the urbanization and industrialization of South Korea by modifying household strategies of labor allocation, migration, and capital investment without sacrificing fundamental principles of family continuity, division of labor, and kinship obligation. Because of this, the functional requirements of households as they are presently constituted determine the limits of rural response to social and economic change. The farmers of Sangongni make use of their productive technology to formulate strategies that will maximize the total rate of return for the labor of those persons included in the patrilineal corporate household. Due to changing circumstances, the means by which this may be done have changed, and this has motivated villagers to modify residence patterns and other aspects of the social organization of their households. Although both native and foreign observers of the contemporary Korean rural family have often been impressed by the dramatic changes in family organization that have appeared in recent years, preoccupation with this change has led many, in my opinion, to ignore some of the deeper continuities in the response of rural residents of central Korea to the urbanization and industrialization of South Korea since 1960.

The Structural Foundation of Sangongni Society

I would contend that most of the social change that can be observed in the Korean household is relatively superficial—change in social organization due to changes in strategy—but that the most fundamental structural features of village life, the basic principles of household social and economic organization, have remained remarkably stable in the face of strong new social and economic forces. These principles include the organization of households as corporate units of both production and consumption, and the provision that households will have a head, a fixed rule of succession through which crucial household roles (such as house head, or house mistress) can be refilled when vacated by the death or retirement of their incumbent, and a fixed membership whose identity is determined by sociocultural rules. The specific form that these rules of household entry and exit take in Sangongni are those common to many classic patrilineal societies: kinship is reckoned agnatically, marriage is virilocal. Succession to the house headship is by male primogeniture, and children other than this successor must leave their natal household one by one as they are ready—usually at or shortly after marriage. The tasks that must be done to maintain the household are divided into the female inside labor and the male outside labor. Together, the males and females of the household can complete most all tasks necessary for the subsistence of the household, so that the flow of energy forms a closed loop within the household.

These rules set up the structure of households and have been quite stable over the past few years. Given a particular level of fertility and mortality, and a particular pattern of timing of the events of the family cycle, the size and structure of the households that will be generated through the operation of these rules can be estimated as we attempted to do in chapter 6. These ideal households, however, were not found in Sangongni in 1977 or 1983, and we have good reason for supposing that they have not been characteristic of the past, either. The cause of the deviation of the size and composition of the households of Sangongni from what would be created by the unmodifed operation of the basic rules of household social structure lies in the kind of functional adaptation of the household to the requirements of production and consumption on the family farm that Chayanov (1966) noted for Russian peasant farms. In Sangongni, however, Chayanov's insights have had to be extended in two important areas: (1) Sangongni's families are not simply "natural" but are organized according to culturally specific corporate, patrilineal principles; (2) just as farm size is shaped by family consumer needs and labor capabilities, land-tenure relations and farm size also shape family size and composition. Because of Korea's culturally constituted division of labor, a fully functioning farm household has had to maintain, at the minimum, one able-bodied female and one able-bodied male. Once this minimum labor requirement for the full functioning of the agricultural household is met, other functional requirements of the farm household depend on aspects of the social, ecological, and economic system that were analyzed in the central chapters of this study: (1) the productivity of land and labor; (2) the subsistence needs for the household; (3) the size and composition of the family labor force; and (4) the amount and tenure status of land available to the household for farming.

The villagers of Sangongni cultivate two different kinds of field: *non,* or fields that have been leveled, diked, and provided with a secure source of irrigation water, and *pat,* fields that depend upon natural rainfall for water. The productivity of irrigated fields is twice that of rainfall fields, yet only the poorest farmers concentrate their holdings in this more productive irrigated land. This is because the return to capital and labor is highest only on land that is cultivated by family labor. The highest labor requirements for rice agriculture are concentrated during a three-week period at the end of May and the beginning of June. Although there are mechanisms for overcoming labor shortages, the amount of irrigated land that can be cultivated by a household tends to be limited by family labor resources during this crucial period. Since the labor peaks of crops grown on rainfall field do not correspond with those grown on irrigated land, however, households can increase the efficiency of their labor use by distributing their hold-ings relatively equally over both types of field. Both kinds of land are necessary for the cultivation of the crops needed to provide an ade-quate diet for household subsistence, moreover, so households orga-nized as family labor farms have a double motivation for spreading their cultivated fields among both types of land. The distribution of land and the crop mix have, for these reasons, come to be partially determined by the functional requirements of the household.

In the past, adaptive requirements may have imposed simple limits on the values of certain variables for some households. Land was short relative to the needs of the peasants, and modern inputs in agriculture were expensive and difficult to acquire in most rural areas. Agricul-tural work outside the household, moreover, is extremely seasonal. With the dendritic marketing system mentioned, villages have been at a disadvantage in the use of exchange relationships to raise their pro-ductivity. Since there were few alternatives for the use of household labor, and since capital was extremely expensive, villagers had few means or incentives to raise the productivity of their labor. Thus, it was rational for villagers to retain labor within the household and apply this labor toward the intensification of cultivation on family landholdings. Before the land reform most peasants could get access to land only through fifty-fifty sharecropping arrangements. With the levels of productivity prevailing at the time such tenant farmers were limited by the productivity of labor. Their households could not make ends meet with a consumer/worker ratio much above three—that is, one able-bodied male could support no more than his wife and two or three children. Many tenant farmers, thus, had to either stretch the spacing between children or maintain those children capable of work in the household because of household adaptive requirements with a given kind of land tenure and level of productivity of labor.

Even in the traditional period, however, adaptive limits usually left householders with a certain amount of choice. If the farmer were a landowner, or if productivity had been higher, for example, no prac-tical limit on the consumer/worker ratio would have been operative. The landowner receives twice the return on his labor that the tenant does. The amount of land that a landowner can manage with his own labor is the same as a tenant, but since his return to labor is higher, he can get by with a consumer/worker ratio as high as six or seven—a ratio that is not naturally found except among widows. Even in the latter case, by renting land out the landowning widow can obtain in-come sufficient for subsistence. Thus, the productivity of land and labor is a limiting factor only for tenant farmers, and even then only because levels of productivity were low due to the unavailability of fertilizer. Large landowners, on the other hand, ran into the opposite problem; the amount of land they owned might exceed what they could cultivate with household labor. In such a case, of course, the land can be rented out, but the return on investment in land is lower than when the land is cultivated with household labor. Where alternatives to subsistence farming and alternatives to investment in land exist, the rural peasant has less incentive to invest his capital resources in land once the amount of land that can be cultivated by family labor is exceeded. In such a situation, which has been approximated in recent years within South Korea, land ownership should be concentrated within a narrow, ecologically defined range.

During the colonial period, those who owned no means of production lacked opportunities for industrial wage labor and, because of high population densities that made land short relative to the size of the agricultural labor force, were driven by consumption needs to pay rents at such high levels that nearly their entire surplus was confiscated. In such a situation, owners of land could make more profit from rental property than from investment in industry (Suh 1978:85), and prices were driven so high relative to productivity that it was virtually impossible for the landless to accumulate enough capital to acquire land. Those with a surplus were likely to invest in rental land, usury, and leisure. The proletarianization that Kautsky thought should be the result of industrialization took place at this time in Korea—not because of industrialization, but because of its lack. We can see, then, that because of the multiple interrelationships between social, economic, and ecological factors, the adaptive requirements of the household imposed by the system do not always lead to simple, invariable results.

As a unit of consumption the household requires land to produce its subsistence needs; as a unit of production it needs land to put household labor to work. If we hold constant other variables, such as the productivity of land or labor, patterns of land tenure, or household organization, we can specify the minimum and maximum adaptive farm sizes. The minimum amount of land a household needs for subsistence is determined by the productivity of land and labor, land-tenure relations, and the number of consumers in the household. There is no maximum amount of land a household can use. Since one gets diminishing returns to capital investment once land has to be rented rather than owner-cultivated, however, the maximum efficient farm size is determined primarily by the productivity of household labor, as Chayanov predicted (1966:92).

Since land-tenure relations determine the amount of labor a household can use at the maximum rate of return, however, they influence the size and composition of household. People are encouraged to migrate when household landholdings are meager, and to remain in the village when household landholdings are more substantial. Improved agricultural techniques introduced since 1955 have enabled villagers to increase their productivity for land and for labor, so farmers can support themselves on less land. A good deal of labor once useful in agriculture has been freed in this way for alternative occupations and more individuals can now migrate from the household without jeopardizing household subsistence. Although this new migration from the household has been a potent force in changing the size and composition of rural households, it does not signal a fundamental change in principles of family organization, but only a change in strategies for the allocation of labor.

We thus find that principles of family organization and the structural requirements of farm households influence the distribution of land, but that the distribution of land also influences the size and composition of farm families. Opportunities for industrial employment outside the village have given people alternatives to farming, moreover, and made it possible to leave agriculture if the return to labor is not adequate. These choices have both encouraged investment in improvements that enhance labor productivity in agriculture, and provided a place for labor released by these investments. Urban opportunities for work are fundamentally different from rural ones because they do not require the same access to capital that the most productive forms of agriculture require. They are not as highly seasonal as agricultural wage labor, and one does not have to be a member of a fully functioning household organized as a unit of production and consumption to take advantage of them. Rural households can make use of urban wage labor opportunities to send surplus household members into productive occupations with little capital expense. This gives them both the means to reduce household size and the incentive to invest in modern agricultural inputs that will increase the productivity of household labor in agriculture. The peasant farmers of Sangongni can now contemplate a host of new strategies for the deployment of labor. They can migrate to the city and become wage laborers, they can diversify and found branches in the city to make use of some household labor and retain other branches in the village to make use of the family lands, or they can remain in the village and adjust their landholdings to the labor force they have available. They have choices in how they will respond to new social forces.

Thus, although Sangongni itself has not been urbanized or industrialized, villagers have been induced to change their strategies for the allocation of household labor and capital. The opportunities provided by industrialization have made considerations of the return on household labor more important than in the past. Even so, it is village social traditions that have made villagers think of the corporate household as the basic unit of accounting, and by defining the basic rights and duties of household members to one another to a large extent determined the functional requirements that shape household adaptive strategies. The migration out of the village that has accompanied urbanization is as much a consequence of the needs of the village household as it is a response to industrialization. Reduction in household size and increase in farm size are strategies only made rational by changes in farm technology within the context of corporate household structure.

Since migration of families and individuals from the village has made possible changes in farm size, and since farm size affects the amount of labor that can be used at the highest return by the household, these strategies designed to deal with present realities promise to induce more change in the future. It is quite possible that if Sangongni farm households remain family labor farms without significant mechanization, rising farm sizes will cause an increase in household size in the future. If significant mechanization is introduced, on the other hand, the relationship between farm size and family size may disappear. Whatever the future holds, however (and we cannot rule out significant structural change), those changes in social organization observed in the immediate past seem to have been due to changes in strategies in the allocation of labor and capital, rather than changes in the rules of social structure. Households are still constituted as corporate, patrilineal, extended families. Many successors to the house headship have migrated from the village, but this is more likely evidence of household diversification or stepwise migration strategies than the breakdown of a social structure based on organized corporate stem families. The obligation of eldest sons to support their parents in their old age, for example, remains legally enforceable in Korea. Unlike modern Japan where the traditional corporate household, the *ie*, has been abolished as a legal entity, the modern Korean legal code preserves the corporate *ka,* even though *chip* strategies of adaptation have been modified in response to new circumstances.

Change and Explanation in Anthropology

Although I would not wish to argue that social structure never changes, it seems likely that Sangongni is not the only place in the world where change in social organization has been the result of changing strategies brought about by changing circumstances within a stable social structure. The findings of this work have a bearing on a number of questions of explanation of general interest to anthropologists.

Systems and Causality

Throughout this analysis of social change in Sangongni we have been at pains to demonstrate the intricate mutual influences of multiple factors upon each other. As mentioned in chapter 1, the establishment of strict linear causality requires that the independent, that is causal variables, satisfy four criteria: (1) they must be contiguous to their effect; (2) they must precede their effect in time; (3) the relationship must be invariant, and (4) the relationship must be asymmetrical, that is, the relationship between cause and effect cannot be reversible, as in feedback relationships (Nagel 1961:74–75). Although some of our variables satisfy the first three criteria, none satisfies all four. We can say with confidence, for example, that the size of landholdings is at least partially a consequence of household size, since the amount of land bought or sold between 1977 and 1983 was proportional to the size of the household in 1977 (thus satisfying criteria 1 through 3). Since migration strategies also are conditioned by the amount of land already owned by the household, however, we can also say that household size is a consequence of the amount of land held. The criterion of asymmetry is not met and neither variable can be considered truly causal, even though there is no doubt as to their correlation.

This difficulty in finding a causal explanation for social change in Sangongni is due to the systems nature of the interrelationships. Rather than being related as independent and dependent variables, the social forces of Sangongni consist of multiple strings of dependent variables connected to each other in a system. Although all variables of the system are mutually adjusted to each other and will readjust if one variable is suddenly changed, this mutual adjustment also has the effect of muting and hindering radical change.

When doing a synchronic study of a social or ecological system, one usually has only one measurement of such factors as productivity or population. This often leaves no choice but to consider these factors constant, even though they may actually be variable. If the system is simple enough, it may appear that these "constants" have, in fact, "caused" some of the characteristics of the social system thought to be variable in the short run. Diachronic study of the same system, however, may reveal these constants or causes to be as variable in the long run as other factors. Once these constants are included as variables in the system their causal status comes into doubt. We showed in chapter 5 how the energy flow of the household consists of systematically related dependent variables, but systems relationships are not confined to the internal structure of the household. In fact, the mutual dependence we find among relevant socioeconomic variables throughout our analysis shows the same systemic characteristics as the variables of internal household organization: none is constant or free from feedback relationships and thus act as the cause of change in the social system. We have criticized Kautsky, Chayanov, and Steward for trying to find linear causal determinants of social change that ranged from forces of production, to family cycle, to technology applied in an environment, yet careful reading of the works of each of these writers shows they had an intuitive grasp of the systemic nature of social organization that was not incorporated into their formal theoretical statements. The tools of systems theory that are now available hold out the possibility of a more rigorous and explicit exploration of causality by multiple variables and feedback relations, yet many of those interested in ecological questions or the causes and consequences of social change have moved in the opposite direction (Harris 1979; Ross 1978). The social system of Sangongni simply cannot be interpreted as the simple effect of a limited number of causes. It is the goals toward which strategies are directed by individual actors that give coherence and direction to change in the social system (Bennett 1976: 21–22).

Adaptation and Choice

Given the mutual dependence of major explanatory variables upon one another, then, it is unlikely that any one factor, such as the need for adaptation—even adaptation to new circumstances—can explain social change. It may be that failure to find the cause of the Sangongni social system in environmental adaptation lies in impractically stringent criteria for causality, rather than the inherent characteristics of the Sangongni socioeconomic system, yet even by the less stringent criteria outlined in chapter 2, we are unable to assign a causal role to adaptation. It will be recalled that these requirements involve establishing that a crucial adaptive problem can be solved by one and only one strategy. Given the number of interrelated variables involved in the adaptive system of Sangongni, of course, precise delineation of adaptive strategies is not simple. If we consider the changes that households in the village went through between 1977 and 1983, however, several strategies can be discerned.

Most households reduced their size and labor force over the study period regardless of their status in 1977. The reasons for this, having to do with increases in the productivity of land and labor, have already been dealt with. Those households that remained in the village and neither bought nor sold land increased their efficiency somewhat as they cultivated the same amount of land with higher productivity and less labor. Other households, however, seemed to follow one of two different strategies: migration or increase in landholdings. Although migrants from the village, as a whole, owned less land than those who remained in the village, it was impossible to predict to a statistically significant level which households would leave the village by 1983 on the basis of the characteristics of those households in 1977. Those households that departed included large landowners, tenants, educated and uneducated, those with close relatives already in town, and those with no relatives already in town. Those households that remained also included houses with these characteristics. When household behavior was considered over the seven-year period from 1976 to 1983, however, some households were clearly gradually selling their land and preparing for departure from the village. Other households that started out with almost precisely similar characteristics in 1977, on the other hand, were clearly adding land to their holdings and increasing the amount of labor they could put to good use. In other words, although the 1977 household circumstances influenced strategies of adaptation, a certain latitude in devising them was allowed. Clear and consistent differences could be discerned in the strategies of households observed over time. Strategies for adaptation are clearly conditioned by the adaptive requirements of the household, but these conditions do not determine which household strategy must be selected. Villagers have a choice in deciding on their adaptive strategy.

It seems then that the conditions within which the villagers of San-gongni live influence but do not determine their response to social forces, even when the shaping effect of social structure is taken into account. This finding puts into doubt the utility of the early cultural ecological approach advocated by Julian Steward in the 1950s. He once defined the goals of this approach as follows: "The problem is to ascertain whether the adjustments of human societies to their en-vironments require particular modes of behavior or whether they per-mit latitude for a certain range of possible behavior patterns."

Freilich (1963) has already observed that Afro-Caribbean and Asian villages in Trinidad with identical technoenvironmental bases need not converge in other aspects of their social organization. The material from Sangongni suggests it is necessary to go further: even within a village with a single cultural tradition and technoenviron-mental base, there is so wide a range of variation in the possible strat-egies of adaptation to the circumstances in which the villagers find themselves that the necessity of adaptation to the environment has low explanatory value.

Ecological Variables in Complex Societies

Does the low explanatory value of the necessity of adaptation to the natural environment in Sangongni mean that ecological variables are irrelevant for the understanding of the social organization of complex societies? It is a truism that human societies have evolved from domi-nation by nature to domination of nature (Bennett 1976:5–6). The more complex the society, then, the less adaptation to the environment should matter. While numerous studies of adaptation to the environ-ment of hunters and gatherers or horticulturalists have yielded impor-tant insights, ecological concepts, when applied to complex societies at all, have tended to be used metaphorically (Barth 1956; Ellen 1982:90–91). This ignoring of ecological variables, however, may be a mistake. If, as Chayanov noted, agriculture on family labor farms is conditioned by family subsistence needs and family labor require-ments (and I think the evidence from Sangongni that this is so is very strong), these needs and requirements can often be most usefully de-fined by reference to the flow of energy in a system, as was attempted in chapters 4 and 5 of this study.

Though the flows of energy do not cause the system, neither are they simply negative constraints. Rather, they are one of a number of interactive elements in a complicated feedback system whose role in the social system must be assessed for a complete understanding of that system to emerge. The peasants of Korea during the colonial period, for example, were certainly alienated from their land partially because of exploitation by the Japanese, but the efficacy of that exploitation in proletarianizing the peasants depended upon a farming system with specific levels of productivity of land and labor and specific rural population densities. The postwar land reforms reversed peasant alienation from the land, but this reversal would only have been temporary if the productivity of land and labor had not improved and if rural population densities had not been reduced by migration from the countryside to take urban jobs. The larger society in which the peasants have been situated has conditioned their adaptations, but the consequences of the influence of the larger society on rural agriculturalists has partially depended on ecological factors.

Adaptation and History

Finally we come to the role of history in conditioning adaptations to the environment. Functionally oriented anthropologists, with their synchronic, holistic approach, have been particularly concerned with the interrelation of social institutions at single time periods. This point of view, of course, has provided us with numerous insights in the way that social, environmental, religious, and cultural institutions are integrated into operating wholes. As has been pointed out by J. Friedman (1974:457) among others, functionalist explanations have a tendency toward circularity and have not been very successful dealing with the questions of explanation or social change. This is not because functional explanations of change are intrinsically impossible, but rather because the necessity of functions can be established only in obvious cases and with the greatest difficulty in synchronic analysis (Dore 1961:845–46).

In one sense, this study is yet another contribution to functional analysis. That is, we have been very interested in the interrelationship of variables that mutually influence each other and how the functional requirements of institutions might limit the amount of change that institutions can undergo in the short run. We have shown, for example, that there is a correlation between farm size and family labor force, and that the size and composition of families observed in Sangongni is partially dependent upon the amount of land available and the tenure conditions under which it can be obtained. In this way, we might be tempted to infer a neat homeostatic system in which farm size, land tenure, and family size all mutually limit one another. In fact, however, the land-tenure patterns of the village are not the effect of processes that can now be observed going on in the village, but rather are an artifact of the past when social, political, and economic conditions were different from those that could be observed in 1977 or 1983. Present land-tenure patterns are not primarily the result of present-day inheritance patterns nor of present-day processes of land acquisition and sale, but rather are the result of a deliberate attempt to foster landholding among farm households through land reform legislation. Although the land reform program itself did not provide most of the present-day farmers of Sangongni with their land, if we can believe villagers' statements of 1983, the depressed price of land that was a direct result of the land reform and rent control first allowed most of the present-day landowners of the village to acquire substantial amounts of land. Those who acquired land during that period are now in a position to continue the acquisition of land, but the landless farmers of 1977 or 1983 are unlikely to even get a first foothold on land, since prices are relatively much higher now than they were in the late 1940s and early 1950s.

The size and structure of households observed in the village in 1977 and 1983 and the strategies of migration or residence in the village during these periods were all seen to be strongly conditioned by patterns of land tenure observable in the village during the fieldwork period. Since these patterns of land tenure were not, in fact, created in response to the conditions of 1977 or 1983, but in response to conditions in the past that were materially different, those institutions observed in 1977 and 1983 that are conditioned by land-tenure patterns are, in fact, conditioned by history. If the land-tenure history of the village had been different from what it actually was, the social organization of the village in 1977 and 1983 would have been different. If the social organization of the village is shaped and constrained by present-day socioeconomic forces, it is also shaped and constrained by past socioeconomic forces. History is, in fact, indispensable for understanding adaptation to the environment and other functional relationships that traditionally have been studied in a synchronic framework.

Appendix
1983 Data for Sangongni Households

Occupation	Age of House Head	Type of Succession	Type of Family	Family Size	Adult Male Equivalents	Adult Worker Units	Land Owned	Land Cultivated
F	47	2	2	2	2.00	2.00	99.30	165.50
F	57	1	3	5	5.00	4.30	99.30	331.00
F	38	1	6	7	4.90	3.10	162.19	162.19
F	44	1	6	7	4.90	2.40	59.58	92.68
M	32	1	7	6	4.30	3.30	112.54	33.10
F	42	2	3	5	3.90	2.70	99.30	99.30
F	68	2	2	2	1.60	0.60	79.44	13.24
F	52	1	4	4	4.00	3.90	251.56	251.56
F	48	1	3	4	3.40	2.80	148.95	215.15
F	73	1	4	8	5.50	3.10	446.85	331.00
M	51	3	6	5	4.60	3.50	231.70	185.36
M	30	1	6	5	3.50	2.00	211.84	33.10
F	52	1	6	5	3.80	2.10	264.80	89.37
F	44	2	3	3	2.80	2.50	92.68	139.02
F	42	2	3	5	3.70	2.60	43.03	125.78
M	50	1	6	6	4.10	2.50	99.30	99.30
F	48	2	3	6	4.60	3.00	0.0	99.30
M	37	1	3	7	5.00	3.40	0.0	46.34
F	45	2	3	5	3.90	2.70	0.0	119.16

Appendix 1983 Data for Sangongni Households (continued)

Occupation	Age of House Head	Type of Succession	Type of Family	Family Size	Adult Male Equivalents	Adult Worker Units	Land Owned	Land Cultivated
F	68	2	4	6	5.00	3.70	0.0	66.20
M	71	4	8	2	1.80	1.00	33.10	59.58
F	69	4	3	2	1.80	1.00	178.74	13.24
F	48	1	5	3	2.80	2.00	264.80	264.80
F	53	2	3	4	3.70	2.90	261.49	261.49
F	25	1	3	4	2.50	2.00	86.06	112.54
F	45	1	2	4	3.70	2.90	205.22	152.26
F	37	1	6	7	4.20	2.70	182.05	182.05
F	57	5	1	1	1.00	0.80	46.34	0.0
F	27	4	2	2	2.00	2.00	0.0	142.33
F	27	1	3	4	2.50	2.00	82.75	115.85
F	43	1	3	4	3.10	2.50	0.0	38.07
M	65	1	6	6	4.40	2.00	0.0	33.10
F	31	1	5	4	3.80	2.90	182.05	182.05
F	50	2	3	5	4.40	3.70	99.30	99.30
F	31	1	7	7	4.70	3.90	112.54	132.40
F	69	2	3	4	3.60	2.20	79.44	145.64
M	50	4	6	3	2.60	1.50	82.75	82.75
F	64	2	4	5	3.70	3.00	105.92	105.92
F	59	2	3	4	3.20	2.00	165.50	165.50
F	30	1	6	7	4.80	3.10	148.95	148.95
F	55	1	3	4	3.80	3.10	33.10	33.10

F	41	6	3	4	3.30	2.60	0.0	92.68
F	56	2	3	3	2.80	2.30	165.50	165.50
F	37	1	6	6	3.40	2.00	99.30	99.30
F	56	1	2	2	2.00	1.90	142.33	142.33
F	45	2	3	5	3.90	2.80	122.47	122.47
F	66	2	3	4	3.60	2.90	59.58	72.82
F	48	2	3	5	3.80	2.60	132.40	191.98
R	71	2	1	2	1.60	0	0.0	0.0
F	60	1	3	3	2.80	2.50	0.0	132.40
R	76	4	1	1	0.80	0	132.40	0.0
R	62	4	1	1	0.80	0.60	0.0	0.0
F	64	2	2	2	1.60	0.60	59.58	59.58
F	57	1	2	2	2.00	1.60	66.20	66.20
F	48	1	6	6	4.90	2.90	148.95	148.95
F	30	1	6	4	3.20	3.00	125.78	178.74
F	41	2	3	5	4.50	3.80	132.40	132.40
F	22	1	5	2	1.80	1.60	46.34	46.34
F	26	1	6	6	3.90	2.80	0.0	99.30
F	51	2	3	3	2.50	2.00	165.50	165.50
F/M	46	1	6	4	3.30	2.00	662.00	522.98
F	47	2	3	3	2.80	2.50	132.30	132.30
F	50	2	3	4	3.80	3.50	139.02	201.91
M	39	2	3	5	2.90	2.00	0.0	0.0
F	56	4	5	2	2.00	1.90	92.68	92.68
M	44	0	3	2	1.40	1.00	3.31	3.31
F	28	4	3	3	2.20	2.00	0.0	52.96
F	45	1	3	3	2.70	2.30	82.75	182.05
F	24	2	3	3	2.20	2.00	0.0	132.40
F	20	1	7	4	3.30	2.60	99.30	115.85

Appendix 1983 Data for Sangongni Households (*continued*)

Occupation	Age of House Head	Type of Succession	Type of Family	Family Size	Adult Male Equivalents	Adult Worker Units	Land Owned	Land Cultivated
F	47	2	3	4	3.70	3.40	0.0	86.06
R	70	1	2	2	1.0	0	211.84	0.0
M	48	1	5	2	1.80	1.00	364.10	0.0
F	46	2	3	3	2.70	2.30	234.18	234.18
F	73	1	4	7	4.90	2.90	19.86	119.16
F	65	1	8	3	2.60	1.40	294.59	228.39
F	56	4	1	1	1.00	1.00	105.92	39.72
F	46	2	3	5	4.20	3.10	19.86	52.96
R	73	2	4	4	2.40	0.70	231.70	0.0
F	39	3	6	5	4.20	3.00	231.70	231.70
F	67	1	4	8	5.60	3.50	0.0	115.85
F	47	1	3	4	3.20	2.30	145.64	165.50
F	38	1	6	7	4.30	2.60	165.50	165.50
F	42	1	3	4	3.00	2.20	0.0	165.50
F	27	2	3	3	2.10	2.00	109.23	109.23
F	70	1	2	2	1.60	0.60	129.09	129.09
F	44	2	3	7	4.80	3.10	168.81	155.57
F	69	1	4	6	4.70	3.10	297.90	297.90
M	43	2	3	4	3.40	2.70	0.0	0.0
M	54	2	2	2	2.00	2.00	0.0	0.0
F	28	2	3	4	2.40	2.00	0.0	112.54
M	58	1	3	4	3.80	3.20	0.0	59.58

| F | 30 | 1 | 3 | 2.30 | 2.00 | 0.0 | 211.84 |
| F | 42 | 1 | 7 | 4.40 | 3.00 | 0.0 | 185.36 |

CODING KEYS

Occupation
F   Farming without significant nonfarm source of income
M   Significant nonfarm source of income
R   Retired

Type of Succession
1. Eldest son succession
2. Younger son *pun'ga*
3. Succession by adoption
4. Legal household-head resides elsewhere
5. Female household head
6. Stepchild *pun'ga*

Type of Family Resident in Household
1. Single person
2. Married couple
3. Married couple and unmarried children
4. Married couple and one married child (with or without grandchildren)
5. Married couple (no children) and husband's mother
6. Married couple (and children) and husband's mother
7. Household with resident collateral relatives
8. Other

NOTE: Land values given in ares

Notes

Chapter 1

1. See Osgood (1951) for detailed descriptions of agricultural implements and work patterns in rural Korea as observed in 1947.

2. See Brandt and Lee (1981:83) for a quantitative measure of this phenomenon in Kyŏnggi and South Ch'ungch'ŏng Provinces.

3. *Studies in the Modernization of The Republic of Korea: 1945–1975* (Cambridge: Harvard University Press).

4. Other aspects of Marxist modeling of societies are discussed in the following chapter.

Chapter 2

1. See Goodenough (1956) and Fischer (1958) on this point, however.

2. It is important to note that the rationality mentioned here is a "rationality of agents" rather than a "rationality of systems" (Godelier 1972:8). As such it is a property of individual actors operating within the social system and is not intended to refer to the social system itself, whose rationality could only be assessed in relation to some external goal.

3. See Janelli and Janelli (1982:129–35) for discussion of the status assertion characteristics of Korean lineages.

4. It is true that in rare cases, where the previous attainment of social status by the lineage allowed the attainment of high office by a lineage mate, the profit from attaining office could be seen as a motivation for lineage organization. In this case, profit goals and social status goals are not mutually exclusive. Chances of this happening were quite small, however, since a small group

249

of lineages in the capital virtually monopolized high office (Wagner 1974). The vast majority of Korean lineages, on the other hand, were located in rural areas and hadn't boasted an officeholder in several hundred years.

5. The point of view outlined here is similar in many respects to that of Anthony Carter who distinguishes "patterns of observable social arrangements" from "cultural principles of household formation and management," calling the former the household structure and the latter the household system (Carter 1984:47–48). His term *household structure* corresponds to my *social organization,* and his *household system* to my *social structure.* As do I, Carter sees the social organization of households (his household structure) as generated by underlying systems of rules and strategies (ibid.:49).

6. I do not mean to deny, of course, the importance of personality and of symbolic behavior, for understanding social life. Such behavior is simply not the focus of this study.

7. Though the models of social structure referred to here are quite similar in concept to mechanical models as defined by Lévi-Strauss (1963:283), I have avoided using this term. The word *mechanical* might give readers a false idea that I believe behavior modeled in such a way to be fully determined. The possibility of multiple goals, however, prevents this.

8. This "fundamentalist" interpretation of Marx is less complex than other explanations that might be inferred from various of his other writings (cf. Rader 1979:56–61), but it has the virtue of being widely regarded as the basis of his theory of history. Since the object of this chapter is to develop a vocabulary and theoretical framework adequate for explaining social change in Sangongni, I have not attempted to encompass all interpretations of Marx and Engels that could legitimately be derived from their works. Rather, I have used certain common interpretations, as found in Kautsky's *Die Agrarfrage,* as a vehicle for introducing the question of how peasants should respond to industrialization and for raising problems of the logic of explanation in anthropology. There are some recent elaborations and interpretations of Marx that address many of the problems I have raised here, but the writings of Marx and Engels are too various for a single unified theory on which everyone could agree. Rader (1979), whose intention was only to try to correctly understand what Marx himself had written, finds three different models of society in Marx's work. If we add the interpretations, revisions, and extensions of Marx's work done by others, the number of possible Marxist theories of society becomes enormous and would require a book-length work to sort out.

9. This correspondence, of course, is an ultimate one. Most Marxist theorists allow a certain amount of time for the relations of production to be transformed to correspond with the level of development of the forces of production. Although it is entirely legitimate to allow for a lag between the development of the forces of production and the transformation of relations of production, the conditions under which this obtains must be specified. If this is not done, the phenomenon of lag might be used to explain away any deviation from what is predicted by Marxist theory. By making falsification of the

hypothesized relation between forces and relations of production impossible in principle, such a procedure would endanger the scientific status of Marxist theory.

10. Steward does not cite Marx in any of his major publications. I am not trying to argue that Steward's concept of cultural core is identical to Marx's idea of the mode of production. My purpose is to show that the logical structure of his explanations is almost identical to that of Marx, with the main difference between the two lying in the importance of the idea of adaptation to the natural environment. Harris recognizes the similarity of Steward to Marx and attributes it to the influence of Karl Wittfogel's ideas of hydraulic civilization, which are derived explicitly from Marx's concept of the Asiatic mode of production (Harris 1968:674).

11. In this work, *causality* is always used to refer to a relationship that meets the above four criteria. Some call this concept of causality *lineal causality* and distinguish it from *circular causality* or *spiral causality*, which is akin to the feedback in closed loop systems. To avoid confusion, I refer to the latter concept either as a "dialectical relationship" (when discussing Marxist frameworks), or a "feedback relationship."

12. White's formula is $E \times T = C$, where E is the amount of energy harnessed per capita per year, T is the efficiency of the tools used, and C represents the degree of cultural development.

13. Although Harris's formula for technoenvironmental efficiency, $E = m \times t \times r \times e$ (where E is the number of calories that a system produces annually, m is the number of food producers, t the number of hours of work per food worker, r the calories expended per food producer per hour, and e the number of calories of food produced for each calorie expended in food production) has potential for use as an operationalization of the concept of adaptation, he has never, to my knowledge, used it that way in any of his numerous articles.

14. Chayanov assumes in his work that farm size can easily be adjusted to family need. In some communities this was done through a periodic redistribution of the land. In other cases Chayanov thought that rental arrangements would serve the same purpose. This point of view, of course, does not take into account that returns to labor are lower on rented than owned land. See chapter 7 for an analysis of this factor for Sangongni.

15. In 1976, the amount of land cultivated per capita per household could be predicted by the following equation: $LPH = 16.7 + 16.5$ (consumers/workers) (significance of $F = 0.0555$). In 1983, it could be predicted by the equation: $LPH = 23.2 + 25.0$ (consumers/workers) (significance of $F = 0.0469$).

16. In 1976, the amount of land cultivated per adult male equivalent per household could be predicted by the following equation: $LPA = 55.8 - 6.1 \times$ adult male equivalents (significance of $F = 0.000$). In 1983, the equation was: $LPA = 66.3 - 6.9 \times$ adult male equivalents (significance of $F = 0.0066$).

17. Villagers who belong to the major lineages that maintain autumn tomb-side ancestral rites (about 68 percent of the households of the village in 1977) consider themselves, and are considered by others in the area, to be of yang-ban (aristocrat) background. Although informants say that in the past there were servile households (*ha-in*) in the village whose members had to defer in all respects to the householders to whom they were attached, such households no longer exist. In the past, aristocrats would not carry the village funeral bier or engage in other demeaning occupations, but today they do. Former aristocrat/commoner distinctions no longer affect everyday interaction in terms of forms of address, clothing, or the bearing of funeral biers. Families that maintain autumn tombside ancestor worship, however, generally avoid inter-marrying with families that don't.

18. By a corporate family, I mean one which has fixed membership and a mechanism of succession. See chapter 6 and Sorensen (1984; 1986:139–41) for more detail.

Chapter 3

1. It is common for hamlets or villages to own ritual paraphernalia such as funeral biers, and there is usually some land or resources around the villages that is considered "village land," but these resources are not great. In San-gongni in 1977, each hamlet had a consumer cooperative run by the hamlet women's association. The three hamlets on the west side of the river main-tained one bier, and Overbridge maintained another. By 1983, the number of cooperatives had been reduced to two with the three hamlets west of the river maintaining one, and Overbridge maintaining another. Village "Buddhists" (*pulgyo*, or Buddhism, is the most common name villagers use to denote the folk religion, though some villagers distinguish Buddhism from folk religious "superstition," or *misin*) worship collectively a number of gods enshrined on the highest peak of a nearby mountain, but this worship involves people from all hamlets.

2. Before 1894, Korean society was divided into four estates (aristocrat, middle person, commoner, and base person) based on descent, education, and life style. There was a certain correlation between one's estate membership and one's economic position, since one's liability to taxes and corvée was partly determined by estate classification, but this correlation was very in-exact. Korean folklore abounds with stories of aristocrats who were so poor they hardly had enough to eat (but would not engage in manual labor), and base people such as shamans who were quite wealthy. Although these four

estates are often called "classes," since economic criteria were secondary in determining status group membership, and since each status group had different rights and duties within the Korean state, "estate" is a more accurate term than "class." In traditional times, three of the four estates were represented in the village, i.e., aristocrat, commoner, and base person. The middle-person estate was found chiefly in administrative centers.

3. For a detailed discussion of local government and rural development in South Korea in the early seventies, see Aqua (1974).

4. In 1976, according to the county statistical yearbook, 7.3 percent of the rice harvested in Sangok Township passed through government hands (5.7 percent through the marketing of the cooperative, with less than 1 percent going for land tax paid in kind and for fertilizer paid for in kind). About half of the total crop would have been consumed at home, so these figures can be doubled to show what proportion of *marketed* rice was distributed through government agencies.

5. Market schedules are known by the last digit of the solar calendar date upon which they convene. Flatland is a 4–9 market; that is, the fourth, ninth, fourteenth, nineteenth, twenty-fourth, and twenty-ninth of any month were market days. Broadmart is a 2–7 market that meets on the second, seventh, twelfth, seventeenth, twenty-second, and twenty-seventh of any month. Thus within any ten-day period, there were markets at either Flatland or Broadmart on those days ending with 2, 4, 7, or 9.

6. See Brandt and Lee (1981:102) for more detailed information on what rural Koreans see as the cause of improving living standards.

7. For example, labor for transplanting rice could be gained through paying wages, through labor exchange, through labor gangs, or through having a live-in agricultural laborer (see p. 69).

8. Although the ordinary Korean language lacks such a word, there are several Sino-Korean coinages that are similar in meaning. *T'oji* (land) includes nonagricultural land such as house sites, and thus doesn't qualify. *Kyŏngji* (plowed land) is quite close, however, as is the word *chŏndap*, which means literally "rainfall field and irrigated riceland." Both of these, however, are literary words that a peasant would not use spontaneously.

9. Actually, there are significant differences in how readily people report on all types of land. Interviewing in 1983, when I was being especially careful to distinguish types of land and whether the land was rented in or out, or had been inherited, people were often surprised at the details I asked for. Very few people refused to tell me about irrigated riceland. Some who told me about their riceland were hesistant to tell me about their rainfall field, however, even though it is less valuable by far than riceland. The reason for this, I think, is that the amount of riceland one owns is a socially significant variable that is widely known and used among villagers to classify their neighbors socially, but other kinds of land, being less socially significant, are less known to one's neighbors and thus something worth keeping to oneself.

10. These measures were inaugurated by Public Law 1778 of April 28,

1966, as amended on May 21, 1968, and were implemented by Presidential Proclamation 2803 of November 11, 1966, as amended on March 22, 1969.

11. Although wood is the commonest fuel in mountain districts where forest is common, alternative fuels must be used in other districts. Rice straw may be used for cooking, though it is difficult to heat a house with it. In those areas accessible to motorized transport, *yŏnt'an,* large bricks of soft coal held together by clay, are the most common fuel.

12. According to the county statistical yearbook of 1976, for Sangongni's township of seventeen villages, the proportion of total seeded land devoted to various types of crops was as follows: 32.9 percent rice, 30.2 percent pulses, 9.6 percent barley and wheat, 7.9 percent vegetables (most important were daikon radish, Chinese cabbage, and red pepper), 6.8 percent miscellaneous grains (most important, maize), 4.8 percent tubers (mostly white potatoes, but including sweet potatoes), 3.9 percent tobacco, 3.8 percent special crops (most important, sesame and perilla), with less than 1 percent each devoted to fruit and medicinal crops. Of these crops, all but tobacco and medicinal crops (and a few of the specialized crops not grown in Sangongni) are processed and used within the agricultural household, as well as sold for cash.

13. *Makkŏlli* is often termed "rice wine" in English, but as it is a fermented drink made of yeast (*nuruk*), wheat, and rice, is it more accurately termed beer (Royal Anthropological Institute 1951:246).

14. These figures were calculated from a sample of 549 farm households from throughout Korea surveyed by the Research Department of the Bank of Korea (Han'guk ŭnhaeng chosabu 1963). According to this survey, households harvested an average of 2,851 *sŭng* of paddy with an average of 855 man-hours of labor. Husked rice (which converts from paddy at a rate of 0.51 by volume) was selling at 13,682 *hwan* per 100 liters at that time and the official exchange rate was 650 *hwan* to the dollar (ibid. 1961). Households harvested an average of 601 *sŭng* of barley with an average of 468 man-hours of work. Husked barley (which converts from unhusked at the rate of 0.55 by volume) was selling at 8,525 *hwan* per 100 liters. Although when figured in money these returns seem exceedingly small, each hour of work on rice at these rates provided enough rice to feed three persons for one day at a time when 80 percent of people's caloric intake depended upon rice and other grains.

15. Agricultural workers have noted resistance to the use of potash by Korean farmers (hence its inclusion in composite fertilizer). Whether this resistance is related to Korean farmers already putting ash manufactured at home on the soil in their *t'oebi* is difficult to tell.

16. Some of the newly introduced strains of high-yield rice are *japonica-indica* crosses.

17. Since the end of World War II, women have gradually taken a larger and larger role in agriculture (Kim Chusuk 1985:213–15). In most periurban areas where male labor is expensive and in short supply, the bulk of rice trans-

plantation is done by women. In outlying areas, however, men commonly still do most of the rice transplantation.

18. Of course, if the division and scattering of fields is too severe, what is gained in timing of labor may be lost in travel from house to field and back. As long as one's fields are not too distant, however, this statement holds.

19. If a September typhoon hits, the rice can be beaten down and washed away by torrential rains, so if a typhoon threatens, it is extremely urgent to get the rice in as fast as possible.

20. The sole exception to this is households made up of single men (all of whom were teachers) who ate their meals in one of the winehouses and thus did not have to prepare their own food.

21. There are adults today in Sangongni and many other Korean villages who, in spite of high native ability, have never made very good farmers. Because of their high status background during the period up through the mid-sixties when agricultural labor was cheap, they often used live-in laborers to do their farm work, and never developed good work habits. It has been a common observation in villages where former yangban and commoners both reside that the commoners have often done better economically than the yangban. Many peasants of yangban background prefer to invest in the education of their children rather than in the improvement of their farms.

22. A survey of four villages in 1957 (Mills 1960) found that approximately 30 percent of the farm households had at least one cow or calf. Several of these were acquired by an arrangement in which a man feeds someone else's female calf until it reaches maturity and receives the first offspring as payment.

23. Bank of Korea, *Results of the Farm Household Economic Survey, 1958–1962*, Seoul. This was first pointed out by Cho (1963:78).

24. Vincent Brandt (1980:274) has noted, however, that there is often considerable village pressure to make loans to poor farmers who may need them for consumption purposes, and that in most cooperatives a certain number of these loans are quietly forgotten.

25. Wages have doubled whether calculated in terms of dollar value or of rice equivalents.

Chapter 4

1. The minimum amount of land necessary for the support of a person varies with the tenure status of that land. This aspect of the system will be dealt with more explicitly in chapter 7.

2. With the changes in the amount of manual labor that rural Koreans do (especially the women), one might assume that there have been changes in caloric need. While this may indeed be so, the amount of change caused by changes in work patterns is relatively small when compared to the total subsistence requirements, and our measurement of general dietary requirements are not, in any case, so precise that these differences will affect the conclusions we will use them for.

3. I have met Koreans who to this day cannot stand the taste of barley because it reminds them of times in the past when they had to substitute it for rice because of poverty.

4. Korean women universally say that *miyŏk kuk* (brown seaweed soup) is a good dish for postpartum mothers. Some women will also recommend meat. Seaweed, in fact, may be the poor woman's substitute for meat in a time of physiological stress. Dietary analysis has showed each 100 grams of dried brown seaweed has 12.7 grams of highly digestible protein (twice that of uncooked rice by weight), with a large number of the essential amino acids, 0.12 grams of thiamine, and 0.14 grams of riboflavin—two of the B vitamins most likely to be short in the rural Korean diet. When fresh, it is also a good source of vitamin C, though in mountain villages it is necessarily purchased in dried form.

5. According to the *Farm Household Economic Survey* for 1960 (Han'guk ŭnhaeng chosabu 1963) the percentage consumption of grains by volume was the following: rice 62.6 percent, barley 18.0 percent, miscellaneous wheats (chiefly wheat and buckwheat) 6.4 percent, pulses 4.6 percent, and miscellaneous grains (chiefly foxtail millet [*Setaria italica*], sorghum, broomcorn millet [*Panicum miliaceum*], sesame and maize) 3.0 percent. Although maize is widely grown in rural Korea, it is not eaten in large quantities. The varieties grown are tough and unpalatable, and used primarily as animal feed. Nevertheless, roast corn on the cob is found in rural areas as an occasional snack.

6. Most of the variation in the amount of consumption of different grains by month in the early 1960s as reported in the *Farm Household Economic Survey* (Han'guk ŭnhaeng chosabu 1963) can be predicted by a linear equation that uses as its independent variable the number of months since the harvest of that crop. As rice is the most important crop, one can get a high correlation coefficient on an equation simply using the number of months since the rice harvest as the independent variable. The equations for the major crop categories are as follows, with c standing for the consumption of the crop in question, and x the number of months since November, the peak of the rice harvest (all values are in liters, except for potatoes, which are in grams); rice $c = 106.2 - 7.0x$, $r^2 = 0.78$; barley $c = 12.8 + 6.1x$, $r^2 = 0.69$; wheat $c = 2.1 + 1.4x$, $r^2 = 0.78$; miscellaneous grains $c = 2.6 + 0.3x$, $r^2 = 0.39$; pulses $c = 9.7 - 1.2x$, $r^2 = 0.36$; potatoes $c = 279 - 17x$, $r^2 = 0.25$; ($p < 0.01$ in all cases).

These figures can be improved if a simultaneous equation using number of months since the rice harvest, and number of months since the barley harvest, and number of months since the main potato harvests in July and October are used as the independent variables, but the values for r^2 in the above equations are already substantial and their interpretation is straightforward enough to make the more complicated equations unnecessary.

When the rice has just been harvested and is abundant, total household consumption during this period is about 106 liters of uncooked rice, but as the time from the end of the rice harvest gets longer, consumption of rice decreases an average of 7 liters per month. Barley is a possible substitute for rice, but is not preferred. Thus barley consumption is inversely proportional to the number of months since the rice harvest: that is, rural Koreans ate 12.8 liters per month even at the peak of the rice harvest, but then ate 6.1 liters more for each month past the rice harvest even though these months (until June is reached) are even further past the barley harvest. Wheat and other miscellaneous grains show the same pattern as barley: they are possible substitutes for rice, but not preferred, so they are consumed increasingly as the rice supply is diminished.

Legumes, on the other hand, are similar to rice in the time of harvest. They are possible substitutes for rice to a certain extent, but their main use is in processed foods such as fermented bean paste (*toenjang*), bean curd, and soy sauce. The seasonality of their consumption depends more on the seasonality of women's labor patterns than anything else. Potatoes are eaten mostly in the winter, so they show the same pattern as rice.

7. Another reason for the heavy rice consumption during this period is that November and December are months of intense ritual activity. Weddings and betrothals are often held during these months, and the annual tombside ancestor worship ceremonies (*sije*) also take place at this time. Not only do the ceremonies themselves require the consumption of rice, but also the visiting of high status lineagemates to take part in local ceremonies can lead to high entertainment costs for prominent lineage elders.

8. The Recommended Daily Allowances used in this study are those in Passmore, Nicol, and Rao (1974) of the FAO for populations of approximately the stature and weight of the Koreans in Sangongni. RDA are conventionally set at about two standard deviations above what is believed to be the physiological minimum requirement, and thus are only an approximate guide to nutrition. Of course, these published requirements take no account of possible racial or adaptational variation in nutritional needs or tolerances.

9. Vitamin B-deficiency diseases such as beriberi were endemic to many rice-eating parts of the world where machine milling of rice was the norm before World War II. Although data for rural Korea on this point are sketchy, it seems that beriberi was not commonly found. There are two main reasons for this: most rural Koreans milled their rice by hand until the sixties, and hand-milled rice, being coarser than machine-milled, has a higher content of B vitamins, and although rural Koreans depend upon rice for a great number

of their calories, rice is habitually stretched by combining it with barley, beans, chestnuts, potatoes, and other food items that provide some of the nutrients that rice is lacking. See Williams (1961:226–27) on this point.

10. Based on observations in the village, I would guess that in most families in 1977, meat (primarily chicken, with occasional beef, pork, or dog) was prepared perhaps ten times a year. Each time meat was prepared (i.e., a chicken butchered, or some meat purchased), the dishes in which it was an ingredient might be consumed for several days, so perhaps 10 percent of the meals included animal protein in the average household.

11. The digestibility of various staples is as follows: rice 97.9; wheat 90.9; potatoes 89.0; buckwheat 82.7; sorghum 76.3; common bean 66.2 (Food and Agriculture Organization of the United Nations 1970).

12. Even as late as 1959, much grain was husked and polished by hand. Since food tables are based on an assumption of machine-polished rice, analysis based on these tables may seriously underestimate the amount of B vitamins actually consumed.

13. *Tchanji* used in this sense is dialectical. In Standard Korean, *tchanji* refers to radishes pickled in brine only.

14. If *kimch'i* is not kept below 9 degrees Celsius, it will lose all of its vitamin C by the third day (Yi Kiryŏl 1976:124). Urban residents often must keep their crocks on balconies where they are susceptible to changes in the weather. One such unseasonable warm spell came in the autumn of 1976 and for a few days urban residents faced the specter of losing their whole winter stock of *kimch'i,* in many cases worth several hundred dollars. Such a loss would have been catastrophic in many a family, but luckily the warm spell ended before this juncture was reached.

15. Fermented bean soupstock (*toenjang*) is a good source of protein, calcium, and, to a certain extent, of B vitamins.

16. Based on the work of Ki Yull Lee (1962), which preceded the data of the *Farm Household Economic Survey* by one year, I have assumed that rice and barley together account for 86.5 percent of the calories consumed in January, 87.5 percent of those consumed in April, 77.8 percent of those consumed in August, and 67.9 percent of those consumed in October. The percentage of consumption of other months was calculated by interpolation from these months.

17. Each 1.8 liters of rice was assumed to contribute 4968 kilocalories to the family, and each 1.8 liters of barley 4921. Monthly figures were converted into daily figures and divided by the mean number of AME per household.

18. Energy expenditure was calculated as $500kcal + 360kcal/hour * W + 100kcal/hour * (16 - W)$ where W is the number of hours worked in agriculture per day. Sleeping time was thus seen as requiring 500 kilocalories per day, the nonworking additional expenditure of energy 100 kilocalories per nonworking hour, and the working expenditure of energy 360 kilocalories per hour. See Passmore, Nicol, and Rao (1974) and Passmore and Durnin (1955). The value of 360 kilocalories per hour was taken from the

indirect calorimetry tests of Freedman (1980:139) on Filipino peasants engaged in rice farming tasks.

19. For the months between January 1960 and June 1962 included in the *Farm Household Economic Survey* (Han'guk ŭnhaeng chosabu 1963), variations in harvest explained little of the variation in consumption. However, if any of these years had been unusually bad or good, a better correlation between variation in harvest and consumption might have been found.

20. These deaths, gleaned primarily from genealogical records, are mostly of adults. Since Koreans must worship ancestors on the anniversary of their death, they generally record the day of death, but this was normally done by the lunar calendar. Lunar dates can only be converted to solar dates if their year is known, however, and the year of death is often not recorded, or was recorded according to the sixty-year cycle of "heavenly stems and earthly branches." These factors limited the size of my sample.

21. See chapter 5, K. K. Lee 1975:95, and Shima 1976:85 for more detail on the distinction between junior and senior households.

22. Of course, during the sixties marginal land that is not cultivated now could have been used. The outlawing of fire field farming did not occur until the late sixties and was not implemented until the seventies in many places.

23. These statements apply primarily to central Korea. In more southerly portions of Korea, it is possible to plant winter barley on the rice paddies in the winter, and this substantially changes the ecological picture we have been painting in this chapter.

Chapter 5

1. Chayanov wrote, for example, "It seems to us that if Rothschild were to flee to some agrarian country given a social revolution in Europe, and be obliged to engage in peasant labor, he would obey the rules of conduct established by the Organization and Production School, for all his bourgeois acquisitive psychology" (1966:48).

2. The closure of the energy loop of rural Korean households of course is relative rather than absolute and varies with the time period under consideration and the economic level of the household. Virtually all households pay some of their produce as tax and exchange what surplus they have. From the time of land reform until recently, however, in most households more energy has flowed through the closed energy loops of the household than has flowed in or out.

3. One night in 1977, for example, several men came down from a village

up the valley to buy cigarettes at a house that sold them as a sideline. Since it was dark they called for Sŏngsik, the eldest son of the house, intending to ask him to bring them the cigarettes. Sŏngsik, however, was in the provincial capital attending high school, and had not lived in the village for several years. Villagers, who all knew this, always called for one of the younger children in the same circumstances, but these men, knowing only that the house head was known as "Sŏngsik abŏji" (Sŏngsik's father), logically called for the son after whom the father had been named, even though they had never met him.

4. Use of given names is much more prominent among men than among women in rural areas. Part of the reason for this is that the intimacy that allows the use of given names is most easily cultivated among childhood playmates. This intimacy involves not only the use of given names, but also the use of verbs uninflected for the relative status of the speakers (a linguistic phenomenon that is virtually confined to persons who grew up together as children). Because most women marry patrilocally and come to the village as adults, they haven't had the opportunity to develop childhood intimacy and are more prone to use teknonymy and other forms of indirect reference than the men.

About half of the women born before 1910 were recorded in residential registration records or family registration records solely by their surnames in a form such as "Kim Ssi" (née Kim), or with the given name of "Kannan," a name arbitrarily given to women for registration purposes. This practice began to die out after 1920, and is not found at all after 1930 in my Sangongni sample. In some cases during my interviews, men would conceal their wives' given names from me in the same manner, but in these cases the residential registration records and family registration records recorded other given names.

5. A leading legal scholar defines the *ka* as follows: hoju rŭl chungsim ŭro hayŏ hoju wa kajok sanghogan e kwŏlli ŭimi e ŭihayŏ pŏmnyulsang yŏn'gyŏl toen kwallyŏmjŏk in hojŏksang ŭi kajok tanch'e (an ideal family group recorded in a family register, centering on a house head and legally connected by mutual rights and duties between the house head and the family members) (Kim Chusu 1984:58).

6. Legally, all Koreans without exception belong to one and only one *ka*, or legal *chip*. In some cases, however, this *chip* is made up of only a single person. If one is engaged in a nonagricultural occupation, it is possible (though inconvenient) to survive as a single person household even in Sangongni. Agricultural households, however, also have to maintain a minimum labor force. Thus, all agriculturalists are integrated into multiperson *chip* organized as units of production and consumption whatever their *ka* membership.

7. Per capita production of rice for agricultural households ranged from 0.96 kg. to 1.27 kg. between 1920 and 1940 (Suh 1978:92), a level similar to contemporary consumption levels. Whether or not farmers could generate a surplus depended very much on external conditions such as weather and pol-

itics. During bad times, such as the mid-fifties when Korean agriculture hadn't fully recovered from the Korean War, even substantial farmers had a hard time generating a surplus (Mills 1960:44,61–64,73–74,95–97). At other times it wasn't so difficult. During the Japanese period, however, the living standard of most of the rural population fell (H. K. Lee 1936:274–80; Grajdanzev 1944:109–21). Farmers became indebted and tenancy rates steadily rose as land passed into Japanese hands. One assumes, then, that during the colonial period the generation of surpluses was difficult, if not impossible, for a large percentage of farmers due to land-tenure relations.

8. During the period of 1915 to 1925, about one-third of the total crop would have been extracted through rents if one assumes a 50 percent sharecrop on all tenanted land (see Zenshō 1929:4–5). In the thirties, tenancy rates skyrocketed and it is likely that as much as half the crop entered the circulation system this way. Exports of rice to Japan alone reached one-third of the total crop in the 1936–40 period (Suh 1978:92).

9. One woman I interviewed claimed that in fact women do all the agricultural tasks that men do, including plowing, but I have never observed women plowing in Sangongni, though I have seen them engaged in most other agricultural tasks.

10. In stem families with an active grandmother in the house, the grandmother may spend the greater part of her time caring for the younger grandchildren. She does this partly out of pure interest in the children and partly so that she can ease the burden of the daughter-in-law and free her to concentrate more on other domestic tasks. Although most grandmothers feel that they should contribute to household labors in this way, it is not something that the daughter-in-law can require of her mother-in-law, and some mothers-in-law prefer other activities, such as agriculture. Thus even with a grandmother in the house, the primary responsibility for the care of the children still rests with their mother.

11. All but the poorest households (mostly those of tenant farmers), have had wells with hand pumps drilled in the courtyards of their houses, so that drawing water for cooking no longer entails a trip to the river or a spring for most families. In those cases where recourse must be made to a spring outside the house, it is the wife's responsibility to fetch the water, although husbands could also be seen doing it.

12. Thus, the baby chick salesman who hiked through the mountains with a rucksack filled with chicks newly hatched from a large commercial hatchery near Ch'unch'ŏn always went from household to household seeking the "housewives" (ajumŏnidŭl), never the husbands.

13. The home manufacture of fabrics had discontinued in Sangongni by 1977 when I first arrived there, although most women who were married before about 1960 could recall weaving and making clothes when they were younger. Cotton was still being grown in the village for home use, but it was not spun. One household, for example, planted cotton in 1977 because of an impending marriage. The members of the household knew they would need

the cotton to stuff the numerous quilts that the new couple would have to have. The fabric out of which the quilts were to be made, however, was to be purchased. During one point in the summer of the same year, there was a man who camped by the side of one of the village streams to process hemp in the pure stream water. This hemp was grown locally, but was intended for sale. As in the case of cotton, the weaving of hemp as a home handicraft has died out.

14. We will follow the diagramming conventions of Howard Odum's "energese" (Odum 1971).

15. Energy diagramming, of course, always requires a certain amount of idealization of energy flows. In figure 5.3, for example, several energy loops and pathways, such as those of domestic animals apart from cattle and the vegetable gardens of the women, have been ignored. As with the females' inside labor, the males' outside labor could have been represented as several pathways if rice fields, rainfall fields, and forest had been diagrammed separately. Exchange relations have also been slighted. Only those energy flows that are important to illustrate the contrast between male and female labor and need to be discussed to understand recent changes have been diagrammed.

16. I do not mean to imply here that the establishment of a steady state is inevitable. Obviously this is not the case, since during droughts in the past, for example, people did starve to death and households died out. The ability to adjust to minor perturbations, however, is a general characteristic of open systems, and follows from the complex interaction of multiple variables with one another.

17. For the time being, we will consider the amount of land available and the tenure conditions under which it is available as an exogenous factor. These factors are discussed further in chapter 7.

18. In my original work (Sorensen 1981a), these figures were calculated in man-hours per *majigi* (a folk/land measure equivalent in this part of Korea to approximately 6.6 ares). I have converted the man-hour calculations to man-days assuming an eight-hour day. For most of the agricultural year, this is a reasonable assumption, although during the rice transplantation season, the standard work day is ten hours. Since working even five days a week at rice transplantation is considered too arduous to consider (unless starvation were a possibility), however, I have used the eight-hour figure for rice transplantation, too. No provisions were made for days off in the calculations. Thus all ten days of any ten-day period were considered potential work days.

19. Villagers would say that a person could transplant one *majigi* of rice in a day. While this was true of a few young and vigorous workers, most of the farmers of the village could not sustain that pace. In addition, even the young and vigorous workers needed others to uproot the young seedlings, transport them to the fields, put on the fertilizer, and make sure the water level of the field was correct to be able to transplant a *majigi* in a single day. The 26.7

man-day per hectare figure for the transplantation of rice quoted here takes all of these factors into account.

20. Pulses, especially, are variable in their time constraints. They are planted any time from March to June, and harvested any time from July through September and October. They were most commonly planted in April and May, however.

21. Brandt (1971:67) records informants from Sŏkp'o as saying that a single male could cultivate approximately 0.4 hectares of riceland and 0.4 hectares of barley. This figure probably reflects the lower efficiency of work during the sixties when labor was plentiful and factor inputs (such as draft animals) short, expectations of fewer hours of work than the maximum possible, and, perhaps, the different labor requirements of an area where a winter crop of barley can be planted in rice fields.

22. The assumptions upon which these calculations are based are the same as those given in table 4.9.

23. The proportion of labor hours in farming supplied by women in Korea increased from 30.3 percent in 1965 to 35.4 percent in 1975 (Nongnimbu 1978). Chun (1984:82), in discussing the division of labor in Hasami, a mixed fishing and farming village in South Chŏlla Province, emphasizes the difference between the female contribution to "plow cultivation" (25 percent) and the female contribution to "hoe cultivation" (67 percent). Plow cultivation seems to refer to irrigated rice agriculture, while hoe cultivation seems to refer to rainfall field agriculture. That the contribution of females to the cultivation of rainfall fields is more significant than their contribution to irrigated rice fields is generally true in Korea (Kim Chusuk 1985:225). The extremely high female contribution to field agriculture as recorded by Chun probably is due to the small holdings of the two houses he investigated (33 ares in one case and 5.3 ares in another), making it likely that vegetable gardens, which are a primary female responsibility, are a large proportion of the rainfall fields.

24. The division of labor into a female inside component and a male outside component is generally found in inland villages in mainland Korea, but in some areas, particularly Cheju Island, male/female roles are almost reversed. See S. Y. Yoon (1977) and H. Cho (1983) for contrasting examples.

Chapter 6

1. The quote consists of interpolated lines from Ode VIII, part II, book 5 (Legge 1960) of the *Shī Jīng*. Most Chinese texts give the character *dé* (virtue)

in place of the *ēn* (parental grace) found in *Myŏng Sim Pogam*. The full poem has been translated by Arthur Waley (1937: poem 283), as well as by Legge.

2. In a survey of 7,366 persons in 1249 farm households in 48 counties in 1931, H. K. Lee reported 36 percent of the males claimed to be able to read Chinese, and 17.7 percent claimed to be able to write it. Only 20.2 percent of the males claimed to read Japanese, though 58 percent claimed to read Korean. Although two-fifths of the women could read Korean, hardly any claimed knowledge of Chinese or Japanese (H. K. Lee 1936:52–54).

3. The translation "parental grace" for the word *ēn* is somewhat unorthodox. Semantically, the word has two poles. Most fundamentally, it refers to parental favor in granting their children life, education, and social status. From this basic meaning comes a second: the debt one incurs due to someone's previous *ēn*. The cognate term in Korea, *ŭn*, is seldom used by itself, except, perhaps, in the explicit discussion of parental favor. The character is found in the compound *ŭnhye*, however, which is commonly used to denote a favor granted by a social superior to a social inferior. In the second sense, the character *ŭn* is found in such compounds as *paeŭnhada* (to carry the debt incurred by a favor), and *poŭnhada* (to pay back the debt incurred by a favor), but these terms are not widely or commonly used in ordinary discourse, and I suspect their use in this sense is of Japanese origin. The Japanese pronounce the same character as *on*, and it is this character that underlies the Japanese concept of indebtedness that Ruth Benedict analyzed with such perspicacity in chapters 5 through 7 of the *Chrysanthemum and the Sword* (1946). The psychology of indebtedness may be similar in Japan and Korea. In Korea, however, the concept of *ŭn* tends to be confined more to the parent-child relationship than in Japan.

4. Although the perspective of Korean women may be more bilateral than men (Kendall 1983:107–8), women understand and uphold the principles of patrilineal organization and succession in the context of the household. When asked if her daughter-in-law had gone to her mother's house for the birth of her first child (a practice that is said to have been common among elite families in traditional times [Imamura 1909:305] but for which I found no evidence in Sangongni), for example, one woman responded that since her daughter-in-law's mother belonged to a different house, the birth of her daughter's child was not her concern. On the other hand, the intricacies of the lineage system are often poorly understood by the women. When agnates gather, the men will usually be able to specify precisely their relationship with other agnates, but the women, while they may know which people in the local area are lineagemates to their marital house and which ones are not, seldom are able to identify distant agnatic kin by name or relationship to the house head of their own household. This partly due to most village women over sixty in both elite and nonelite families being illiterate—especially in Chinese, the language of the genealogies and ritual handbooks.

5. The centrality of the value of filial piety was also emphasized by Janelli

and Janelli (1982:50) for Twisŏngdwi, though they also report folkloristic material that reveals more ambivalent feelings (ibid.:51–52).

6. According to the 1912 Decree on Korean Civil Affairs (*Chōsen minji rei*), under which Korea was governed during the colonial period, most affairs were to be adjudicated according to the Japanese Civil Code (which had been enforced in Japan from 1898). Section 11 of the Decree on Korean Civil Affairs, however, made Korean custom the basis of family law (Chŏng Kwanghyŏn 1967:22). During the colonial period, modifications were introduced to Korean family law through interpretations of administrative bodies and courts, and by decree. Many of the innovations of the colonial period that were objectionable to Koreans (such as the decree of 1940 requiring Japanese names) were removed after liberation (1967:65–67), but a thorough revision of Korean civil law did not emerge until the introduction of the New Civil Code (*Sin Min Pŏp*) in 1958. Parts four and five of the New Civil Code (as amended in 1962, 1964, and 1977), and various laws regulating family registration introduced from 1960 on form the legal foundation of the Korean kinship, marriage, and inheritance systems (Kim Chusu 1985:7–11).

7. Adoption of the son of an agnate was by far the most common solution to sonlessness in rural Korea in the past, but this custom may be dying out. Although adoptions to died-out lines that entailed the inheritance of property without the obligation of nurturing the former owners of the property continued through the seventies in Sangongni, the last adoption in which an adoptee moved in with his wife to succeed to the headship of a continuously operating household was in 1969. Although this household was in full operation in 1977, by 1983 the adoptee had moved from the village and the widow of the former house head accompanied by her unmarried youngest daughter inhabited the house. A son-in-law who had been well established elsewhere in the village for years now cultivates their land for them in a tenancy agreement.

8. The New Civil Code (sec. 826) recognizes a kind of uxorilocal marriage similar to the Japanese type known as *ippuhon*, in which the wife stays in her natal home, succeeds to the house headship and can pass this headship on to her children. This is not a traditional Korean institution, however, but was an innovation of the colonial period. It has never been very common, and I know of no cases for any period in Sangongni.

9. Strictly speaking, unmarried daughters have a right to one-half of what a son inherits, and married daughters have a right to one-fourth, but this right never leads to the transfer of land to a married daughter when there is a son available. One sonless family has not made an adoption, however, and the widow says that the land will go to her daughters on her death. Although the descendants of the house head will receive the land, legally speaking, with the death of the widow the house will be extinguished. The 1958 revision of the civil code, however, does allow the married daughters to hold the land in their own right. They do not have to pass it to the control of their husbands as would have been the case before 1958.

10. The legal formula for inheritance is much more complicated than this rule of thumb, and includes provisions for widows and daughters. For a more detailed description and analysis of this legal rule, see Sorensen (1981a:156–61).

11. For comparison with Japan see Sorensen (1984).

12. Before the war, there was some question as to whether it was possible for an unmarried son to split from his natal household. In 1921 the Customs and System Investigation Committee (*Kanshū oyobi seido chōsa iinkai*) decided that this was not possible according to traditional Korean custom. However, in 1916 or 1917 the head of the Justice Office (*Hōmukyokuchō*) of the colonial government had issued an opinion that it was possible. Since the colonial government legislated by decree, this opinion had the force of law. (Chŏng Kwanghyŏn 1967:24). Current family law in South Korea allows all adults of both sexes except the legally designated successor to the house headship (i.e., the eldest son) to split from the family whether married or unmarried (Kim Chusu 1985:83).

13. Cases of joint family organization in fact are rare even in the pre-1966 ethnography on Korea. One of the few ethnographers to mention joint families is Osgood (1951:41–42) who found one joint family (3.7 percent of the total) in Sŏndup'o, with about 5 percent of the families in neighboring villages exhibiting joint organization. The one family that was nominally of joint type in Sangongni in 1977 (the Chin family, which is also mentioned in the section on family migration strategies) had, in the course of following a family diversification strategy, maintained joint form over three generations. One of the three brothers of the original family had died, leaving a widow and three children. She lived in the village in a separate house within the same compound as her older brother-in-law. Although it could be said that she had set up separate housekeeping (*segan natta*), the official splitting of the households (*pun'ga*) had not taken place, and the households were still legally in joint form in 1977. The widow received protection and assistance from her brother-in-law, but her household economy was separate from that of the *k'ŭn chip*. She arranged for the cultivation of her own land, and had her own cow for plowing (though her eldest nephew did the actual plowing for her). See Sang-bok Han (1977:91) for another example.

14. The age of marriage for males and females in Sangongni changed rapidly between 1918 and 1977. For females, the mean age of marriage ranged from 16.4 for the 1920–29 birth cohort to 20.3 for the 1950–59 birth cohort. For males it ranged from 20.9 for the 1920–29 cohort to 24.3 for the 1940–49 cohort. The figure given in the text is the mean for the marriages among the twenty-five Sangongni sample families during the relevant portions of their family cycle.

15. In all cases in the Sangongni sample except one, all male and female siblings within the same family were married at the same age. The age at which children were married off, however, varied from family to family.

16. The method for computing labor is taken from T. C. Smith (1977:136).

Age 0–10, no units. Age 11–19, add 0.1 unit for each year. Age 20–55, one unit. Age 56–65, subtract 0.1 unit for each two years past 55. Age 66–70, subtract 0.1 unit for each year past 65 to reach 0 at the age of 70. Over 70, no units. Smith subtracts 0.5 units from each woman who has a child under 4. In a previous work (Sorensen 1984) this method was used in unmodified form. Since the sexual division of labor in Korea is different from Japan, however, I have here computed male and female contributions to labor separately. Care of children has been considered part of female *annil* rather than a distraction from productive work.

17. Taylor and Hudson (1972:249–51) found crude birth rates for the period around 1960 to range from a high of sixty-one (Mali) to a low of thirteen (Hungary). The majority of developed countries had crude birth rates between fifteen and twenty (the United States CBR was nineteen). With crude death rates estimated at sixteen per thousand for South Korea, a CBR of forty-five would imply an annual growth rate of 2.9 percent.

18. Although it is true that in most cases the whole family accompanies the house head if he moves, there are exceptions. In a very few village families, the house head has established long-term residence in the city and his family has remained in the village. In a more common pattern, a widow may remain in the village when her son, the legal house head, migrates to town. In some of these cases, she will follow him to town after he has established himself. In others, especially if the household owns some village land that the widow can manage or live off, the widow may remain in the village until she is no longer able to live alone.

19. Comparison of the education level shows that those who have migrated have, in general, attained one level of education higher than those who have remained in the village, even when one controls for age. It is difficult, however, to see education as an independent pull factor. That is, although educational success may induce certain individuals to migrate who would otherwise remain in the village, others pursue education precisely because they have already decided to migrate to the city for reasons having to do with their structural position in the household. Although the acquistion of education is an extremely important part of most people's migration strategy, it cannot be seen uniformly as either a cause or effect; it is both.

20. These figures have been calculated excluding the households of teachers whose families are not from Sangongni. Thus the total number of households used in these calculations was 111 in 1977 and 93 in 1983.

21. It is difficult to compare the total fertility rates of the village between 1977 and 1983 because the residents are not the same in the two time periods, and the age distribution of women was different. However, there is no difference between 1977 and 1983 in the number of children between zero and four divided by the number of women between twenty and thirty-nine, an indication of similar fertility rates at the two times. In 1977 the ratio was 1.07 and in 1983 it was 1.10.

22. It is not necessary for my argument here that the family head necessarily

manage this income communally. Sometimes this is the case, but communal management of family resources when family members are dispersed is unusual. In some families, unmarried children who have jobs are expected to send remittances back home, but even this is probably done today in fewer than half the cases.

23. But not brother and sister, a combination common in Ireland.

24. Even house heads who acknowledged the receipt of remittances conceded that to do so was no longer a matter of course. Mintz (1977) found similar data among working girls in Seoul, where only about 25 percent of her sample reported giving their family part of their salary, 15 percent explicitly denied giving their family any of their salary, and the disposition of the salaries of the rest was left unmentioned. The contrast here with the behavior of Chinese women in Hong Kong and Taiwan, who seem universally to give a substantial part of their salary to their family (Salaff 1981:6), is especially striking. One reason for this low frequency of remittances may be that the legal code no longer recognizes the right of the house head to manage the property of all family members as in the old civil code (Kim Chusu 1984:66), but it also seems to be related to most migrated children being the potential founders of independent houses and thus in the process of establishing their independence.

25. For reasons of space I have omitted such interesting cases as younger son succession (there was, in 1983, one case of a younger son returning from the city to form a stem family with his parents), and the splitting of older sons from their natal household despite remaining in the village (two cases). Although these latter two cases on the surface seem very significant, upon closer inspection their significance is hard to judge. In both cases the fall in village population has made it easy for them to find land to rent and thus form separate households, but the structural reasons for their splitting were different. In one case, the father had remarried after the death of his wife who had been the mother of his children, and the son who had split from his father's household cited this as an explicit reason. Tension between stepmothers and sons was quite common in the past, and I know of one similar case where the eldest son split from his natal household before the revision of the legal code, so this particular case probably does not indicate a new pattern. In the other case, the daughter-in-law said they did not get along in the stem household and cited that reason for the split (they had formed a stem household, but later had broken it up). Again in traditional times it was possible to find anomalous cases like this, so it is hard to generalize from a single case. In addition, it is quite possible the two sections of the stem family will amalgamate later in the family cycle when old quarrels seem less important.

Chapter 7

1. The total number of male and female workers per household in 1977 was 2.28 in 1977 ($SD = 0.967$, $N = 91$) and 2.21 in 1983 ($SD = 0.837$, $N = 84$). This difference is not statistically significant. Differences in the distribution of workers in the household, however, may be statistically significant. Thus I found fewer workerless households in 1983 than 1977 and more two male-worker households in 1983. Although the difference in workerless households may be due to inaccuracies in land-tenure data (e.g., I may have included in my workerless category households who rent out all or most of their land) the difference in the number of two worker households is more difficult to explain.

2. The chief limitation of the land reform was on the total size of agricultural landholdings (three hectares excluding orchard and forest) and on long-term rental of land. Recent interpretations of land-tenure law in legal circles hold that the provisions of the land reform were limited to that period and no longer apply (Kuramochi 1985:2), though this interpretation has not been universally held in the past (see, for example, Pak 1966:241). Farms larger than three hectares are for economic reasons, however, still rare.

3. See, for example, the figures published for several villages by Pak Ki Hyuk (1975) and No Changsöp et al. (1964).

4. Land-tenure and farm-size data was acquired through direct interview with householders. Although there was some underreporting of landholdings for both riceland and rainfall field (especially by female interviewees), I have reason to believe that this problem was more serious for rainfall field than riceland. Had my land-tenure data been perfectly accurate, it seems likely that the proportion of rice and rainfall fields for individual households would be very similar to the proportion of these types of fields in the village as a whole: 45 percent irrigated riceland, and 55 percent rainfall field.

5. One informant thought that one male could cultivate an hectare each of irrigated riceland and rainfall field. This estimate is 25 percent larger than mine. This particular informant, however, had substantially more land than he could cultivate himself and was accustomed to hiring a good deal of extra labor. In addition, his wife put more effort into agriculture than in most households. When we combine this information with the effect of using round numbers, one is inclined to discount the importance of this discrepancy. Pak (1966:226) sees two hectares as the limit on farms cultivated with family labor. This seems reasonable to me, though it must be kept in mind that in this case all family members are included rather than a single adult male.

6. The land distribution curves are not of normal shape. All of them are skewed to the left with high kurtosis. This means that most values cluster to the left of the mean with a few extreme values to the right. The high kurtosis describes a curve with values much more closely concentrated around the mean than in a normal distribution. In other words, most landholdings are

slightly smaller than the means given in table 7.2, and there are a few extremely large landholdings that skew the mean to the right and increase the standard deviation.

7. Land was considerably cheaper in relation to its productivity in the 1945–55 period.

8. None of the twenty-four landless farmers of 1977 had bought any land by 1983.

9. Tenancy arrangements of all types are known as *sojak*. Sharecropping arrangements are technically called *t'ajak*, though this term is seldom actually heard in the village. The most common terms for sharecropping (as opposed to fixed rate rental arrangements) are *pyŏngjak* or *panjak*. Both of these terms assume an equal division of the crop between landlord and tenant.

10. Although the 50:50 sharecropping rate was standard in 1977 and in 1983, rental rates may be falling. I found several cases of rentals in the 30 percent range in 1983. Renters cited the poor quality of the land. A few such cases were between related households. One of these households had moved to town, and the closeness of the kinship tie may have had something to do with the low rental rate.

11. This comes to approximately a 25 percent rate at the average level of productivity prevailing on good land in 1983.

12. This comes to approximately a 30–40 percent rate at prevailing levels of rainfall field grain crop productivity.

13. The government had provided the village with a large number of chestnut trees to reforest a steep hillside denuded by fire and in 1977 a caretaker (who doubled as a ferryman) was paid by the village to tend the trees. The new bridge over the river took away the need for a ferryman at that particular crossing, and when the caretaker left he was not replaced.

14. The number of households used in the calculation of the means in table 7.2 is not the same for landowners and farmers. The landownership figures include only those households that own land (thus excluding tenant farmers), while the farm-size figures include only those who cultivate some land (thus excluding those who rent all their land out). Since long-term renting out of land is still thought by some to be illegal, several of the largest landowners claimed to cultivate all of their land themselves even when they have twice or more what a single male can cultivate. In some cases I was able to find the tenants of these landowners, but not in all. This kind of error undoubtedly has skewed the distribution of farm size to an unknown extent. If all my data were completely accurate, it is likely that the means and especially standard deviations of amounts of land cultivated would be reduced more than they are in table 7.2.

15. For 1983, the difference between household landholdings (amount of land owned) and household farm size (amount of land cultivated whether it was owned or not) was negatively correlated with the size of the landholding, and positively correlated with the number of adult male equivalents, the num-

ber of male work units and the number of female work units in the household. The significance of these correlations was at the 0.6 percent level or better for all of these variables. This corresponds to the common-sense assumption that the larger the landowner, the more land he will rent out, and the smaller the landowner, the more land he will rent in. A large male or female labor force or a large number of consumers in the household will all encourage the renting in of more land. This model of the factors that condition household rental strategy can be tested by multiple regression analysis with the difference between landholding and farm size as the dependent variable and the number of consumers, the number of male workers, and the number of female workers as the independent variables. When this is done, 60 percent of the variation in the amount of land rented in or rented out is accounted for with a significance better than 0.0001.

The same procedure can be done for 1976–77. For this period, however, many of the correlations are not statistically significant. The regression, however, accounts for 28 percent of the variation and again has a significance better than 0.0001. The difference between the amount of variation accounted for in 1977 and 1983 is probably not related to changes in village social structure or agricultural economy, but rather the quality of the data. The 1976 data was collected by a team of Korean anthropologists in the course of a survey done for other purposes, and they did not systematically distinguish between farm size and landholding for those who both owned and rented land. The 1983 data, on the other hand, were collected specifically to distinguish between landholding and farm size. Thus each householder was asked how much land was owned and cultivated, rented in, and rented out in each of three land categories (irrigated riceland, rainfall field, and forest land). This information on land was then correlated with social data collected at the same time.

16. During the late forties after the Korean peninsula had been organized into two competing states, guerrilla groups were discovered trying to infiltrate down from the north on several famous occasions. Several of these groups holed up for a while in the high mountains not too far from Sangongni. The most serious guerrilla activity centered near Chiri Mountain in South Kyŏngsang Province, the coastal regions of North Kyŏngsang Province, and Cheju Island (Cumings 1979:201; Merrill 1980). Although guerrilla warfare was never successfully set up in this part of Korea, some of the older village residents could remember instances of "reds" (*ppalgaengi*) trying to transit through the area (though none claimed to ever have actually seen them until the occupation of the village by the North in the summer of 1950).

17. The actual price eventually came to about 180 percent of the annual crop because official productivity figures were arbitrarily reduced by 40 percent (Ban, Moon, and Perkins 1980:288).

18. Exceptions are made for small amounts of ancestor land (*wit'o*) located near tombs, and for orchard land. Forest was never included in the land re-

form. Landholdings of forest are very concentrated, and often in the hands of lineages or lineage elders. Even quite poor farmers who come from well-established lineages may have shares in or access to large tracts of forest.

19. One of the largest landowners of the village (who owned 3.5 hectares of irrigated riceland, 1 hectare of rainfall field and 15 hectares of forest in 1983), however, claimed to have received nothing from his family and began to acquire land even in the thirties (he was born in 1910 and thus was thirty-five at liberation). Although he has gradually increased his holdings until he is one of the two or three largest landowners in the village, he says that he got no land at all through private sale or government purchase during the land reform period.

20. At the levels of productivity prevailing at that time, it would have taken four to six hectares of irrigated riceland to produce 200 bags of rice. Thus, the holdings of the largest landowners might have ranged around ten hectares, if both irrigated and unirrigated land is considered. Three households with ten-hectare holdings would have accounted for almost a third of the land in the village.

21. Recognition (*inji*) is a legal step a man can take to legitimize a child by someone other than his wife (New Civil Code, sec. 855).

22. Although I questioned each household on the source of its land, there were many households in which the interviewee professed ignorance of the amount of land received in inheritance. This problem was complicated in the case of siblings not only by the chances that one of the siblings may have not answered the questions on inheritance, but also by few younger sons having remained in the village, and among those sibling pairs that remain, many of even the eldest sons received nothing.

23. In 1976, 46.7 percent of the houses were headed by eldest sons and 35.0 percent were headed by younger sons, with the remainder headed by adoptees, widows, etc. In 1983, 48.9 percent of the houses were headed by eldest sons and 36.2 percent headed by younger sons. In 1977, houses headed by eldest sons had a mean landholding of 104.5 ares, and those headed by younger sons of 82.8 ares. The figures for 1983 were 158.5 and 106.4, respectively. Thus in 1977, younger sons had a mean landholding size 79.3 percent of the mean main house landholding size, while in 1983 it was only 67.2 percent of the mean main house landholding size. The reasons for the fall in the relative position of the branch houses are obscure, since there was no uniform tendency for larger landholders to acquire more land than smaller landholders. However, the characteristics of households that acquired land between 1977 and 1983 better fit main houses than branch houses, and it may be that the larger size of main houses, the larger amount of labor available to them, and their firmer commitment to remaining in the village explain the difference in their acquisition of land.

24. In earlier work (Sorensen 1981a:568–69) I assumed present landholding patterns were largely a function of inheritance patterns. I have since become more aware of the important amounts of land that are bought and sold,

and no longer think it possible to infer inheritance patterns from present land-tenure patterns. All the data presented here are taken from direct interviews on how much of informants' land was acquired by various methods. Only those interviews in which I obtained specific ares for each method of land acquisition for each type of land have been used for quantitative assessment.

25. Even if a holding were split equally, it would take a holding of 2 hectares to provide two sons with the 103.6 ares of land that was the mean holding in 1983, and only thirteen households (14.3 percent) of the farm households in the village in 1983 had holdings of this size or larger. Although farms with holdings smaller than 1 hectare can clearly survive, even thrive, in the village, the competition from city life and urban occupations make anything but a substantial farm a weak incentive to remain in the village.

26. Thus, there was no systematic correlation between acquisition of land and whether the eldest son was present in the village or not. Nor was there a correlation with changes in labor supply or family type. This is because one cannot predict, with sufficient accuracy, whether the eldest son will return to the village or not based only on village data. Whether he will return is obviously partially determined by his success in town.

27. The correlation between the number of adult male equivalents in the household in 1977 and the amount of land bought or sold between 1977 and 1983 was 0.2254 (p = 0.036). This and the size of households in 1977 were the only household factors with a significant correlation to the amount of land bought or sold between 1977 and 1983.

28. If we compare the characteristics of the households that left in 1977 with the 1983 characteristics of the households that sold land between 1977 and 1983, none is significantly different except household size. The difference of this characteristic is undoubtedly related to the mean household size of the total village falling one full person between 1977 and 1983.

29. Of course the Gini index for farm size (amount of land cultivated) is smaller than for land tenure (amount of land owned), since the mechanisms we have been discussing that affect farm size select against extreme values. The tendency for increasing inequality is also less marked for farm size where the 1977 coefficient was 0.291 and the 1983 one 0.315. This increase is half what it was for landholdings. Because of rental in and out, then, household income is probably more equal than household assets as evinced in land tenure. One's return from labor, however, is directly correlated to the amount of land one owns relative to one's family labor supply.

30. The mean Gini index for the land distribution of fifty-four countries in the late fifties and early sixties collected by Taylor and Hudson (1972) was 0.670 with a high of 0.933 (Peru) and a low of 0.351 (Finland). In that collection, South Korea was the second lowest at 0.307, and the United States fairly high at 0.710. Even the recent higher figures calculated for Sangongni would qualify for the lowest quintile of land concentration in that collection.

Guide to Romanization

abŏji 아버지
ach'im pap 아침밥
aengdu 앵두
  der. fr. 櫻桃
ajubŏni 아주버니
ajumŏnidŭl 아주머니들
anbang 안房
an chuin 안主人
annil 안일
chaenggi 쟁기
chagŭn chip 작은집
ch'albyŏ 찰벼
ch'amkkae 참깨
ch'ammil 참밀
ch'an (panch'an) 饌（飯饌）
changdoktae 醬독臺
changma 장마
ch'apssal 찹쌀
ch'apssal ttŏk 찹쌀떡
chesa 祭祀
ch'ilk 칡
ch'in'gatchip 親家집
chip 집
chipt'ŏ 집터

chŏlgu 절구
chŏmsim pap 點心밥
chŏndap 田畓
chŏn'ga 傳家
chŏnse 傳貰
ch'ŏnsudap 天水畓
chŏnyŏk pap 저녁밥
Chōsen minji rei (J.)
  朝鮮民事令
chuin 主人
chumin tŭngnok 住民登錄
Ch'unch'ŏn 春川

dé (C.) 德
ēn (C.) 恩 *see* ŭn
fēnjīa (C.) 分家 *see* pun'ga

haepssal 햅쌀
haepssal pap 햅쌀밥
ha-in 下人
Han'guk ŭnhaeng chosabu
  韓國銀行調查部
Hoengsŏng 橫城
hoesa 會社

275

hojŏk chedo 戸籍制度

Hongch'ŏn 洪川

hwajŏn 火田

hwan 圓

Hwasŏng 華城

hyo 孝

hyodo rŭl chik'ida
　孝道를 지키다.

hyoja 孝子

hyonyŏ 孝女

hyŏng (dial. sŏng) 兄

ie (J.) 家 *see* chip, ka

ilban pyŏ 一般 벼

Inje Kun 麟蹄郡

inkyo (J.) 隱居 *see* chŏn'ga

insam 人參

ippuhon 入夫婚

ipssal 입쌀

iptong 入冬

jīa (C.) 家 *see* chip, ka

ka 家

kaekt'o 客土

kajogwŏn 家族員

kama (kamani) 가마 (가마니)

Kangnam k'ong 江南콩

Kangwŏn 江原

kanjang 간醬

Kanshū oyobi seido chōsa iinkai
　(J.)
　慣習及制度調査委員會

k'i 키

kidun chesa 기둔 祭祀

kije 忌祭

kim 김

kimch'i 김치

kimjang 김장

kisul 技術

kisul sujun i najŭnikka
　技術水準이 낮으니까

kiuje 祈雨祭

kkaktugi 깍두기

koch'i 고치

koch'u 고추

koch'ujang 고추醬

kŏmŭnkkae 검은깨

kongi 공이

kongmuwŏn 公務員

kŏt pori 겉보리

kuk 국

kuksu 국수

kumŏng kage 구멍 가게

kun 郡

k'ŭn chip 큰집

kwangmok 廣木

Kyŏnggi 京畿

kyŏngji 耕地

li 里

lǐ (C.) 理

mandu kuk 饅頭국

majigi 마지기

makkŏlli 막걸리

mebyŏ 메벼

meju 메주

memil 메밀

mepssal 멥쌀

min myŏnŭri 민며누리

minari 미나리

Miryang pyŏ 密陽 벼

miso (J.) 味噌 *see* toenjang

miyŏk 미역

miyŏk kuk 미역국

mo 모

monaegi 모내기

mŏru 머루

mŏsŭm 머슴

muk 묵

mumyŏng 무명

Munhwa kongbobu
文化公報部

myŏn 面

Myŏng Sim Pogam 明心寶鑑

myŏngju 明紬

myŏnjang 面長

nat 낫

nattō (J.) 納豆 *see* meju

non 논

nongbŏn'gi 農繁期

Nongnimbu 農林部

Nongŏp chidoso 農業指導所

Nongŏp hyŏptong chohap
農業協同組合

nongsa ch'ŏnha taebon
農事天下大本

nuruk 누룩

oi kimch'i 오이김치

oksusu 玉수수

ŏmma 엄마

ŏmŏni kage 어머니 가게

oryun 五倫

paech'u kimch'i 배추김치

paeŭn-hada 背恩하다

pakkannil 바깥일

pakkat chuin 바깥主人

pan 瓸

panjak 半作

p'anmitk'ong 팥밑콩

pap 밥

pap mŏgŏ 밥 먹어

pat 밭

p'at 팥

p'o 脯

pon'ga 本家

Ponggwang pyŏ 봉광벼

pŏpchŏng pun'ga 法定分家

porit kogae 보릿고개

porit kogae rŭl nŏmgyŏtta
보릿고개를 넘겼다

posint'ang 補身湯

pŏt 빗

ppalgaengi 빨갱이

ppallae t'ŏ 빨래터

puch'u kimchi'i 부추김치

p'umasi 품앗이

p'ump'ari 품팔이

p'umsak 품삯

pun'ga 分家

p'uppasim-hada 풋바심하다

pyŏ 벼

pyŏngjak 並作

pyŏt 볏

Sa eich'i kurakpu 四 H 俱樂部

Sae maŭl undong 새마을 運動

saellŏri maen 샐러리맨

saengjihwang 生地黄

sahu yangja 死後養子

sallim 山林

sallim ŭl naeda 살림을 내다

sam 삼

sambe 삼베

san kŏnnŏ san itta

　山건너 山있다

sangch'i 상치

San'gongni 山谷里

san namul 山나물

segan-nada 세간나다

Shī Jīng (C.) 詩經

sije 時祭

sijip 媤집

simsim-hada 심심하다

Sin Min Pŏp 新民法

singmo 食母

soban 小盤

sŏdang 書堂

sojak 小作

soju 燒酒

sokkyŏri 숫결이

sok'uri 소쿠리

sot 솥

ssal 쌀

ssam 쌈

ssŏre 써레

sŭng 升

susu 수수

tadŭmijil 다듬이질

Tae porŭm 大 보름

T'aebaek sanmaek 太白山脈

taech'u 대추 der. fr. 大棗

T'aegŭgi pyŏ 太極이벼

teril sawi 데릴사위

t'ajak 打作

tambae 담배

tan 段

tchanji 짠지

tidil panga 디딜방아

tŏdŏk 더덕

t'oebi 堆肥

toenjang/t'ojang 된醬 / 토醬

togŭp 都給

toji 賭地

t'oji 土地

t'ong kimch'i 통김치

tongch'imi 동치미

T'ongil pyŏ 統一벼

tongjok purak 同族部落

top'o 道袍

tubu 豆腐

tŭlkkae 들깨

ture 두레

ŭmbok 飲福

ŭn/ŭnhye 恩 / 恩惠

uri myŏnŭri 우리 며누리

wit'o 位土

wŏn 元

Wŏnju 原州

xiào (C.) 孝 *see* hyo

Xiào Jīng (C.) 孝經

yangban 兩班

yangbun i chot'a 養分 이좋다   Yŏngsŏ 嶺西

Yangju 楊州   yŏnt'an 煉炭

yŏlmu kimch'i 열무김치   Yusin pyo 維新 벼

Yŏngdong 嶺東

A Note on Weights and Measures

All quantities in tables and in the text have been given in metric units except in quotes from informants.

Land is measured in hectares (2.47 acres) and ares (119.6 square yards). One hectare is equivalent to 100 ares. Koreans measure land in *p'yŏng* (3.95 square yards) and *chŏngbo* (2.45 acres). One *chŏngbo* equals 3000 *p'yŏng*. One hectare equals 3025 *p'yŏng*. In Korean government publications, *chŏngbo* are sometimes treated without conversion as hectares, but I have avoided this practice except in discussion of the limit on landholdings imposed by the Land Reform Act of 1949 where I have substituted "three hectares" for what is actually "three *chŏngbo.*" Peasants often count landholdings in terms of *majigi*. In Kangwŏn Province a *majigi* is equal to approximately 200 *p'yŏng* (6.6 ares or 0.16 acres).

I have expressed productivity and yield in terms of metric tons (1000 kg). In government reports, and in discussing productivity with villagers, the standard units of measure are of volume rather than weight. The most common village measures of grain are the *toe* (3.81 pints), *mal* (4.77 gallons) and *kama*, or "bag." Ten *toe* are equivalent to one *mal*. The *kama* is usually figured as 54 kilograms of unhusked rice, or 60 kilograms of polished rice, though 90 kilogram bags are also found in Korea. Government figures are usually expressed in *sŏk* equivalent to 10 *mal*. One *sŏk* equals 180.39 liters, or 5.12 bushels.

I have converted volume to weight using the following conversion factors: 1 *sŏk* of unhulled rice = 100 kilograms = 74 kilograms of polished rice; 1 *sŏk* of polished rice = 144 kilograms; 1 *sŏk* of barley = 105 kilograms = 74 kilograms of polished barley; 1 *sŏk* of polished barley = 141 kilograms.

The standard Korean unit of weight is the *kŭn* of 601 grams.

References

Adams, Richard N.
  1975 *Energy and Structure: A Theory of Social Power.* Austin: University of Texas Press.
  1981 "Natural Selection, Energetics, and 'Cultural Materialism.'" *Current Anthropology* 22(6):603–8 (December).
Alland, Alexander
  1970 *Adaptation in Cultural Evolution: An Approach to Medical Anthropology.* New York: Columbia University Press.
Allison, Paul D.
  1978 "Measures of Inequality." *American Sociological Review* 43:865–80 (December).
Aqua, Ronald
  1974 *Local Government and Rural Development in South Korea.* Ithaca, N. Y.: Rural Development Committee, Center for International Studies, Cornell University.
Ban, Sung Hwan, Pal Yong Moon, and Dwight H. Perkins
  1980 *Studies on the Modernization of The Republic of Korea: 1945–1975: Rural Development.* Harvard East Asian Monographs, no. 89. Cambridge: Harvard University Press.
Banaji, Jairus
  1976 "Chayanov, Kautsky, Lenin: Considerations Toward a Synthesis." *Economic and Political Weekly,* October 2:1594–1606.
Barth, Fredrik
  1956 "Ecological Relationships of Ethnic Groups in Swat, North Pakistan." *American Anthropologist* 58(6):1079–89 (December).
  1967 "On the Study of Social Change." *American Anthropologist* 69:661–69.
  1981 *Process and Form in Social Life: Selected Essays of Fredrik Barth.* London: Routledge and Kegan Paul.
Bartz, Patricia M.
  1972 *South Korea.* Oxford: Oxford University Press.
Beardsley, Richard K., John W. Hall, and Robert E. Ward
  1959 *Village Japan.* Chicago: University of Chicago Press.

Benedict, Ruth
  1946   *The Chrysanthemum and the Sword.* Boston: Houghton Mifflin.
Bennett, John W.
  1976   *The Ecological Transition: Cultural Anthropology and Human Adaptation.* New York: Pergamon Press.
Bertalanffy, Ludwig von
  1969   *General System Theory: Foundations, Development, Applications.* New York: George Braziller.
Boas, Franz
  1911   "Handbook of American Indian Languages." *Bureau of American Ethnology Bulletin* no. 40, pt. 1. Washington, D. C.
Boserup, Ester
  1965   *The Conditions of Agricultural Growth: The Economics of Agrarian Change under Population Pressure.* New York: Aldine.
Brandt, Vincent S. R.
  1971   *A Korean Village Between Farm and Sea.* Cambridge: Harvard University Press.
  1980   "Local Government and Rural Development." In Ban, Moon, and Perkins 1980:260–80.
Brandt, Vincent S. R. and Man-gap Lee
  1981   "Community Development in the Republic of Korea." In Ronald Dore and Zoë Mars, eds., *Community Development: Comparative Case Studies in India, the Republic of Korea, Mexico and Tanzania.* London: Croom Helm.
Buckley, Walter
  1967   *Sociology and Modern Systems Theory.* Englewood Cliffs, N. J.: Prentice-Hall.
Cancian, Francesca
  1960   "Functional Analysis of Change." *American Sociological Review* 25(6):818–27 (December).
Cancian, Frank
  1966   "Maximization as Norm, Strategy and Theory: A Comment on Programmatic Statements in Economic Anthropology." *American Anthropologist* 68:465–70 (April).
Carter, Anthony
  1984   "Household Histories." In Robert McC. Netting, Richard R. Wilk, and Eric J. Arnould, eds. 1984:44–83.
Chayanov, A. V. [Aleksandr Vasil'evich Chaîanov]
  1966   *Peasant Farm Organization.* Trans. R. E. F. Smith. In Danial Thorner et al., eds. *A. V. Chayanov on The Theory of Peasant Economy,* pp. 29–270. Homewood, Ill.: The American Economic Association (Russian original 1925).
Cho, Haejoang
  1983   "The Autonomous Women: Divers on Cheju Island." In Kendall and Peterson, eds. 1983:81–96.

Cho, Yong Sam
1963 *"Disguised Unemployment" in Underdeveloped Areas with Special Reference to South Korean Agriculture*. Berkeley and Los Angeles: University of California Press.

Ch'oe Chaesŏk
1966 *Han'guk kajok yŏn'gu* [A study of the Korean family]. Seoul: Minjung Sŏgwan.

Ch'oe Paek
1981 "Han'guk ŭi chip—kŭ ŭi kujo punsŏk" [The Korean household—its structural analysis]. *Han'guk Munhwa Illyuhak* 13:119–35.

Chŏng Kwanghyŏn
1967 *Han'guk kajok pŏp yŏn'gu* [A study of Korean family law]. Seoul: Seoul National University Press.

Chŏng Yŏngil
1984 "Han'guk nongŏp ŭi hyŏnhwang kwa tangmyŏn kwaje" [The present conditions and problems confronted in Korean agriculture]. In Pak Hyŏnjae et al., ed. *Han'guk nongŏp munje ŭi saeroun insik* [New knowledge on Korean agricultural problems], pp. 35–66. Seoul: Tol Pegae.

Chun, Kyung-soo
1983 "We Are Nourished by Virtue of Our Ancestors: Ancestor Worship and Nutrition in a Korean Village." *Ecology of Food and Nutrition* 13:267–76.
1984 *Reciprocity and Korean Society: An Ethnography of Hasami*. Seoul: Seoul National University Press.

Cohen, Myron
1976 *House United, House Divided: The Chinese Family in Taiwan*. New York: Columbia University Press.

Cumings, Bruce
1979 "Political Participation in Liberated Korea: Mobilization and Revolt in the Kyŏngsang Provinces." *Journal of Korean Studies* 1:163–203.

Donham, Donald L.
1981 "Beyond the Domestic Mode of Production." *Man*, n. s. 16:515–41 (December).

Dore, Ronald P.
1961 "Function and Cause." *American Sociological Review* 26(6):843–53 (December).
1978 *Shinohata: A Portrait of a Japanese Village*. New York: Pantheon Books.

Durrenberger, Paul E., ed.
1984 *Chayanov, Peasants and Economic Anthropology*. New York: Academic Press.

Eisenstadt, Shmuel N.
    1965   *Modernization: Protest and Change.* Englewood Cliffs, N. J.: Prentice-Hall.
Ellen, Roy
    1982   *Environment, Subsistence and System: The Ecology of Small-Scale Social Formations.* Cambridge: Cambridge University Press.
Ember, Melvin and Carol Ember
    1983   *Marriage, Family and Kinship: Comparative Studies of Social Organization.* New Haven: Human Relations Area Files Press.
Embree, John F.
    1936   *Suye Mura: A Japanese Village.* Chicago: University of Chicago Press.
Engels, Friedrich
    1968   "Brief an Paul Mehring, 14. Juli, 1893." In *Karl Marx, Friedrich Engels Werke* 39:96–100. Berlin: Dietz Verlag (English version in Tucker 1972:648–50).
Firth, Raymond
    1951   *Elements of Social Organization.* London: Watts and Co.
Fischer, J. L.
    1958   "The Classification of Residence in Censuses." *American Anthropologist* 60(3):508–17.
Food and Agriculture Organization of the United Nations
    1970   *Amino-Acid Content of Foods and Biological Data on Proteins.* Nutritional Studies, no. 24. Rome.
Fortes, Meyer
    1958   "Introduction." In Jack Goody, ed., *The Developmental Cycle in Domestic Groups,* pp. 1–14. Cambridge: Cambridge University Press.
Foster, George M.
    1973   *Traditional Societies and Technological Change.* 2nd ed. New York: Harper and Row.
Freedman, Stephen M.
    1980   "Modifications of Traditional Rice Production Practices in the Developing World: An Energy Efficiency Analysis." *Agro-Ecosystems* 6(2):129–46 (September).
Freilich, Morris
    1963   "The Natural Experiment, Ecology and Culture." *Southwestern Journal of Anthropology* 19(1):21–39.
Friedman, F. G.
    1953   "The World of 'La Miseria'." *Partisan Review* 20(2):218–31 (March–April).
Friedman, Jonathan
    1974   "Marxism, Structuralism and Vulgar Materialism." *Man,* n.s. 9(3):444–69 (September).

Fukutake, Tadashi
1982 *The Japanese Social Structure: Its Evolution in the Modern Century.* Tokyo: University of Tokyo Press.
Gallin, Bernard and Rita Gallin
1982 Socioeconomic Life in Rural Taiwan: Twenty Years of Development and Change." *Modern China* 8(2):205–46 (April).
Godelier, Maurice
1972 *Rationality and Irrationality in Economics.* New York and London: Monthly Review Press.
Goode, William J.
1963 *World Revolution and Family Patterns.* New York: Free Press.
Goodenough, Ward H.
1956 "Residence Rules." *Southwestern Journal of Anthropology* 12:22–37 (Spring).
1961 "Comments." *Daedalus* 90:521–28 (Summer).
1971 *Culture, Language and Society.* Reading, Mass.: Addison-Wesley.
Gragert, Edwin Harold
1982 *Landownership Change in Korea under Japanese Colonial Rule: 1900–1935.* Ph.D. Diss. Columbia University.
Graham, G. G.
1975 "Effect of Deficiency of Protein and Amino Acids." In *Improvement of Protein Nutriture,* pp. 109–37. Washington, D. C.: National Academy of Sciences.
Grajdanzev, Andrew J.
1944 *Modern Korean.* New York: John Day.
Greenhalgh, Susan
1985 "Is Inequality Demographically Induced? The Family Cycle and the Distribution of Income in Taiwan." *American Anthropologist* 87(3):571–94 (September).
Han, Sang-bok
1977 *Korean Fisherman: Ecological Adaptation in Three Communities.* Seoul: Population and Development Studies Center, Seoul National University.
Han'guk ŭnhaeng chosabu [The Bank of Korea Research Department]
1958 *Kyŏngje yŏn'gam* [Economic yearbook]. Seoul.
1961 *Kyŏngje t'onggye yŏnbo* [Economic statistical yearbook]. Seoul.
1963 *Nongga kyŏngje chosa chonghap pogo: 1953–1962* [Summary report on the farm household economic survey]. Seoul.
Hanks, Lucien M.
1972 *Rice and Man: Agricultural Ecology in Southeast Asia.* Chicago: Aldine-Atherton.
Harrell, C. Stevan
1981 "Effects of Economic Change on Two Taiwanese Villages." *Modern China* 7(1):31–54 (January).

Harris, Marvin
  1966 "The Cultural Ecology of India's Sacred Cattle." *Current Anthropology* 7(1):51–56 (February).
  1968 *The Rise of Anthropological Theory: A History of Theories of Culture.* New York: Thomas Y. Crowell Co.
  1971 *Culture, Man and Nature.* New York: Thomas Y. Crowell Co.
  1979 *Cultural Materialism: The Struggle for a Science of Culture.* New York: Random House.
Harrison, Mark
  1975 "Chayanov and the Economics of the Russian Peasantry." *Journal of Peasant Studies* 2(4):389–417 (July).
  1977a "Resource Allocation and Agrarian Class Formation." *Journal of Peasant Studies* 2(2):127–61 (January).
  1977b "The Peasant Mode of Production in the Work of A. V. Chayanov." *Journal of Peasant Studies* 4(4):323–36 (July).
Hasan, Parvez
  1976 *Korea: Problems and Issues in a Rapidly Growing Economy.* Baltimore: The Johns Hopkins Press.
Hegsted, D. M.
  1963 "Variation in Requirements of Nutrients: Amino Acids." *Federation Proceedings* 22:1424–30.
Henry, Louis
  1961 "Some Data on Natural Fertility." *Eugenics Quarterly* 8(2):81–91 (June).
Heston, Alan
  1971 "An Approach to the Sacred Cow of India." *Current Anthropology* 12(2):191–97 (April).
Hsu, Francis L. K.
  1943 "The Myth of Chinese Family Size." *American Journal of Sociology* 48:555–62 (March).
  1959 "The Family in China: The Classical Form." In Ruth Anshen, ed. *The Family: Its Function and Destiny,* pp. 123–45. New York: Harper and Bros.
Hu, Tai-Li
  1983 "The Emergence of Small-Scale Industry in a Taiwanese Rural Community." In June Nash and Maria Patricia Fernandez-Kelly, eds., *Women, Men and the International Division of Labor,* pp. 387–406. Albany: State University of New York Press.
Imamura Tomo
  1909 *Chōsen fūzoku shū* [An anthology of Korean customs]. Keijō: Shidōkan.
Itō Abito
  1973 "Kankoku nōson shakai no ichimen" [One view of Korean village society]. In Nakane, ed. 1973:147–59.

Janelli, Roger L. and Dawnhee Yim Janelli
 1982 *Ancestor Worship and Korean Society.* Stanford, Calif.: Stanford University Press.
Johnson, E. A.
 1970 *The Organization of Space in Developing Countries.* Cambridge: Harvard University Press.
Kautsky, Karl
 1899 *Die Agrarfrage: Eine Übersicht über die Tendenzen der modernen Landwirthschaft und die Agrarpolitik der Sozialdemokratie.* Stuttgart: Dietz Verlag.
Keidel, B.
 1980 "Regional Agricultural Production and Income." In Ban, Moon, and Perkins 1980:112–59.
Kendall, Laurel
 1983 "Korean Ancestors: From the Woman's Side." In Kendall and Peterson, eds. 1983:97–112.
 1985 *Shamans, Housewives, and Other Restless Spirits.* Honolulu: University of Hawaii Press.
Kendall, Laurel, and Mark Peterson, eds.
 1983 *Korean Women: View from the Inner Room.* New Haven, Conn.: Eastrock Press.
Kim Chusu
 1984 *Chusŏk ch'injok sangsok pŏp, chŏnjŏng chŭngbo p'an* [Annotated family and inheritance law, rev. and enl. version]. Seoul: Pŏp Mun Sa.
Kim Chusuk
 1985 "Nongch'on yŏsŏng kwa il: kŭ ch'egye wa posang" [Farm women and work: system and compensation]. In *Han'guk yŏsŏng kwa il* [Korean women and work], pp. 213–46. Seoul: Ehwa Women's University Korean Women's Study Center.
Kim, Dong-hi
 1979 "Issues and Strategies for Agricultural Growth in Korea." *Journal of Rural Development* 2:15–37.
Kim Namje
 1985 "Han'guk kajok chedo ŭi pyŏnhwa: kajok yuhyŏng kwa kajok yŏkhal ŭl chungsim ŭro" [Changes in the Korean family system: centering on family form and family roles]. In *Han'guk sahoe ŭi pyŏndong kwa paljŏn* [Korean society's change and development], pp. 411–309. Seoul: Seoul National University Social Science Research Center.
Kim T'aekkyu
 1964 *Tongjok purak ŭi saenghwal kujo yŏn'gu* [A study of the cultural structure of a one-clan village]. Taegu: Ch'ŏnggu University, Silla-Kaya Yŏn'guwŏn.

Ko Ponggyŏng, Yi Hyojae, Yi Man'gap, and Yi Haeyŏng
1963 *Han'guk nongch'on kajok ŭi yŏn'gu* [A Study of the rural Korean family]. Seoul: Seoul National University Press.

Koo, Hagen and Doo-seung Hong
1980 "Class and Income Inequality in Korea." *American Sociological Review* 45:610–26 (August).

Kuramochi Kazuo
1985 "Kankoku ni okeru nōchi kaikoku to sono go no kosaku no tenkai" [The land reform in Korea and subsequent developments in tenancy]. *Ajia kenkyū* 32(2):1–33 (July).

Kwon, Taihwan, Haeyoung Lee, Yunshik Chang, and Euiyoung Yu
1975 *The Population of Korea.* Seoul: The Population and Development Studies Center, Seoul National University.

Leach, Edmund
1954 *Political Systems of Highland Burma: A Study of Kachin Social Structure.* Cambridge: Harvard University Press.
1961 *Rethinking Anthropology.* London School of Economics Monographs in Social Anthropology, no. 22. London: Athlone Press.

League of Nations
1932 "Conference of Experts for the Standardization of Certain Methods Used in Making Dietary Studies." *League of Nations Health Organization Quarterly Bulletin* 1:477–83.

Lee, Hoon K.
1936 *Land Utilization and Rural Economy in Korea.* Chicago: University of Chicago Press.

Lee, Ki Yull et al. [Yi Kiryŏl]
1962 "Dietary Study of Korean Farmers: A Dietary and Nutritional Status Survey of a Rural Community in South Korea, Including Four Seasons, from July 1959." *Journal of Home Economics* 54(3):205–11 (March).
1963 "Dietary Survey of Weanling Infants in South Korea." *Journal of the American Dietetic Association* 43(5):457–61 (November).

Lee, Kwang Kyu [Yi Kwanggyu]
1975 *Kinship System in Korea.* 2 vols. New Haven: Human Relations Area Files.

Lee, On-jook
1980 *Urban-to-Rural Return Migration in Korea.* Seoul: Seoul National University Press.

Legge, James
1960 *The Chinese Classics.* Vol. 4: *The She King, or The Book of Poetry.* Hong Kong: University of Hong Kong Press.

Lenin, Vladimir Ilich
1964 *Collected Works.* Vol. 3: *The Development of Capitalism in Russia.* Moscow: Progress Publishers (Russian original 1899).

Lévi-Strauss, Claude
  1963 *Structural Anthropology.* New York: Basic Books.
Llobera, Josep R.
  1979 "Techno-economic Determinism and the Work of Marx on Pre-capitalist Societies." *Man,* n.s. 14(2):249–70 (June).
Lotka, Alfred
  1922 "Contribution to the Energetics of Evolution." *Proceedings of the National Academy of Sciences* 8:147–51.
McArthur, Margaret
  1974 "Pigs for the Ancestors: A Review Article." *Oceania* 45(2):87–123 (December).
McGough, James P.
  1984 "The Domestic Mode of Production and Peasant Social Organization: The Chinese Case." In Durrenberger 1984:183–201.
McFarlane, Hylton
  1976 "Nutrition and Immunity." In *Nutrition Review's Present Knowledge in Nutrition.* 4th ed. New York: The Nutrition Foundation.
Malinowski, Bronislaw
  1922 *Argonauts of the Western Pacific: An Account of Native Enterprise and Adventure in the Archipelagoes of Melanesian New Guinea.* New York: E. P. Dutton.
Marx, Karl
  1969 "Der Achtzehnte Brumaire des Louis Bonaparte." In *Karl Marx, Friedrich Engels Werke* 8:111–207. Berlin: Dietz Verlag (English version in Tucker 1972:436–525).
  1971 Vorwort, *Zur Kritik der Politischen Ökonomie.* In *Karl Marx, Friedrich Engels Werke* 13:7–11. Berlin: Dietz Verlag (English version in Tucker 1972:3–6).
Marx, Karl and Friedrich Engels
  1955 *The Communist Manifesto.* New York: Appleton Century Crofts.
Mattielli, Sandra, ed.
  1977 *Virtues in Conflict: Tradition and the Korean Woman Today.* Seoul: Royal Asiatic Society, Korea Branch.
Mintz, Barbara
  1977 "Interviews with Young Working Women in Seoul." In Mattielli, ed. 1977:169–89.
Mason, Edward S. et al.
  1980 *The Economic and Social Modernization of the Republic of Korea.* Cambridge: Harvard University Press.
Meillassoux, Claude
  1981 *Maidens, Meal and Money: Capitalism and the Domestic Community.* Cambridge: Cambridge University Press.
Merrill, John
  1980 "The Cheju-do Rebellion." *Journal of Korean Studies* 2:139–97.

Mills, John E., ed.
  1960   *Ethno-Sociological Reports of Four Korean Villages.* Rev. ed. San Francisco: United States Operations Mission to Korea, Community Development Division.
Munhwa kongbobu [Ministry of Culture and Information of the Republic of Korea]
  1979   *Han'guk minsok chonghap chosa pogosŏ: Kangwŏn p'yŏn* [Report of the general investigation of Korean folk customs: Kangwŏn section]. Seoul: Munhwajae Kwalli Kuk [Office of Cultural Resources Management].
Murdock, George Peter
  1949   *Social Structure.* New York: Macmillan.
Na Sejin
  1964   "Han'guk minjok ŭi ch'ejil illyuhakchŏk yŏn'gu" [A physical anthropological study of the Korean people]. In *Han'guk Munhwa Sa Taegye,* pp. 87–233. Seoul: Korea University Press.
Nagel, Ernest L.
  1961   *The Structure of Science: Problems in the Logic of Scientific Explanation.* New York: Harcourt, Brace and World.
Nakane, Chie
  1967   *Kinship and Economic Organization in Rural Japan.* New York: Humanities Press.
Nakane Chie, ed.
  1973   *Kankoku nōson no kazoku to saigi* [Ritual and the family in Korean agricultural villages]. Tokyo: University of Tokyo Press.
Netting, Robert McC., Richard R. Wilk and Eric J. Arnould, eds.
  1984   *Households: Comparative and Historical Studies of the Domestic Group.* Berkeley and Los Angeles: University of California Press.
No Changsŏp, Kim Chongsŏ, and Han Sangjun
  1964   *Kaebal kwajŏng e innŭn nongch'on sahoe yŏn'gu* [A study of rural society in the process of development]. Seoul: Ehwa Women's University Press.
Nongnimbu [Ministry of Agriculture and Forestry of the Republic of Korea]
  1966   *Nongŏp sensŏsŭ* [Agricultural census]. Seoul.
  1977   *Nongnim t'onggye yŏnbo* [Agricultural statistical yearbook]. Seoul.
  1978   *Nongnim t'onggye yŏnbo* [Agricultural statistical yearbook]. Seoul.
Nongŏp Hyŏptong Chohap [Agricultural Cooperative Federation]
  1978   *Nonghyŏp yŏn'gam* [Cooperative yearbook]. Seoul.
Norbeck, Edward
  1978   *Country to City: The Urbanization of a Japanese Hamlet.* Salt Lake City: University of Utah Press.
Nornis, T.
  1949   *Dietary Surveys: Their Technique and Interpretation.* Nutritional Studies, no. 4. Rome: Food and Agricultural Organization of the United Nations.

O Hosŏng
1981   *Kyŏngje paljŏn kwa nongji chedo* [Economic development and the
       agricultural land system]. Seoul: Han'guk nongch'on kyŏngje yŏn'-
       guwŏn.
Odum, Howard T.
1971   *Environment, Power and Society.* New York: John Wiley and Sons.
Osgood, Cornelius
1951   *The Koreans and their Culture.* New York: Ronald Press.
Pak, Ki Hyuk
1966   *A Study of Land Tenure System in Korea.* Seoul: Land Economics
       Research Center.
1975   *The Changing Korean Village.* Seoul: Shinhung Press.
Passmore, R., and J. V. G. A. Durnin
1955   "Human Energy Expenditure." *Physiological Reviews* 35:801–40.
Passmore, R., B. M. Nicol, and Narayana Rao
1974   *Handbook on Human Nutritional Requirements.* Nutritional Stud-
       ies no. 28. Rome: Food and Agricultural Organization of the United
       Nations.
Popkin, Samuel L.
1979   *The Rational Peasant: The Political Economy of Rural Society in
       Vietnam.* Berkeley and Los Angeles: University of California Press.
Potter, Jack
1968   *Capitalism and the Chinese Peasant: Social and Economic Change
       in a Hong Kong Village.* Berkeley and Los Angeles: University of
       California Press.
Radcliffe-Brown, A. R.
1965   *Structure and Function in Primitive Society.* New York: Free Press.
Rader, Melvin
1979   *Marx's Interpretation of History.* New York: Oxford University
       Press.
Ross, Eric
1978   "Food Taboos, Diet and Hunting Strategy: The Adaptation to Ani-
       mals in Amazon Cultural Ecology." *Current Anthropology* 19(1):1–
       36 (March).
Royal Anthropological Institute
1951   *Notes and Queries on Anthropology.* 6th ed. London: Routledge
       and Kegan Paul.
Salaff, Janet
1981   *Working Daughters of Hong Kong: Filial Piety or Power in the
       Family?* Cambridge: Cambridge University Press.
Sahlins, Marshall T.
1972   *Stone Age Economics.* Chicago: Aldine.
Scott, James C.
1976   *The Moral Economy of the Peasant: Rebellion and Subsistence in
       Southeast Asia.* New Haven: Yale University Press.

Shanin, Teodor
  1972   *The Awkward Class: Political Sociology of Peasantry in a Develop-
         ing Society, Russia 1910–1925.* Oxford: Oxford University Press.
Shima, Mutsuhiko
  1976   "Dōnai (chib-an) no bunseki: Kankoku Zenra Nandō ni okeru jirei
         no kentō" [An analysis of the *tangnae* (*chiban*): an investigation of
         an example in South Chŏlla Province, Korea]. *Minzokugaku
         kenkyū* 41(1):75–90 (June).
Skalweit, August
  1924   "Die Familienwirtschaft als Grundlage für ein System der Sozial-
         ökonomik." *Weltwirtschaftliches Archiv* 20(2):231–46.
Sloboda, John E.
  1980   "Off Farm Migration." In Ban, Moon, and Perkins 1980:316–82.
Skinner, G. William
  1964   "Marketing and Social Structure in Rural China, Part I." *Journal of
         Asian Studies* 24(1):3–43 (November).
  1965a "Marketing and Social Structure in Rural China, Part II." *Journal
         of Asian Studies* 24(2):195–228 (February).
  1965b "Marketing and Social Structure in Rural China, Part III." *Journal
         of Asian Studies* 24(3):363–99 (May).
Smil, Vaclav
  1979   "Energy Flows in Rural China." *Human Ecology* 7(2):119–31
         (June).
Smith, Carol A.
  1976   "Regional Economic Systems: Linking Geographical Models and
         Socioeconomic Problems." In Carol Smith, ed. *Regional Analysis*,
         pp. 3–63. New York: Academic Press.
Smith, Robert J.
  1978   *Kurusu: The Price of Progress in a Japanese Village, 1951–1975.*
         Stanford, Calif.: Stanford University Press.
Smith, Thomas C.
  1977   *Nakahara: Family Farming and Population in a Japanese Village,
         1717–1830.* Stanford, Calif.: Stanford University Press.
Solomon, Susan Gross
  1977   *The Soviet Agrarian Debate: A Controversy in Social Science,
         1923–1929.* Boulder, Colo.: Westview Press.
Song, Ch. D. and Lee, O. H.
  1970   "Study in Improving Workspace for the Rural Homemaker." *Ka-
         jŏng Kwalli Yŏn'gu* [Journal of home management] 1:7–14.
Sorensen, Clark W.
  1981a *Household, Family and Economy in a Korean Mountain Village.*
         Ph.D. Diss. University of Washington.
  1981b "Marketing and Social Structure among the Peasantry of the
         Yŏngsŏ Region of South Korea." *Journal of Korean Studies* 3:83–
         112.

1983 "Female, Male; Inside, Outside; The Division of Labor in Rural Central Korea." In Kendall and Peterson, eds. 1983:63–79.

1984 "Farm Labor and Family Cycle in Traditional Korea and Japan." *Journal of Anthropological Research* 40(2):306–23.

1986 "Migration, the Family, and Care of the Aged in Rural Korea: An Investigation of a Village in the Yŏngsŏ Region of Kangwŏn Province 1918–1983." *Journal of Cross Cultural Gerontology* 1(2):139–61.

Steward, Julian R.
1938 "Basin-Plateau Sociopolitical Groups." *Bureau of American Ethnology Bulletin*, no. 120. Washington, D. C.

1955 *Theory of Culture Change: The Method of Multilinear Evolution.* Urbana: University of Illinois Press.

Street, John
1969 "An Evaluation of the Concept of Carrying Capacity." *Professional Geographer* 21(2):104–7 (March).

Suh, Sang-chul
1978 *Growth and Structural Change in the Korean Economy, 1910–1940.* Cambridge: Harvard University Press.

Taylor, Charles Lewis and Michael C. Hudson
1972 *World Handbook of Political and Social Indicators.* New Haven: Yale University Press.

Tucker, Robert C.
1972 *The Marx-Engels Reader.* New York: W. W. Norton and Co.

United Nations Korean Reconstruction Agency
1954 *Rehabilitation and Development of Agriculture, Forestry, and Fisheries in South Korea.* New York: Columbia University Press.

United States Department of Agriculture
1963 *Composition of Foods.* Agriculture Handbook, no. 8. Washington, D. C.: Consumer and Food Economic Institute, Agricultural Research Service.

Wagner, Edward W.
1974 "The Ladder of Success in Yi Dynasty Korea." *Occasional Papers on Korea* 1:1–8.

Waley, Arthur
1937 *Book of Songs.* Boston: Houghton, Mifflin Co.

White, Leslie A.
1949 *The Science of Culture: A Study of Man and Civilization.* New York: Farrar and Strauss.

Williams, Robert R.
1961 *Toward the Conquest of Beriberi.* Cambridge: Harvard University Press.

Wirth, Louis
1938 "Urbanism as a Way of Life." *American Journal of Sociology* 44:1–24 (July).

Wolf, Arthur
1985 "Fertility in Prerevolutionary Rural China." In Susan B. Hanley and Arthur P. Wolf, eds., *Family and Population in East Asian History*, pp. 154–85. Stanford, Calif.: Stanford University Press.
Wolf, Arthur and Chieh-shan Huang
1981 *Marriage and Adoption in China: 1895–1945*. Stanford, Calif.: Stanford University Press.
Wolf, Eric R.
1966 *Peasants*. Englewood Cliffs, N. J.: Prentice-Hall.
Wolpe, Harold
1980 "Introduction." In Wolpe, Harold, ed., *The Articulation of Modes of Production*. London: Routledge and Kegan Paul.
Yi Hŭisŭng
1971 *Kugŏ Tae Sajŏn* [Great dictionary of the Korean language]. Seoul: Minjung Sŏgwan.
Yi Kiryŏl [Ki Yull Lee]
1976 *Han'guk in ŭi sik saenghwal* [The culinary life of Korean people]. Seoul: Yŏnsei University Press.
Yi Kwanggyu [Kwang Kyu Lee]
1975a "Ŭngŏ chedo ŭi punp'o wa yuhyŏng e kwanhan yŏn'gu" [A study of the type and distribution of retirement systems]. *Han'guk Munhwa Illyuhak* 7:1–19.
1975b *Han'guk kajok ŭi kujo punsŏk* [A structural analysis of the Korean family]. Seoul: Ilji Sa.
1981 *Han'guk kajok ŭi simni munje: kobu munje chungsim ŭro* [Psychological problems of the Korean family: centering on the mother-in-law-daughter-in-law problem]. Seoul: Ilji Sa.
Yi Kwangsu
1975 *Hŭlk* [Soil]. Seoul: Samjungdang Mun'go (original 1933).
Yi Tuhyŏn, Chang Sugŭn, and Yi Kwanggyu
1974 *Han'guk minsokhak kaeron* [An introduction to Korean folklore]. Seoul: Minjung Sŏgwan.
Yoon, Soon Young S.
1977 "Occupation, Male Housekeeper: Male-Female Roles on Cheju Island." In Mattielli, ed. 1977:191–207.
Zenshō Eisuke
1929 *Chōsen no kosaku kanshū* [Korean tenancy customs]. Keijō: Chōsen Sōtokufu.

Index

CPSIA information can be obtained at www.ICGtesting.com
Printed in the USA
BVOW032322240413

319052BV00002B/32/P